The
9-to-5
Cure

Work on Your Own Terms and Reinvent Your Life

Kristin Cardinale, Ph.D.

jist
Works
America's Career Publisher®

THE 9-TO-5 CURE

© 2011 by Kristin Cardinale

Published by JIST Works, an imprint of JIST Publishing
7321 Shadeland Station, Suite 200
Indianapolis, IN 46256-3923

Phone: 800-648-JIST   Fax: 877-454-7839
E-mail: info@jist.com   Web site: www.jist.com

Quantity discounts are available for JIST products. Please call our Sales Department at 800-648-JIST for a free catalog and more information.

Visit www.jist.com for information on JIST, free job search information, tables of contents, sample pages, and ordering information on our many products.

Acquisitions Editor: Susan Pines
Development Editor: Jennifer Lynn
Production Editor: Stephanie Koutek
Book Designer and Layout: Aleata Halbig
Proofreaders: Laura Bowman, Jeanne Clark
Indexer: Kelly D. Henthorne

Printed in the United States of America

15 14 13 12 11 10   9 8 7 6 5 4 3 2 1

Library of Congress Cataloging-in-Publication Data
Cardinale, Kristin, 1970-
  The 9-to-5 cure : work on your own terms and reinvent your life /
Kristin Cardinale.
       p. cm.
  Includes bibliographical references and index.
  ISBN 978-1-59357-807-7 (alk. paper)
  1. Flexible work arrangements. 2. Part-time employment. 3. Career
development. 4. Quality of work life. 5. Job satisfaction. I. Title.
II. Title: Nine-to-five cure.
  HD5110.C37 2011
  650.1--dc22
                              2010045777

We have been careful to provide accurate information throughout this book, but it is possible that errors and omissions have been introduced. Please consider this in making any career plans or other important decisions. Trust your own judgment above all else and in all things.

ISBN 978-1-59357-807-7

TABLE OF CONTENTS

Preface

We all have a dream for our lives. We may not have the dream all mapped out, but on some level we all have a vision dancing in our heads of what we would like our life to be. That dream is comprised of images of a particular lifestyle, which likely includes a thriving career. What does *your* dream look like? What really stands out for you? You will be asked to explore this dream as you read this book, and I want you to really get in touch with what matters most to you. Is it being home with your kids during the day? Getting home early enough to cheer at the soccer games? Pulling in a certain amount of money each year? Or perhaps doing work that you love?

Whatever the cornerstones are of your dream lifestyle and dream career, I want you to hold those images in mind as you read through this book. That vision for your life is possible. It is! Instead of sweeping that dream to the back of your mind as some fantasy that will never come true, allow it to come to the front of your mind. Be open to the possibility that your dreams can become a concrete reality. In Zen Buddhism this openness is called adopting a *beginner's mind,* which is eager and open to new ideas and free from assumptions or foregone conclusions. The more experience you have in the workplace, the more challenging it can be to assume the beginner's mind because you may have some strongly held beliefs about who gets ahead, why, and how. However, you have to ask yourself if the paradigm that you currently subscribe to is benefitting you. In other words, are you happy with your work and your lifestyle? If the answer to that question is no, now is the right time to stop and reconstruct the dream that you have for your life. Invest in yourself and develop your dream lifestyle. Don't just think about it; make it happen!

In this book you will follow me through a step-by-step process for defining the lifestyle that you long for with a career to match. For more than twenty years, I have been designing my dream and expecting results from myself and the world at large, in part by developing an annual ritual that makes tailoring a life plan and sticking to it more routine than anything else. I'll describe how you, too, can systematically develop a vision for yourself and create a constructive plan for getting results. I feel so passionate about sharing this 9-to-5 Cure with you because I know from firsthand experience that you can become the dream that is in your mind's eye. If you will invest in yourself by doing the preparation, you can step away from the rat race and into your dream, whatever that dream may be for you. Don't settle for surviving—start thriving!

If you hesitate to take a chance because you have been disappointed before by other people or your own inaction, I say to you at the top of my voice:

> Take the most important lessons that you learned from those negative experiences and leave the rest behind!

Take the energy of that shame, humiliation, rage, resentment, or whatever it may be and channel it into getting on with your life. Use that force that pulses within you for something that will bring you up instead of drag you down. Dig deep and rediscover your passion for life, for your dreams. And dream big! This time, dream bigger than you ever dreamed before. Give yourself the opportunity to learn about the transformational power of reconstructing your career in a way that lets you get in alignment with your dreams. Go ahead, get your hopes up!

Acknowledgments

I am grateful to so many people who contributed to the success of this project, including

> Sue Pines, Jennifer Lynn, and the entire team at JIST Publishing, for believing in the concept and helping to shape the content masterfully.

> Ken Horn and Jennifer Mulchandani, for sharing countless hours of your time and talent with me.

> My wonderful family and amazing friends, for cheering me on throughout this process and loving me always and in all ways.

> My daughter, for inspiring me to work on purpose; I love you.

> My husband, for your unwavering love and support now and always; I am so blessed to be on this journey with you.

About the Author

Dr. Kristin Cardinale is an optimist, columnist, adjunct college professor, technology instructor, career coach, consultant, seminar speaker, owner of a small technical support business, and serial entrepreneur. She is living the life of her dreams, working on her own terms, and thankful for her many blessings. Previously, she worked as an international educator and went on to own and operate a national seminar business, which served her colleagues in hundreds of colleges, universities, government agencies, and public corporations. Dr. Cardinale has lived, worked, studied, and traveled in more than twenty countries in every corner of the globe and hopes to someday visit the last continent on her list, Antarctica. Dr. Cardinale holds a Ph.D. in Educational Administration from the University of Wisconsin–Madison and an M.Ed. in Adult Learning and Development from Cleveland State University.

"Make your work to be in keeping with your purpose."

—*Leonardo da Vinci*

PART I

Escape Your Reality

CHAPTER 1

The Life of Your Dreams

I have a secret to share with you. It's something that has changed my life—forever. It is a groundbreaking career strategy that is based on freedom, choice, and abundance. No matter what your employment situation is or has been, you can apply this strategy in your everyday life to bring you the work—and the lifestyle—for which you are searching:

- If you are seeking job security that is infallible, this is it.

- If you are seeking freedom of choice regarding where you work, when you work, and who you work with, this is it.

- If you desire the flexibility to sample new occupations regularly in a way that is productive and beneficial to your overall career success, this is it.

- If you simply want to bring balance to your life and know that any special event or important moment in your personal life will not require approval from your boss before you can commit, this is it.

This is it; this is the moment when you first learned that work and time can be yours in abundance. Either your boss can be in complete control of your career, or you can. The 9-to-5 work world is a choice, but it is not the only choice.

Can you imagine a lifestyle other than the infamous 9-to-5 version? Typically we think there are only two choices to toggle between: either the 40-hour workweek or the 0-hour workweek that immediately follows winning the lottery. We dream of abandoning work as we know it and cashing in. What is it about winning the lottery that is so appealing? The money, of course! Right?

Well, I have news about that angle of the argument. *Forbes* reported that there is "virtually the same level of happiness between the very rich individuals on the Forbes 400 and the Maasai herdsmen of East Africa."[1] Seriously.

The first time I read that information, I thought to myself, "Yeah, right!" After all, I have gone on those tourist trips to spend a day in the Great Rift Valley with the Maasai in Kenya and Tanzania. The people are beautiful, talented, and kind; the culture is deep, complex, and marvelous; but the reality is that they wear a red woven garment for clothing and sandals made from cowhide, live in mud huts, and are penniless by most American standards. So at first blush, the premise seems outrageous at best: that a nomadic shepherd roaming the land could rival the happiness level of, say, Bill Gates, one of the richest men in the United States, and all that his wealth affords him?

The underlying hypothesis is absolutely shocking and flies in the face of all that the 9-to-5 lifestyle represents. After all, isn't the 9-to-5 lifestyle characterized by a thirty-year span of "work" with the endgame being the accumulation of "wealth" of some measure? And with that being the case, do we all really work the prime years of our lives in order to be as happy as—or perhaps less happy than—a Kenyan shepherd?

Okay, but what if at this moment you *did* have in your hands the winning Powerball ticket that could give you a taste of the lifestyle that Bill Gates enjoys? *Would* you be happier? For a short time perhaps. However, research indicates that within five years of winning the lottery, you would return to your current level of happiness. Think about that for a minute. How happy are you *right now?* This is about as happy as you would be if you were a multimillionaire, after the initial period of elation. Did you get that? You are as happy right now as your multimillionaire self would be.

At first glance that might be a depressing thought, but I invite you to instead think about it as liberating. To get there, think about it like this: If your happiness doesn't depend on accumulating excessive amounts of wealth that may be beyond your reach anyway, then this theory of your present self being as happy as your millionaire self brings achievement of a happy lifestyle closer into range, doesn't it? Furthermore, a medical study at Emory University found that people who actually earned their money were more satisfied with the wealth they accumulated, however great or small, than those who received it through happenstance such as an inheritance or the lottery.[2] So you see, earning a living *can* be rewarding.

If you're not exactly jumping out of bed in the morning on a workday—and trust me, you're not alone—there is an alternative framework, a "cure" if you will, that I can't wait to tell you about. It's the big secret I alluded to right at the start. But before we jump in, let's look at one more reason why we all dream about the winning lottery ticket.

Let's take the vision that we all have about winning the lottery one step in another direction. Aside from the unimaginable wealth, what is so attractive about that lifestyle? Do images of sipping a fruity drink at a cabana near the ocean come to mind? Or spending a month in the South of France at a vineyard? Or perhaps touring the country on your Harley-Davidson motorcycle with a riding club? Now, with those visions in your mind of what your lottery lifestyle would be like, can you guess what they all have in common? Freedom! They represent freedom.

Freedom is what winning the lottery really represents to most people. The winning ticket is a ticket, literally, to various freedoms that in traditional terms only great wealth affords you, including the ability to do any and all of the following:

- Create your own schedule
- Associate with people you like
- Disassociate from people who annoy you
- Sample different experiences and lifestyles
- Enjoy extended periods of free time
- Pursue your interests at will
- Get passionate about your life
- Have a lifestyle that others envy
- And more

So what does all of this have to do with you? After all, you haven't won the lottery—yet. Well, that's true, and yet it isn't. Although you haven't won the lottery officially, I would challenge you to believe me when I tell you that I have good news along those lines. This is some of the best news you might hear all day:

> **There *is* a cure for the 9-to-5 lifestyle that can make you feel in many ways like you *have* won the lottery.**

(And it may make you as happy as a nomadic shepherd.)

The 9-to-5 Cure is real. It is tangible. It is a systematic strategy that anyone with any level of education, any skill set, and any work history can apply to his or her own life and enjoy the same freedoms that are traditionally afforded only to lottery winners and the ultra riche. Although excessive wealth may or may not become part of the formula for you depending on a number of factors, the ability to earn a good living, enjoy an abundance of freedom, and know job security as a way of life is a given. If you do the work, you can realize success.

There *is* a 9-to-5 Cure. This is it.

Endnotes

[1] Matthew Herper, "Now It's a Fact: Money Doesn't Buy Happiness," *Forbes*, September 23, 2004, http://moneycentral.msn.com/content/invest/forbes/P95294.asp (accessed September 2, 2010).

[2] The Associated Press, "Are Lottery Winners Really Less Happy?" May 13, 2004, www.msnbc.msn.com/id/4971361 (accessed September 2, 2010).

CHAPTER 2

Realizing That Old Dream Isn't Worth Realizing

It is 3 a.m. I am in Manaus, deep inside the Brazilian rainforest. A crowd of college students is gathering on the main floor of a dilapidated Amazon riverboat about half a mile away. I am downstream with a guide, floating along in a hollowed-out tree trunk used as a makeshift canoe. The guide handles the long stick-like paddle skillfully, which is demonstrated by the fact that while the water churns and we push forward, there is utter silence. I listen to the sudden and sometimes deafening shrieks of the rainforest animals as we progress in the pitch-dark night toward an area where crocs are known to gather. We scan the edges of the riverbank with a pocket flashlight, looking for the gleaming eyes of a small croc so that we can catch it and bring it back to the riverboat to discuss the habits of nocturnal animals.

As we near the target area, the canoe slows to a stop, and we turn on the flashlight. There before us, just a few feet away, are at least thirty pairs of bright white croc eyes staring back at us. The guide calmly paddles closer to the riverbank as my heart begins to pound so loudly that I am sure that both the guide and the crocs can hear it. My mind is racing, frenetically reviewing the instructions from the impromptu training earlier that day. Now it's up to me.

Slowly, I lean out of the canoe, which is nearly level with the river water, quickly grab the croc's jaws with one hand, and then immediately grab his tail with my other hand as he begins to flail upon being lifted out of the water. "We got him! We got him!" I yell. All at once the students on the riverboat upstream begin to shout with excitement.

The guide helps me ease back into place in the canoe; after all, this is no place to fall in and take a swim. I hold the croc in place on my lap while the guide paddles quickly to the riverboat. Minutes later we float up along the side of the riverboat to the sound of rousing cheers. I hand the croc to the onboard guide and climb onto the old riverboat, feeling flush with adrenaline. In this moment I think to myself, "I have to do this again—and soon!"

That Amazon trip was one of many moments of high adventure in my global nomad graduate student life, but ultimately, racing into the 9-to-5 matrix presses on us all and we walk into the structure in lockstep. I was no different. But what if we chose a different path? What if we created our own rules about how we spent our days? Now, I'm not saying that floating down the Amazon River every day is a realistic way to earn a living, but the experience did lead me to an epiphany years later when I realized that doing short stints of work that I loved was the key to Lifestyle Design staring me in the face, waiting to be recognized. But I'm getting ahead of myself.

There would be two decades of running the traditional 9-to-5 circuit of getting degrees, sending out resumes, going on interviews, and all of that boring and exhausting stuff before I would be able to see my career outside of the 9-to-5 construct.

Chronology of a 9-to-5 Career

Like many other people, I graduated from high school with plans for going to college and someday landing that dream job. However, years later I became completely disillusioned. Have you ever been disillusioned by your own career choices? If so, you might relate to one or more of the following scenarios:

- Did you invest a lot of time and money pursuing an education only to realize years later that it was a poor use of your time?

- Or perhaps you landed a job with that prized company, but that job didn't pay off in the way you hoped?

- Maybe the company you worked for went bankrupt after you dedicated twenty years of your blood, sweat, and tears to the place.

- Or you were replaced on the assembly line by a new high-tech device.

We all have a story, I imagine. Mine begins with a lot of college and ends with a lot of disappointment—followed by my greatest success. Before we charge ahead, let me give you a little background on my journey to this point.

Starting at Point A: Eyes on the Prize

I was a seriously career-minded student; you have no idea. I went to class, then straight to work on campus at the International Education office, and then straight home to study until all hours of the night. I did that for four years of undergraduate school and two years of graduate school. I was driven to someday be "The Director" (cue the harps) of an International Education office somewhere in the United States. Six years of college was just the beginning of the long road ahead; it would be almost ten years before I was able to get from Point A to Point B. My decade of real-world preparation looked like this:

> **1994:** Graduate with a master's degree and land an entry-level job on the other side of the country. I pack my belongings in a shiny, brand-new subcompact car that was now scratched beyond belief by my belongings and drive for thirteen hours to this not-very-exciting new city. I report to the office the afternoon before I am to begin working only to discover that my new boss never set up the temporary housing she promised me, so I sleep in my car the first night. On day one my boss walks in, sits down, takes a look at me, and point blank asks what my religious persuasion is. She then proceeds to lecture me about the stupidity (her word) of religion, and me by extension. It's only 9:15 a.m. I managed to find the one atheist living in the Bible Belt.

> **1995:** Continue to work for the oddball boss, clocking the time on my resume so that making a move to a new employer doesn't look suspicious in my job history. In the meantime I give professional presentations at state and regional conferences to build credibility and become more marketable in the work world. Hiring season arrives, and I apply for jobs everywhere in the United States and overseas.

> **1996:** Land a new job on the other side of the country, this time at a Big Ten university. This job is considered a huge leap forward in my career, but what do I do? I turn the job down six times during the salary negotiation process. I'm finally hired on, but am now making significantly more than my soon-to-retire counterpart, which ticks off my co-workers before I even arrive. The job is interesting and rewarding—for a while.

1997: Begin to realize that being "The Director" seems relatively easy and pays twice the salary, but requires a doctorate. I prep for the GRE test, apply to the stellar doctoral program on campus, and land an assistantship that pays for college. I quit my regular job and begin classes. My 9-to-5er parents think I'm nuts to give up job security. My 80-year-old Italian grandmother cries actual tears while saying, "No man will want to marry a woman who is smarter than him! You will be ruined!" I wonder if this is some tricky reverse psychology tactic.

1998: Work a helluva lot during year one of the doctoral program, but find it surprisingly easy. I finish the required on-campus courses and decide it's time to pursue my dreams of travel in a way that allows me to also earn college credit for some valuable work and research experience that will ultimately pad my resume for the next big job search. I apply for internships overseas; I apply everywhere!

1999: Land an internship working for the Australian government and within weeks pack up and move there. I continue my studies at an Australian university while pursuing my research. I write a paper that gets published by the Aussie government and meet the prime minister during a private meeting with about thirty of my fellow interns. A few weeks later, I receive a phone call from a university travel program that I applied to for five years running. They ask me to work on their cruise ship, and I accept on the spot. The moment the semester ends, I drop off my belongings at the DHL office for shipment back to the United States; the boxes don't surface again for nearly a year. With a few months to spare before the ship sets sail, I throw on my backpack and hit the trails, trekking across Australia, New Zealand, and Fiji. (After all, comprehensive travel experience is a must in order to land a job as "The Director"!) I climb the world's tallest steel bridge in Australia, jump out of planes in New Zealand, have an unexpected encounter with a great white shark while snorkeling in Fiji, and darn near stress out my parents by e-mailing home about all of these adventures.

2000: Race home, pack my bags, and set sail on the cruise ship. I circumnavigate the globe working as an onboard travel agent for one hundred days. I earn money while working to cover my expenses back home. I enjoy breathtaking, life-changing travel experiences like a big-game safari by hot air balloon at sunrise over the Serengeti. A few months later, I am back on campus. I move into a rented house for the summer and proceed to write my entire dissertation from cover to cover and graduate by year's end.

2001: Apply eagerly for director-level jobs nationwide. I land a job as director at a nearby university.

Now, you may think that the punctuation is wrong at that end of that last entry. It should be an exclamation point instead of a period, right? After all, that was the ultimate goal that propelled me through decades of college classes, overseas work, and research, right? In 2001 I finally realized the dream that I had chased and dreamed about for so many years. Finally landing that dream job should have been cause for rejoicing. As it turns out, no. That job, my so-called "dream job," which was the focus of many years of my life, broke me. It shattered my world; it was devastating. And it turns out that it was the most liberating thing that could ever happen to me.

Arriving at Point B: The Illusion of Security

When we are sitting at Point A and plotting a way to get to Point B, doesn't Point B seem like the be-all and the end-all? When Point B is a specific job or career position, we dream of the perks that come with being hired on as a 9-to-5 employee, including the salary, paid vacation days, paid sick leave, and health insurance benefits. We dream of luxuriating in the security of being a salaried employee. That is the goal; it's the golden ticket. Growing up, I remember hearing my grandfather talk about how he never enjoyed a single day of paid vacation in his entire life. The message from his generation was to look for one of those jobs that paid regular benefits, and if you landed one, oh boy, hang on and endure whatever comes your way because those benefits are worth it, baby!

This mindset continues in our present-day world where, in fact, due to the currently high rate of unemployment, previously choosy employees are now willing to do more for less money in order to hold on to their benefits, dwindling though those benefits may be. I understand their reasoning. And I deeply respect them for getting up every day and going to work in order to support their families. Likewise, I realize that companies can sometimes have good intentions, but simply must cut back in order to remain solvent. I empathize with everyone involved. However, I have discovered that all of this round-robin misery is optional. It's optional! Do you hear me? IT'S OPTIONAL!

Contrary to popular belief, being a career employee is *not* the answer to a lifestyle of freedom and security. Walk into any unemployment office and take a good look around. Do all of those previously salaried employees look like they are enjoying the freedom and security that they imagined going into the job on day one? No. They are miserable, they feel helpless, and their entire life is out of control. Allow me to illustrate my point.

When I landed my dream job as "The Director," I had no idea that eight people before me had been offered the job and flatly rejected it because the salary was low and the department was in disarray following an unpopular merger that resulted in ferocious infighting among veteran employees. Nonetheless, blinded by my wanting to at long last assume the title of Director, I naively accepted the position and jumped right into the thick of it. That job became my identity. I worked day and night to the point of exhaustion for about two years before I took a breath to prepare for my impending wedding.

At 10 a.m. on the first day of my vacation, I was busily packing for the wedding when my cell phone rang; it was my boss. She called to inform me that she was in the process of reorganizing my office and would be holding a staff meeting later that day to inform everyone of the situation. She apologized for the last-minute notice and told me that the candidate we mutually agreed to hire for another position would only sign on at the director level, so she decided to reconfigure the organizational chart.

After two years of tireless work to create a cohesive team in the aftermath of the hellish merger, the team was re-divided and the office was reorganized—in an instant and without my consent. To add insult to injury, I had effectively been demoted with no prior notice. And my team felt betrayed, believing I knew this was happening and deliberately failed to tell them before leaving for an extended vacation.

I was angry and deeply saddened in these days just prior to my wedding. Instead of being occupied with details about the flowers and the cake, all I could think about was work. On the day of my wedding, an entire table at the reception stood empty because team members had boycotted the event. By the time I returned to work, I was seething. This job that had been my life's work for the two years prior was now merely a hot potato that I had to get rid of as fast as possible. My dream job turned out to be a "bad boyfriend" job, as it's referred to in colloquial terms—one that you dedicate your heart and soul to only to be dumped suddenly and without warning.

This story illustrates the naked truth about why being a career employee is risky business. The rules of the game can change or be thrown out the window at any moment. In a heartbeat the organization can make sweeping changes, or on a whim the boss can reassign you, increase your workload, change your hours, decrease your salary, or terminate your employment. And no matter how high you climb the career ladder, you are always vulnerable— everyone answers to someone. The 9-to-5 career is merely the illusion of security that society chooses to accept as reality. In reality, changes can come at any time, no notice required. In my case, I was being effectively demoted soon after receiving a significant merit-based raise. Go figure.

This experience at my dream job and the stories from countless others just like mine posted on Internet message boards for job seekers caused me to panic. *Was this what I had to look forward to for the next thirty years?* I thought to myself. Was this my wake-up call to the reality that Point B is merely surviving the rat race until age 67? So many thoughts raced through my head during those days, but it was no time for deep introspection. It was time to find a new job that would pay the bills, and the clock was ticking!

OMG, I Need a Job!

When you are readying yourself for certain unemployment or are desperate to change jobs for some other reason, you develop a unique ability to focus. Most people in this situation work their regular job by day and carry out an "OMG-I-need-a-job" search at night. During the first few weeks, they frantically search all the job postings online and e-mail or call any friends or trustworthy colleagues who might have a possible job connection. Around the second month, the real panic sets in when all of the obvious leads have gone cold. It is in those weeks, months, and for some people—regrettably— years that the search process requires creative thinking in order to keep generating new job possibilities. In the meantime, job seekers continue to scour the Internet for job postings at prime companies or on popular job search engines. They also scan the want ads in their local Sunday paper in which many of the notices state the nature of the work but not the name of the company.

If enough time passes, people in desperation mode will apply for anything that pays. Have you ever responded to a blind ad only to receive an auto-reply message thanking you for your interest in being a salesperson in a multilevel pyramid-scheme company? Or better yet, have you applied for a job only to find yourself on a spam list that advertises products that you cannot afford because you are either unemployed or about to be? And as if all of the fun and games are not enough, some vacancies require the exhausting business of racing around in person and filling out tedious and redundant application forms at local Human Resources offices. Does any of this sound familiar? Have you been there? I sure have.

Well, when you finally run out of networking leads and you respond to all of the position vacancies that are out there, you become willing to negotiate nearly everything that matters to you in a job. As the days and months march by, you drudge up that belief that society has embedded in you: I need to be a salaried employee at all cost! You become willing to work practically anywhere, on any shift, with any commute time, and at a lower salary than ever before. You just need a J-O-B!

The J-O-B Is Not the Answer

Are you in the thick of needing a job right now, as you read this book? If you are, please let me tell you from experience that the J-O-B is not the *answer*. Instead, it's the *addiction*. We crave the so-called security of the salaried job, but in reality that job may end at any time and begin again the cycle of job loss. Aren't you tired of the rat race? Seriously, haven't you had enough? If you are stuck in the job-loss cycle as you read this book, please know that this period of trial and tribulation can be the greatest learning opportunity of your life. I know that it's hard to hear, but believe me when I say that unemployment or career dissatisfaction can be life-changing in a good way! It can be the greatest motivator you have ever known, causing you to dig deep and find courage that you never knew you had.

There is a better way; that is what this book is all about. It's time to break out of the chains holding you prisoner in the 9-to-5 world and be free.

$$\mathcal{EO}$$

My intention is to inspire you and bring you into a new season of your life, one filled with hopes and dreams instead of the realities you currently accept and that pollute the vision you have for yourself. It's time to cure your 9-to-5 addiction, to break free from the chains that weigh you down in this lifestyle in which your job drives your lifestyle instead of the other way around. Say no to the 9-to-5. It's time for you to T-H-R-I-V-E-!

CHAPTER 3

Charting a New Course

Let's face it, most people are not thriving; they are 9-to-5ing—often because either they don't know of a better way or they are afraid to take the leap of faith. Can I just say it? Take the leap already. Jump in and embrace your life! It's the only one you have. Your life can thrive. It can! Maybe you're thinking, "Well, that sounds good, but what does *thrive* mean exactly?" Good question; let's take a look at what it means to *thrive*.

> **Main Entry: THRIVE**[1]
> Pronunciation: \thrīv\
> Function: intransitive verb
> Etymology: Middle English, from Old Norse thrīfask, probably reflexive of thrīfa to grasp
> Date: 13th century
> 1 : to grow vigorously : flourish
> 2 : to gain in wealth or possessions : prosper
> 3 : to progress toward or realize a goal despite or because of circumstances
> — thriv·er \thrī-vər\ noun

According to Merriam-Webster, "thriving" is a word that has been in existence since the 1400s. It may be a coincidence, but I was struck by the fact that the word originated in Old Norse, the extinct language of Scandinavia, where today thriving is a way of life. Survey after survey shines the light on this region as the one with the happiest citizens on Earth. Perhaps thriving has been embedded in their culture for generations; they reach out and "grasp" it as the etymology dictates. In other words, they take hold of their dreams in a very literal sense.

What is it that keeps any one of us from grabbing hold of opportunities to turn our own lives around? The answer may be that we stay stuck because we think about change as one giant step out of our comfort zone into an unfamiliar reality. In truth, however, change is usually a series of small, manageable steps that over time guides us toward a new reality. Many people view the phrase *positive change* as an oxymoron that pushes and pulls them in opposite directions, unable to move ahead because they are afraid of what might be up ahead. This push-pull struggle can cause them to stagnate and miss out on, well, their lives! If you are feeling indecisive about whether to stay put or shrug off your old 9-to-5 lifestyle, my advice to you is to take a chance. Simply open your mind.

This departure from the 9-to-5 lifestyle that you know so well will require a complete paradigm shift away from "surviving" with an eye on "thriving," so consider yourself forewarned. But you can make this positive change happen in your life. You can take small steps toward greatness and use stepping stones, which are small changes made with clear outcomes that lead you in a positive direction. Make the transition from a just-get-by mentality to a set-my-sights-high mentality in which anything you can imagine can be yours if you put your mind to it.

If a fear of failure is holding you back, think about how scary it would be to instead waste your life shackled to the 9-to-5 lifestyle. Know that you will undoubtedly face a number of small failures along the way, just like everybody else. So just accept the fear and move on. You can let fear define your life, or you can conquer it and redefine yourself through it. Rewrite history—today! Chart a new course for your life and set sail toward a bright future.

The Business of Navigating

Have you ever charted a course on a map while you were out in the open water? If you own a boat, you may have done this many times. Sea captains do this every day in order to navigate their ships from Point A to Point B. I remember working on that cruise ship that was circumnavigating the globe (described in the previous chapter). We were all floating around in the middle of the high seas with no land in sight for days. I wondered how on Earth the captain knew where we were on the map when there was only ocean and clouds for as far as the eye could see.

One day I went on a tour of the ship's bridge, which was filled with fancy GPS (global positioning system) equipment that worked very much like the Garmin or TomTom devices on the dashboard in so many of our cars today. However, if your GPS device is like mine, it has probably lead you astray at least once. The same is true of the GPS equipment on today's huge ocean cruise ships; even all of that fancy equipment can fail and cause the ship to arrive at the wrong destination. So how does a captain double-check the GPS directions while out there in the middle of the open water? He puts the 2nd Mate in charge of plotting the course by hand.

The duties of the 2nd Mate, in part, are to plot each leg of the journey from Point A to Point B on a nautical map well in advance of the journey. Then once at sea, the 2nd Mate regularly confirms that the ship is on course and suggests repositioning instructions to the captain when necessary. The 2nd Mate uses age-old seafaring techniques and tools such as identifying fixed objects in the sky (the sun or stars), on land when available (coastal shorelines), and at sea (the horizon) as reference points. Then, using a sextant, the 2nd Mate plots the ship's location on the nautical map and compares it to the course charted prior to the voyage. This process all sounds very calculated and straightforward, but navigating isn't always easy. Currents, tides, winds, and unexpected storms can throw the ship off course at a moment's notice. Sometimes the changes in direction are monumental, but the more dangerous changes are the subtle, unrecognized movements away from the destination that happen over a long period of time.

Beware of Subtle Changes

This business of navigating is also a constant in our own everyday lives back here on land in the 9-to-5 work world. At times we float around, unsure of our direction. We struggle to get our bearings. When our careers go off track, we look to the Internet and other forms of technology to help guide us in the right direction. We look to those timeless, fixed markers of so-called success—such as money, power, and recognition—to set our course and steer us in that direction. However, so many of us still lose our way; after all, navigating our careers is not a simple task. The process is quite complex, with pressures and responsibilities all pushing and pulling us in different directions and causing us to go off track at times. For most people it is those subtle career changes that take them off course and steer them in directions they never intended. Have any of the following scenarios ever happened to you?

- When you graduated from school, were you planning to pursue a career in one field but took the first job that came along as a "temporary" measure and now look back years later only to realize that your first job out of the gate defined your career?

- Did your boss change your job responsibilities at one point in time—for example, adding bookkeeping—and years later you now realize that those duties lead you to land the next few jobs and ultimately changed your career into something completely different, such as becoming a bookkeeper?

- Have you ever taken on a part-time job simply to bring in some extra money for your household to cover luxuries or to bridge a small gap in your expenses only to have your spouse fall ill or become injured? Did that part-time job suddenly turn into a full-time career position out of necessity instead of as a calculated career move?

These and many other examples not listed here can take your career in a new and unintended direction. The small movements to and fro, forward and backward add up over time and gradually may lead you to an unintended destination such as a desk located somewhere in a sea of cubicles on the 23rd floor of a rundown building or standing for hours by the cash register at a local retail store. And before long, you are lost in the rat race.

Set Sail on Your Journey

While the saying goes that all those who wander are not lost, let's face it—some of them are. Are you one of them? Do you feel like your career is adrift? Are you looking for some direction? To chart a course in the right direction, whatever it may be, you simply need to learn how to navigate. The word *navigate* in Latin means "to set sail," and so at this moment, you can think of yourself as setting sail in the direction of your career horizon.

To get started you need to know three things, as any good sailor will tell you:

1. Where you are starting from

2. Where you are going to

3. The resources you have on hand to help you get from Point A to Point B

The course you travel may not be a straight line from A to B, but how many of life's journeys are? You may misjudge your starting point or the correct destination for yourself along the career spectrum, but rest assured that the first rule of navigation both at sea and here in the work world is that "all navigators make mistakes."[2] To get your bearings, begin by triangulating the following three important reference points:

1. **Your emotional state:** Are you emotionally ready and able to take on a career change? Would you like to leap out and begin doing work that is completely different from what your current skill set dictates, or would you like to take those skills and simply make subtle changes about how you apply them? Dig deep and find the courage to take your life in a new and exciting direction.

2. **The state of your physical health:** Can you handle the nervousness, anxiety, and plain old hard labor that often coincides with a new business startup process? Do you have any medical conditions, such as a heart condition or high blood pressure, that warrant careful consideration as you look ahead? You can make changes in small, manageable steps in order to balance your health with your dreams; go for it!

3. **The state of your finances:** Do you need to be conservative, or can you literally afford to take some big risks? Whatever your financial state, you can make The 9-to-5 Cure work for you! The strategy described in this book can cost as much or as little as you choose to invest in the startup process. You are in complete control.

As you begin to think about each of these three important reference points for this journey toward a new career paradigm, it's time to expand your vision beyond a few generalizations about the career you *really* want. Let's get specific. Let's map out your goals; let's get a vision for your life.

A Vision for Your Life

Visualization is so powerful; in my estimation it is the *most* powerful career preparation tool available. After all, career preparation is an inside job. Although people in your life may make suggestions or demands about how you should manage your career, ultimately only you know what will fulfill your heart's desire. The idea of *visualization* is to deliberately and carefully craft an objective and then focus your energy and thoughts on that goal in order to achieve it.

We humans are complicated creatures; we juggle so many competing priorities. Our lives are an intertwining of various priorities, responsibilities, hopes, dreams, and needs, and we are charged with sorting and arranging them to align with the vision in our minds. This process can be messy business, and the thing is, no one else can do it for us. Maria Shriver addressed this point with new college graduates during a commencement speech years ago by saying, "Your life is like a mosaic, a puzzle. You have to figure out where the pieces go and put them together for yourself."[3]

> **Explore an Array of Resources**
>
> Visualization can take many forms, both general and specific in nature. Numerous books and DVDs are available to teach you how to condition your mind for good results. My favorite resource, *The Secret* by Rhonda Byrne, is available in print and on DVD.

But many people have been so busy just surviving their lives that the big picture, the vision, has gone fuzzy or disappeared altogether. Bringing this vision back into focus through regular practice is the starting point of truly navigating toward your dreams, in your career and in the bigger picture.

Map Out Your Goals

The magic of visioning occurs over time; good ideas need to simmer. For example, I have been editing a simple goal sheet since childhood. Each year I add new aspirations, both big and small, to the list and check off others that have been completed. And once in a great while, I cross off goals that no longer align with my long-term vision. Throughout the year, whenever I feel like I'm adrift in any of the four fundamental areas of career, education, relationships, and finances, I refer back to that goal sheet to identify the next item on my list of priorities. Writing down each goal helps make it more concrete. I feel more committed to the goal when I see it in writing, a phenomenon that many studies have proven to be true.

Take some time to reflect on the sample goal sheet included here. Then, fill it in as an initial draft; you can freely edit this sheet at any time in the future. As you work through this important exercise, here are a few things to keep in mind:

- **Goal statements should contain action verbs.** Goal statements that are merely a collection of nouns and adjectives are not a call to action, challenging you to accomplish your goals. Instead, begin your statements with action verbs such as *speak, publish, learn, plan,* and *save.* In other words, instead of a goal being written as "magazine article," make it specific and action oriented, such as, "Publish an article in *Wired* magazine." Set your sights high; challenge yourself!

- **Goals should be quantifiable.** You must be able to know when you accomplish the task at hand; otherwise, the goal statement is of little value. For example, if your goal statement is "Save money for Web site design course," that means that saving a penny satisfies your stated goal. However, the statement "Save $750 for Web site design course" is quantifiable and allows you to know when you reach the goal.

- **Goals should have no boundaries.** Goals need not be limited only to what you *know* you can accomplish (although there should be many of those on the list). Set your sites higher than you ever imagined; dare to set a goal that is seemingly impossible. As Walt Disney once said, "It's kind of fun to do the impossible."

PRELIMINARY GOAL SHEET

CAREER	EDUCATION
Publish an article in *Wired* magazine	Learn the fundamentals of Photoshop

RELATIONSHIPS	FINANCES
Plan a cabin getaway with the kids	Save $750 for Web site design course

How does your initial goal sheet look? Wait, don't tell me! It's a private account, for your eyes only, so go ahead and list whatever it is that really matters to you without worrying about how anyone else will judge it. There are no right or wrong answers. There is no magic number of goals you must maintain or account for. The goal sheet is a completely organic representation of your vision, your dreams.

Develop Goals That Energize You

How do you feel when you look at your goal sheet? Each time I look at mine, I become reenergized and imagine what it would be like to accomplish one or all of these goals. For example, a few years ago one of my goals was to write a newspaper column. Each time I looked at that goal, I imagined pitching my ideas to editors, having an editor hire me, working on drafts, and seeing my writing in print. The dream invigorated me, which fueled my action plan. It was those moments of visioning that gave me both new excitement and new ideas about how to make my goal a reality.

The creative freedom to dream without anyone else passing judgment about the ideas that surface is powerful. Have you ever had a great idea while you were in the shower? I think it is based on a similar principle of creative license to think freely. Let me reiterate a call to action that I learned from the inspirational Joel Osteen, "Get a vision for your life!" Make it your own and really own what you make it.

CHANGE IS GOOD

The framework you develop for your goals will change over time. This transformation is completely normal and, in fact, is a sign of progress. After all, with each new success or failure you will want to shape your vision based on your experience in order to attain your goals or reach new heights. To get started I suggest that you set aside as much time as you can in one single day to develop your initial vision. Find a place far away from your everyday life, far away from people or noise. Be still. Think. Dream. Imagine. Vision!

What works for me is going away each year on my birthday to a place where I can be in nature and have no concerns about the time. I make arrangements in advance and protect my time that day from all other commitments. I have been doing this for about twenty years; it is my annual "vision quest" of sorts. A mentor suggested this idea to me just after high school. He learned this ritual from local people while living in Liberia as a teacher. It is powerful, magical, and simple.

And, hey, if you think that no one else in the business world is doing this, consider that Bill Gates of Microsoft has done something just like this each year since 1994; he calls it "Think Week."[4] He uses the time for business purposes, to read, and to reflect and think about the future. If the success of Microsoft is any indication, this technique is worth a try.

Revisit Your Goals Periodically

What are you waiting for? Go away as soon as you can and begin reworking the preliminary goal sheet you created, only this time really get in the zone, away from any distractions. Then revisit it periodically in the months ahead and plan for a complete overhaul each year on a specific date, perhaps on *your* birthday. Last year I drove to a monastery and spent the day high in the wooded hills on the surrounding property. It was quiet, the view was spectacular, and I felt inspired. Choose a location near you that offers little distraction and inspires you. Turn off your cell phone, computer, and any other device that allows others to interact with you. Once you find an inspirational location, start reflecting, evaluating, brainstorming, and adjusting your goals for the year ahead.

Consider purchasing a journal dedicated to this ongoing project. This journal is a great place to brainstorm, reflect, and look ahead. I do all of this in the form of a letter that I write to myself each year. The letter idea may sound odd at first, but quite honestly it is my favorite part of this annual ritual. I write about the past year, how I feel about it, and what I would like to see happen in the coming year. Over the course of twenty years, I have created a healthy collection of letters that reflect how I feel about my career, my relationships, finances, education, and more. I enjoy having all of these important thoughts in one place, cataloging my progress and setbacks over time. Plus, I find it interesting to see how my priorities have changed from year to year and how some goals that seemed paramount five or ten years ago now seem trivial, even laughable.

Although purchasing a journal is not necessary, it is critical to keep all of your notes in one location, such as a file folder or loose-leaf binder. The perspective that a collection of notes provides over time, even over the course of a single year, can be highly instructional.

Once you finish crafting your goal sheet and perhaps a journal entry for the year, type the most meaningful goals on your sheet in list format and place it in a location where you can readily see it daily. This list represents

> **Dare to Daydream**
>
> Consider creating a theme for each new year to help shape your vision (Celebration or Expansion, for example). This really can add life to your ideas and can bind the individual goals on each list in a meaningful way. Similarly, if there is a song that resonates with how you feel about the coming year, find a copy of it for your MP3 player and play it in the background to help get yourself in the zone. If you feel intimidated by the task of setting off to create this goal sheet, let me share with you some sage advice that I received when I was getting started: just daydream a little. Give yourself permission to revert to the childhood activity of dreaming about what-if.

the vision you have for your soon-to-be-thriving self, and you want to keep these goals at the forefront of your mind to remain committed to them.

One of the many benefits of visioning is the newfound confidence that springs forth from having a goal in mind. Your vision is a roadmap that guides you in the direction of your dreams. Once you chart a course for your career and your life and then begin taking steps in that direction, you begin to build momentum. One success leads to another. And with each new success comes more confidence, and with more confidence, more successes readily spring forth. The momentum that builds is astounding.

As you begin to progress rapidly toward your goal, you may find that your vision expands or takes new direction. What you never before thought was possible is suddenly a reality, and that gives you the courage to dream an even bigger dream. This confidence is one of the building blocks of a successfully thriving person. Have the courage to develop a vision for your career and see it through to fruition. In the next chapter, you'll see how The 9-to-5 Cure can help make your dreams a reality.

> **Concentrate on the Present**
>
> Be sure to write your journal entry for the present year before reviewing entries from previous years. Doing so can adversely affect your feelings and emotions about the present year in comparison or simply rouse emotions that are counterproductive to the task at hand.

Endnotes

[1] *Merriam-Webster Online*, s.v. "Thrive," www.merriam-webster.com/dictionary/Thrive (accessed August 30, 2010).

[2] *Wikipedia*, s.v. "Second Mate," http://en.wikipedia.org/wiki/Second_Mate (accessed August 30, 2010).

[3] Maria Shriver, *Ten Things I Wish I'd Known Before I Went Out into The Real World* (New York: Warner Books, 2000), 67.

[4] Bill Gates, "How I Work: Bill Gates," *Fortune*, April 7, 2006, http://money.cnn.com/2006/03/30/news/newsmakers/gates_howiwork_fortune (accessed September 2, 2010).

CHAPTER 4

The 9-to-5 Cure Equation

Cure is a powerful word. It evokes images of medical miracle drugs, such as penicillin, that end epidemics or of people who are disabled in some way and who are suddenly restored to full health. These events are life altering, changing the course of a person's future forever in a positive way.

Now considering all of that, the thought of labeling my strategy a "cure" was intimidating at first blush. However, it is exactly the right word to describe the career strategy that I am about to share with you. My cure is, in fact, one that can be "life altering, changing the course of a person's future forever in a positive way." And it's funny, but when I was researching the possibility of using the word *cure,* I opened the dictionary with expectations of references to medical examples but was pleasantly surprised to discover that the definition referenced a usage example that was employment related:

> **Main Entry: cure**[1]
> Pronunciation: \ kyu r\
> Function: noun
> Etymology: Middle English, from Anglo-French, from Medieval Latin & Latin; Medieval Latin cura, cure of souls, from Latin, care
> Date: 14th century
> 1 : a complete or permanent solution or remedy <seeking a cure for unemployment>

You see, even Merriam-Webster believes there is a *cure* for your career woes! So, with that, let's get down to the business of discussing the 9-to-5 Cure Equation, a formula for career success.

Solving the 9-to-5 Cure Equation

The 9-to-5 Cure Equation could save your life—literally! It could save you from working your life away without any time available to spend on the other things that *also* matter to you. It could be the difference between thirty-plus years in the rat race or a lifetime of relatively effortless balance. It could alter how your children and grandchildren think about "work" as they grow older. It could liberate you from the bondage of the 9-to-5 lifestyle and usher in a new era of personal freedom into your life. I want that for you.

Let's dive in and take a look at the equation in its entirety:

THE 9-TO-5 CURE EQUATION

Lifestyle Design + The Patchwork Principle = The 9-to-5 Cure

or

Quality of Life + Enjoyable Work in Abundance = The 9-to-5 Cure

I've structured this book around the two fundamental parts of the 9-to-5 Cure Equation. First, I talk about how to live the life of your dreams by defining and exploring the concept of Lifestyle Design in Chapter 6, "The Framework—Lifestyle Design," including what it means, why it matters to you, and how it can shape your career. I also describe how it can set the tone for everything in your personal life and everything work related, from the jobs you accept to the hours you keep. You will work through practical exercises that yield information you can apply directly to your career endeavors going forward.

Then, in Chapter 8, "A New Strategy—The Patchwork Principle," I describe the Patchwork Principle, which is an entrepreneurial career strategy that has much to offer, including doing work that you love on your own terms, in your own time, and at a rate that you choose. Until then, I provide the second line of the equation as a simple translation of these concepts into everyday terms to give you a sense of what lies ahead.

❦

It may sound impossible to you right now. In fact, I'm hoping that you are a little bit skeptical at this juncture because that disbelief will make it all the more exciting when you reach the end of the book and think to yourself, "Hey! I can do this!" And you can. You can!

Let's get started by jumping right into the next section of the book, which details the fundamentals of Lifestyle Design within the context of the 9-to-5 Cure.

[1] *Merriam-Webster Online*, s.v. "Cure," www.merriam-webster.com/dictionary/cure (accessed July 6, 2010).

PART II

Live the Life of Your Dreams

CHAPTER 5

Career Myopia and Other Misperceptions

Recently I read an article about how myopia in children is growing at an alarming rate. Myopia is a structural problem that develops in the eye and causes objects in close proximity to appear clear while those in the distance appear blurry, commonly known as *nearsightedness*. According to this article, a growing number of children are developing myopia because of their constant use of computers and other electronic gadgets that require focusing on objects at a close range, while their distance vision, which is used in activities such as outdoor play, is diminishing.[1] The facts of the article are alarming for parents of young children, but the story also seems to be a great metaphor for something that I call *career myopia*.

Career Myopia: Putting Work in Perspective

If you didn't already know, American workers suffer from *career myopia*, which is a loss of function in our imagination resulting from an inordinate amount of time spent focusing on our work life. We lose the ability to even visualize the big picture for lack of exercising those muscles in our imagination. As a result, our field of vision narrows, and the big picture becomes fuzzy. We lose sight of our dreams and instead fixate on merely *surviving* instead of *thriving*.

If you don't believe me, just watch an episode of NBC's hit show *The Office*. The sitcom is incredibly popular because it allows millions of viewers each week to commiserate about the drudgery of work. There are the incompetent annoying boss and the quirky employees, the pointless meetings, and the endless infighting and mindless gossip that must be endured in the workplace setting for at least forty hours each week. We laugh at the program because it is a cathartic release. But instead of laughing at the drudgery that we commit ourselves to day in and day out, we should be asking ourselves an important question: *Why? Why do we all so readily accept this as the only way to spend the prime days of our lives?* The answer is simple: We do so because we must—or so we think.

Aside from a few career renegades, we are conditioned to accept this situation as our way of life; mind-numbing work that dominates our days is the norm. Don't get me wrong; work matters, but the bigger picture matters more! So often it takes a life-changing crisis to put things in perspective, but I beg of you, don't wait for a crisis. Create your own wake-up call. Remind yourself of the big picture—life—and put work into proper perspective. Let's do that right now.

How Long You Live and Work

Let's take a look at work relative to the proverbial *big picture*. Here are some sobering statistics:

> The average life cycle for someone born in 1970 is 70 years,[2] or 25,550 days.
>
> The average *career* life cycle is 30 years, or 7,200 work days.
>
> That means you work for approximately 43 percent of your life!

Unfortunately, that's a best-case scenario—most people work longer than 30 years. If you begin working when you are 20 years old, for example, retiring 30 years later (at age 50) would mean that you would be ineligible for full Social Security benefits for another 17 years and would need to have saved enough money to live for presumably many more decades. Therefore, most people do not retire until they can draw all or most of their Social Security benefits. So let's look at the realistic scenario:

> A typical career life cycle is 47 years (an average career life cycle of 30 years plus 17 additional years to qualify for Social Security benefits), or 11,280 work days.
>
> That means you would work for approximately 67 percent of your life!

Of course the typical worker then would collect full benefits at age 67 and die 3 years or 1,095 days later at age 70, according to U.S. Government life expectancy data.

How Much You Really Live During Your Working Career

Perhaps the statistics about how much Americans work are not surprising to you. After all, the numbers reflect what we have all come to accept as our shared reality. We work—a lot. Perhaps not as much as people in a few other countries, but we certainly don't lead the charts in terms of how much we truly "live" either.

So, how much do Americans actually "live" during their working careers? How many days are spent away from workplace responsibilities and instead are dedicated to leisurely pursuits? In other words, how much time does the typical American lifestyle allow for what truly matters? Let's answer those questions by taking a look at the facts:

> The average worker has 16 days of paid holiday and vacation leave each year of their career[3] to pursue their wildest dreams, which is 752 days total over the course of 47 years of work.

> However, the average worker *voluntarily* relinquishes 4 of the 16 days of paid leave *each* year because they feel that there is too much work to do, that the company could not function without them, or that a leave of absence may jeopardize their job. The loss of these 4 days each year subtracts 25 percent from the total amount of paid leave that workers take over the course of their lifetime, bringing the total number of vacation days in a lifetime to 564 days.[4]

> Because 6 of these 12 days off each year are holidays, as opposed to flexible time off, only 6 of the remaining days of each year are actual at-will vacation days.

> Those 6 days multiplied by 47 years of service brings the grand total of at-will leave for a lifetime to 282 days, or approximately 9 months. (In fairness, however, the average worker does have an additional three full years after retirement but before death to pursue their passion for travel and leisure, if their health and finances allow for it.)

> So the average American worker spends a **total of 9 months** between the ages of 20 and 67 enjoying freedom that is otherwise only associated with weekends or unimaginable wealth.

However, that data appears to be changing, according to a study in a recent issue of *Harvard Business Review* which found that "47 percent of Boomers—whose median age is currently 54—see themselves as mid-career,"[5] due in part to financial losses associated with poorly performing investments and other important factors that resulted from a significant decline in the U.S. economy. This study seems to imply that working until one is physically unable to is what about half of Boomers expect to do. In fact, Sun Life Financial maintains something called the *Unretirement Index*, which tracks the number of people who continue to work after becoming eligible for full retirement benefits. Sun found that record numbers of Americans past age 67 plan to work full time out of uncertainty about their investments and current economic necessity.[6]

How depressing. Is that really what you want for *your* life? A work-until-you-die mentality? Is that the example you really want to model for your children to follow as they grow older? America, what are we doing with our lives? Well, before I get too carried away, let me mention that Americans are neither the only nor the biggest offenders of the work-before-life mindset.

How the World Works

If you think Americans work a lot, take a look at the following chart, which shows the findings from a comparative survey of the work year in thirty countries. The broad brushstrokes of the findings seem to demonstrate that while the Czech Republic, Greece, Hungary, Korea, and Poland are seemingly above average when it comes to the number of hours workers spend on the job each year, the countries of France, Germany, Luxembourg, The Netherlands, Norway, and Sweden are well below it. Korea stands out as the country with the most demanding work year by far.

Employees living in countries with a relatively shorter work year clocked approximately 1,400 hours each year, while those living in countries on the other end of the spectrum clocked closer to 2,000 hours. Korea has the absolute longest work year, with employees working 2,316 hours each year, or 46.6 hours weekly. Canada claims the title of "exactly average" at 1,736 hours, and the United States comes within range at 1,794 total hours.

These statistics look at the work year, but how about zooming in for a closer look at the work *week?* How many hours do employees in other countries clock each week on average? Although the Netherlands can boast a light schedule of just 30-hour weeks, the worldwide average is just over 38, which again places the 40-hour American work week well within range and amounts to a seemingly reasonable amount of time dedicated to laboring.

Average Hours Worked Per Year*

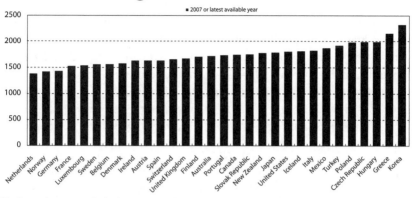

* This figure does not include data on several major countries, most notably China and India, because it is representative of only OECD member countries.

Source: OECD Factbook 2009.[7]

Now if we were all living in Korea and working their 46-hour weeks, perhaps we would have reason to protest, but alas—little did you know that your work schedule was so luxurious comparatively!

So how about the average work *day* in comparison to other countries around the world? We of course withstand the 9-to-5 work day in our American society. However, consider this excerpt from *Forbes*, which provides a snapshot of the average day in a Korean worker's life:

> If you thought you worked long hours, consider 39-year-old Lee from South Korea. A civil servant at the ministry of agriculture and fisheries, Lee gets up at 5:30 a.m. every day, gets dressed, and makes a two-hour commute into Seoul to start work at 8:30 a.m. After sitting at a computer for most of the day, Lee typically gets out the door at 9 p.m., or even later.
>
> By the time he gets home, it's just a matter of jumping in the shower and collapsing into bed before starting the whole routine all over again about four hours later. This happens six days a week and throughout almost all of the year, as Lee gets just three days of vacation. That's right. Three days.
>
> And did we mention Lee has a wife and three teenage kids? "I get to see them for 10 or 15 minutes a week, and then just on the weekend," he says of his children before adding that, on weekends, he usually gets interrupted to go to the office.[8]

Unbelievably, because work is ingrained so deeply in Korean society, its citizens are willing to clock 600 *more* work hours each year than employees in the United States.[9] Therefore, it is not surprising that both Korea and the United States, incidentally, never make it onto the *Forbes'* list of countries with the happiest citizens. Those countries that consistently do—Denmark, Finland, and the Netherlands—are also those countries either with the shortest work year or among the shortest.[10] But less work is not always an indicator of happiness in and of itself, as any unemployed person can tell you. In fact, unemployment results in a significantly lower level of happiness as many scientific studies have proven, pointlessly I imagine.

So where are we then? We know that we want to be somewhere on the employment spectrum between unemployed and overworked. However, Americans are not slaving away in comparison to workers in some other countries, and yet still we feel consumed by our 9-to-5 lifestyle. What is the missing link? The answer: freedom.

The No-Vacation Nation

Ironically, in a country like America where *freedom* is a word that resonates so strongly with its citizens, freedom is the very thing lacking in the 9-to-5 lifestyle. The big, unattainable dream for most of us is having the freedom to enjoy more time away from work to pursue leisure activities without jeopardizing our employment. Certainly we Americans are jealous of our European counterparts who are well known for long and leisurely periods of vacation that can total as much as six weeks of *additional* time off each year. To us, that amount of vacation time seems beyond our imagination; instead, we trudge along and await our six *days* of at-will vacation leave each year. In fact, America is what one study called a *no-vacation nation* relative to the rest of the world; here is an excerpt from that enlightening report:

> The United States is the only advanced economy in the world that does not guarantee its workers paid vacation. European countries establish legal rights to at least 20 days of paid vacation per year, with legal requirement of 25 and even 30 or more days in some countries. Australia and New Zealand both require employers to grant at least 20 vacation days per year; Canada and Japan mandate at least 10 paid days off. The gap between paid time off in the United States and the rest of the world is even larger if we include legally mandated paid holidays, where the United States offers none, but most of the rest of the world's rich countries offer between 5 and 13 paid holidays per year. In the

absence of government standards, almost one in four Americans have no paid vacation and no paid holidays.[11]

Now consider the reality that few Americans are fully aware of: We have a much different opinion about taking time off than many other countries in the world. Perhaps it hearkens back to the Industrial Revolution, but whatever the origin we are certainly behind the curve. In fact, we're off the charts, as shown in the following chart:

Mandatory Paid Vacation Days for Employees, Required by Federal Law

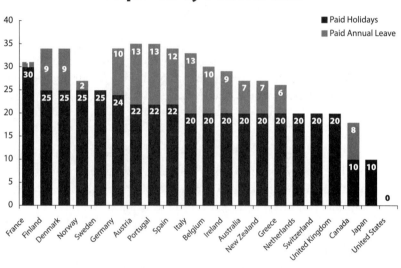

Source: No Vacation Nation. Rebecca Ray and John Schmitt. May 2007. CEPR: Center for Economic and Policy Research.

American workers are not legally guaranteed any paid vacation by law, unlike nearly every other modern economy on Earth. Zero. Despite the fact that our quality of life *is* most certainly connected with this coveted time off because it allows us the opportunity to pursue our interests, strengthen social bonds with our family and friends, and focus on personal development and identity formation separate from our work.[12] Somehow we Americans fit all of this into our six days of vacation a year. Or do we? As a nation we are most certainly not awash in happiness according to any number of polls and studies. The reasons are varied and complex, but one of the key factors to happiness that we so obviously lack in our 9-to-5 lifestyle is this freedom, or personal control, that leads to empowerment, which results in better coping skills and living more happily overall.[13]

The Deliberate Lifestyle

Are you thinking to yourself, "But what is the alternative? After all, I *do* have to earn a living." And to that I say, "Thank you for asking!" The alternative to your current 9-to-5 reality is deliberately designing your lifestyle, beginning with customized work weeks that ultimately create a made-to-order work year.

Would you like more than nine months off during the course of your lifetime? Of course you would! Okay then, how much exactly? What is the magic number? What number would make you feel free? What number would make you feel wealthy, rich with time? I urge you to give this some serious thought because ultimately that is the time you allot to really "live" your life. The amount of time you dedicate to work versus the amount of time you dedicate to leisure determines your overall so-called work-life balance, or lack thereof. How many weeks of vacation time in a calendar year would make you feel like you were able to really "live" your life? Seriously, think about it for a moment and write that number here:

_____ weeks of vacation each year

For me the magic number is 18. On average I take 18 weeks of vacation each year—and by the way, business is *still* booming. My career is undeniably on track and clients are clamoring to get me onto new projects even with the knowledge that I have a limited schedule of availability.

Contrary to popular belief, an organization *can* live without an employee for long periods of time, and the employee *can* enjoy job security in the interim if the expectations are clearly defined from the beginning. Also, my business has the potential for increase because, should there be a year when money is more important to me than free time, I can choose to open up additional days or weeks on my calendar.

But before we venture from our discussion about vacation time in order to escape work, let's spend a moment discussing vacation time specifically intended to improve our work that once was reserved for only a select few in American society but need not be anymore.

BALANCE IN CONTEXT

Have you heard about the concept of work-life balance? It's a concept founded with good intentions but is what I believe to be an erroneous term. For me the idea of work-life balance brings to mind images of a young, preteen girl poised on the end of an Olympic balance beam ready to begin the acrobatic routine of her lifetime. There is only a small margin of error; one wrong move spells disaster. She struggles to balance her work life (being a gymnast) with her personal life (being a scared eleven-year-old girl). It's all so stressful!

Balance. What does it really mean? What could it mean?

Within the context of this book, the word *balance* will be used to describe a lifestyle in which you determine what factors are relevant to you and to what extent you give each priority. In other words, there will be no balancing act, per se. Balance is not stifling one part of yourself in order to satisfy some other part. Nor is it settling for less because you have no other choice.

Although balance is traditionally composed of advice like "avoid unnecessary activities," such as watching television, chatting with the neighbors for too long, and so on, this book describes a different interpretation. In my view, balance means maximizing the time you spend on living and minimizing the time you spend on earning with the activities you choose to spend your time on being your own, free of judgment about whether it's a waste of time or not.

The Power of Time Off

The famous designer Stefan Sagmeister has deeply held beliefs about the power of taking time away from work to do what he calls "experiment" with new ideas, explore, and create. Every seven years he closes his high-profile studio in New York City for one full year in order to reignite his creative energy. In a talk he gave for TED Talks called "The Power of Time Off," Sagmeister explained that he initiated this year-long sabbatical idea after noticing that all his company's design ideas were beginning to look the same, for lack of creative rejuvenation.[14] He thinks about these periods of time off in a way that may provide a helpful new perspective for you as well, as you begin to entertain either a subtle or radical shift from your 9-to-5 mindset to a lifestyle by design.

Sagmeister's rationalization for taking time off is that it is simply borrowed time, a few years of retirement taken earlier in life in small segments. He essentially takes five years of his anticipated retirement and "intersperses" them, as he says, back into his working years to the benefit of his company and society at large. The illustration in his presentation was represented like this:[15]

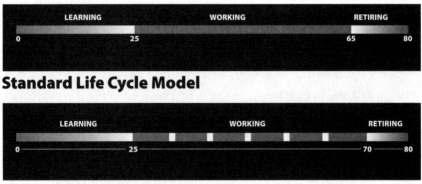

Standard Life Cycle Model

Interspersed Retirement Model

At first glance, in the preceding interspersed retirement model, the amount of time spent working appears to have lengthened whereas the amount of time in retirement appears to have been reduced. However, upon careful inspection, the color coding indicates that the amount of time spent in each category is exactly the same—only the sequence has been rearranged. It's a little bit of retirement right now (every seven years).

Is this a radical idea from which only an artist can benefit? No. Both 3M and Google allow their design engineers to take time off to pursue their own interests, and it pays off! Both Scotch Tape and Post-it Notes were the result of projects pursued by 3M employees during this free time.[16] Also, Google's Innovation Time Off policy for engineers encourages them to take one day off each week "so that they're free to work on what they're really passionate about," which has resulted in wonderful new ideas like Orkut and RechargeIt.[17]

One engineering manager at Google told ABC News that the "20 percent time," as it's called colloquially, gives people new freedoms for creativity. He said, "People who are given free time to think, without pressure, often see further down the road, because they're not focused on today's immediate problems. They can be more visionary." Also, the engineering manager points out, "When you're passionate about something and it's an idea you believe in, you're bound to work harder on it," and as a result, "just about all the good ideas here at Google have bubbled up from 20 percent time, or something like 20 percent time, where people have their own idea and run with it."[18]

Both 3M and Google do something similar to what Sagmeister, Inc., does, which is provide free time for creative thinking as a regular part of the employee's career cycle with the company. As you consider designing your own career lifestyle, consider the benefit of building in a regular period of time off in order to recharge and rejuvenate. Although you may think that you cannot afford to take any time off, perhaps that is the very key to your next breakthrough. Still, these examples are very counterculture. The idea of regular time off seems reserved only for a radical few corporations, but this is a misperception. Many organizations and professions revere the idea of time off and have done so for generations.

In academia, for example, the idea of taking a sabbatical is a long-held tradition among tenured professors who may request an extended leave of absence approximately every seven years in order to work on a project of interest to them, such as writing a book. However, the goal of this time off isn't "accomplishing"; instead, it is simply a time of resting the body, mind, and spirit, or "ceasing," the literal translation of the Latin *sabbaticus.*

This concept is also represented in other ancient cultures, including the Greek *sabbatikos* and Hebrew *Shabbat.* In Judaism there is a great deal of reference to sabbatical including the sabbatical year, a period of rest for the land from planting every seven years, and Jubilee, which celebrated a sevenfold-seven cycle whereby the seven years of rest had been observed seven times over a period of fifty years. This period of Jubilee was a time when all land was returned to its ancestral owners and Hebrew slaves who had chosen to remain in service after the biblical six-year maximum were released.[19]

What's my point? The point is that from the very beginning of time, taking regular periods of rest has been not only recommended but also *required* for the good of the people, nature, and the goods that were produced. The one holdover today that we enjoy from the biblical *Shabbat* refers to Sabbath, "a weekly period of rest," and is in fact the origin of the modern-day weekend that we all know and love.[20]

Time and Money in Abundance

You may be thinking that this is all well and good for a famous designer or a professor on paid leave who can afford to take long periods of time off, but what about the average person? This circles back to the big picture idea that is so troubling for the myopic masses. The question about taking time off is not, "Can you do it?" but instead, "What is holding you back from it?" The answer for most people is twofold: time and money.

As this book illustrates in the chapters ahead, you absolutely can enjoy regular periods of rest and relaxation as part of an entrepreneurial career model called the Patchwork Principle. We'll get to the business of earning and working in the second half of the book, but for now let me give you a preview: You can have time and money—both in abundance. When you are the boss and fully design your own work year, you can take a very short or a lengthy period of time off, based on your priorities. A leave of absence can be something as short as a few hours scheduled into your day to brainstorm or daydream, a day off to bike across the city, or a week off to attend a seminar series.

The 9-to-5 Cure begins with remedying your career myopia by focusing on the big picture and then diving into the Patchwork Principle, which is a business strategy that helps you find work that you enjoy in abundance. Are you ready to dive in and start developing a blueprint for your new life? Here we go!

Endnotes

[1] *Los Angeles Times,* "Booster Shots," December 14, 2009, blog, http://latimesblogs.latimes.com/booster_shots/2009/12/myopia-nearsightedness-trends.html (accessed September 1, 2010).

[2] U.S. National Center for Health Statistics, National Vital Statistics Report, "Expectation of Life at Birth," www.census.gov/compendia/statab/2010/tables/10s0102.pdf (accessed January 5, 2010).

[3] Stephanie Rosenbloom, "Please Don't Make Me Go on Vacation," *New York Times,* August 10, 2006, www.nytimes.com/2006/08/10/fashion/10vacation.html (accessed September 1, 2010).

[4] Kathy Gurchiek, "U.S. Workers Continue to Leave Vacation Unused," *HRMagazine,* August 1, 2006, www.allbusiness.com/sector-92-public-administration/administration-human/1191833-1.html (accessed September 1, 2010).

[5] Sylvia Ann Hewlett, "Reward Older Workers with What They Really Want," *Harvard Business Review,* September 4, 2009, blog http://blogs.hbr.org/hbr/hewlett/2009/09/salute_your_older_workers_this.html (accessed September 1, 2010).

[6] Sun Life Financial, January 20, 2009, www.sunlife.com/us/v/.

[7] OECD, "Economic, Environmental and Social Statistics," *OECD Factbook 2009,* www.sourceoecd.org/vl=1390616/cl=17/nw=1/rpsv/factbook/06/03/02/06-03-02-g1.htm (accessed September 1, 2010).

[8] Parmy Olsen, "The World's Hardest-Working Countries," *Forbes,* May 21, 2008, www.forbes.com/2008/05/21/labor-market-workforce-lead-citizen-cx_po_0521countries.html (accessed September 1, 2010).

[9] *Wikipedia*, s.v. "Working Time," http://en.wikipedia.org/wiki/Working_time#South_Korea_and_Japan (accessed September 1, 2010).

[10] Lauren Sherman, "World's Happiest Places," *Forbes*, May 5, 2009, www.forbes.com/2009/05/05/world-happiest-places-lifestyle-travel-world-happiest.html (accessed September 1, 2010).

[11] Rebecca Ray and John Schmitt, "No Vacation Nation," CEPR: Center for Economic and Policy Research (May 2007), report, 2, www.cepr.net/documents/publications/NoVacationNation_asofSeptember07.pdf (accessed September 2, 2010).

[12] Greg Richards, "Vacations and the Quality of Life: Patterns and Structures," *Journal of Business Research* 44, no. 3 (March 1999): 189–198.

[13] David Myers and Ed Diener, "Who Is Happy?" *Psychological Science* 6 no. 1 (January 1995): 10.

[14] Stefan Sagmeister, "The Power of Time Off," TED Conferences, October 2009, www.youtube.com/watch?v=MNuOmTQdFjA (accessed September 2, 2010).

[15] Stefan Sagmeister.

[16] Stefan Sagmeister.

[17] Google, "The Engineer's Life at Google," www.google.com/jobs/lifeatgoogle/englife (accessed September 2, 2010).

[18] Erin Hayes, "Google's 20 Percent Factor," *ABC News*, May 12, 2008, television interview, http://abcnews.go.com/Technology/story?id=4839327&page=1 (accessed September 2, 2010).

[19] Answers.com, s.v. "Sabbatical Year," www.answers.com/topic/sabbatical-year (accessed September 2, 2010).

[20] *Wikipedia*, s.v. "Shabbat (Talmud)," http://en.wikipedia.org/wiki/Shabbat_(Talmud) (accessed September 2, 2010).

The Framework—Lifestyle Design

As we begin to explore Lifestyle Design, the story of the Mexican fisherman (author unknown) is a good starting point for our discussion:

The Mexican Fisherman

An American investment banker was at the pier of a small coastal Mexican village when a small boat with just one fisherman docked. Inside the small boat were several large yellow fin tuna. The American complimented the Mexican on the quality of his fish and asked how long it took to catch them.

The Mexican replied, "Only a little while."

The American then asked why he didn't stay out longer and catch more fish.

The Mexican said he had enough to support his family's immediate needs.

The American then asked, "But what do you do with the rest of your time?"

The Mexican fisherman said, "I sleep late, fish a little, play with my children, take siesta with my wife, stroll into the village each evening, where I sip wine and play guitar with my amigos. I have a full and busy life."

The American scoffed, "I am a Harvard MBA and could help you. You should spend more time fishing and with the proceeds, buy a bigger boat. With the proceeds from the bigger boat, you could buy several boats, and eventually you would have a fleet of fishing boats. Instead of selling your catch to a middleman,

CHAPTER 6: THE FRAMEWORK—LIFESTYLE DESIGN

you would sell directly to the processor, eventually opening your own cannery. You would control the product, processing, and distribution. You would need to leave this small coastal fishing village and move to Mexico City, then LA, and eventually NYC, where you will run your expanding enterprise."

The Mexican fisherman asked, "But how long will this all take?"

To which the American replied, "15 to 20 years."

"But what then?"

The American laughed and said, "That's the best part. When the time is right…you would announce an IPO and sell your company stock to the public and become very rich. You would make millions."

"Millions…. Then what?"

The American said, "Then you would retire. Move to a small coastal fishing village, where you would sleep late, fish a little, play with your kids, take siesta with your wife, stroll to the village in the evenings, where you could sip wine and play your guitar with your amigos."[1]

This story captures the essence of the two fundamental and opposing perspectives about work on a continuum. On one end is the mindset of the typical 9-to-5 worker, preoccupied with earning in order to someday have the money available to afford time off to finally pursue his interests. On the other end of the continuum is the life-centered perspective, like the one put forth in this book, where making time available throughout one's life is paramount and guides all of the other core elements of life including career-related choices.

Earning is important to people on both ends of the continuum; the emphasis is simply different with the one more often focused on surviving and the other on thriving. Let's start by looking at the first half of the 9-to-5 Cure Equation—Lifestyle Design, which is a concept dedicated to factors related to quality of life—and then begin working through some practical exercises to determine what "quality of life" means to you in practical terms. Because the equation is central to your understanding of the 9-to-5 Cure, it is repeated here for your reference:

THE 9-TO-5 CURE EQUATION

Lifestyle Design + The Patchwork Principle = The 9-to-5 Cure

or

Quality of Life + Enjoyable Work in Abundance = The 9-to-5 Cure

An Introduction to Lifestyle Design

Lifestyle Design is a concept that I have been exploring and experimenting with for many years, but it was only when I sat down to write this book that I discovered Timothy Ferriss had coined the term and defined it as "escaping the 'deferred-life' plan," where instead of waiting until retirement to pursue your wildest dreams, you make life a priority over work—beginning right now.[2]

The term *Lifestyle Design* has become part of mainstream consciousness in recent years, but the concept has been part of the American culture for generations. Take, for example, the surfers that descended on Hawaii in the 1950s to ride the waves and live hand-to-mouth in order to follow their passion. That certainly was a Lifestyle Design that suited them, but in mainstream America it's what we typically think of as a fringe-of-society way of life.

Okay, how about a more mainstream example of Lifestyle Design? Let's look at an industry that is growing exponentially and the people who work in it: online universities. These virtual institutions of higher education are packing in students at a growth rate that outpaces brick-and-mortar campuses 2:1 for a number of reasons, with convenience topping the list. In 2007, 3.94 million students enrolled in at least one online course, and where there are students, there are professors.[3]

The duties and responsibilities of an online professor vary from institution to institution, so let's talk in general terms. What would your opinion be about the Lifestyle Design of a woman who quit her 9-to-5 job in the corporate world in order to accept a position as an online professor? You may think that it seems like a reasonable choice because there is prestige and mystique tied to the title of "Professor." Now what if I told you that she accepted that position so that she could backpack around the world with her laptop in tow in order to periodically log in to her classroom and teach? Would that change your judgment about this woman's Lifestyle Design? Perhaps.

I think this piece about seemingly unlimited travel or leisure or pursuit of our passion is what causes trouble. Those of us raised in the American society are not conditioned to accept it as normal or acceptable behavior because, quite frankly, if we were all running around pursuing our wildest dreams, who would fill those 9-to-5 jobs in office buildings, factories, and warehouses? Who would work at places like those portrayed in *The Office's* Dunder Mifflin if people had a chance to make the same money (or more) and live life on their own terms? No one, that's who. If every 9-to-5er rejected their current work life and instead embraced a form of employment like the one I describe, "Nobody would be left to round out the workforce and execute the business plan," as Bill Rancic, winner of Donald Trump's show *The Apprentice,* once said. However, is that really how you want to spend your life? Being a cog in the corporate machine? Of course not!

Lifestyle Design is about living life on your own terms by clearly defining what it is that really matters to you and then fitting important slices of your life into that bigger picture, a piece of which includes making a satisfactory amount of money on a regular basis. Lifestyle by design doesn't have to be about travel. In fact, for most people it has nothing to do with travel. But what it does always refer to is the unique freedom to work when, where, and with whomever you choose. It is the greatest gift you can give yourself.

But what would your ideal work year look like if you *could* change your routine? Would you work a different schedule during the weekdays? Or during the winter months? How would it look different? What goals would you prioritize and construct your schedule around? In the next section, you will start building a foundation for your ideal lifestyle by design by mapping out your ideal work year.

Your Ideal Work Year

Let's define what the ideal work year looks like for you—separate from the financial gain associated with it. Let's just focus on what "perfect" looks and feels like for you in this initial section. As you read through each workday component, jot down some notes, and then we'll pull them all together.

Okay, let's get in the zone! During this brief exercise, I want you to forget about the realities of the 9-to-5 world that you know all too well. Instead, give yourself permission to dream a little, no holds barred. If money wasn't a factor and you were going to design an ideal work year, what would it look like? Now, before we go any further, I have to let you know I realize that money *is* a factor—an important one! For now, though, let's agree to just walk through this visualization and see what you come up with. You might be surprised.

EXERCISE: IF ONLY I HAD MORE TIME

Get in touch with all of the times you have thought about your 9-to-5 work year and said to yourself, "If only I had more time, I would _____ *(fill in the blank)*." This is *that* moment. I want you to go to the land of "IF ONLY!" for the duration of the following brief exercise and answer these questions while you are in that state of mind. Think about how you would structure your work year in order to make time for the other priorities in your life.

FREQUENCY

How many days of the week would you *choose* to work in a typical week if you could determine this for yourself? Would it be Monday–Friday, only Monday-Wednesday-Friday, only Tuesday and Thursday, only weekends, or some other combination? Would the days you work vary from week to week based on another priority in your life? Would the hours vary by season (for example, summer hours are different from winter hours)?

Write About It

_____

_____

_____

DURATION

How many hours would you work on a typical workday? Would you work two-hour days? Eight-hour days? Four-hour days? How many hours would you aim for in a given week? Forty hours? More? Less? When you take money out of the equation, what is it about the amount of work each day or each week that matters most to you?

Write About It

_____

_____

_____

PACE

Would your workday be fast-paced or slow and steady? Would you work in short segments throughout the workday or straight through? What words come to mind when you think of the pace you would like to set for yourself during a typical workday?

Write About It

_____

_____

_____

CONSISTENCY

How many weeks of each month would you work? How many total weeks would you work each year? What would determine which weeks or months you worked or didn't? In a calendar year, what important events in your personal life would you give priority?

Write About It

_____

_____

_____

Congratulations! You have done what few adults in the world ever take time to do—think about how they would ideally like to work, which ultimately translates into how they would like to live. This is a great first step toward creating the ultimate product of Lifestyle Design, which is your own lifestyle by design.

EXERCISE: PUTTING IT ALL TOGETHER, MAD LIB STYLE

Now let's put all your ideas together and fill out a Mad Lib about your ideal work year. Using your notes from the preceding exercise, fill in the following blanks. (Seriously! Why does figuring things out always have to be so dry and boring?)

In one word, I would describe my ideal work year as

_____! I work a total of _____

  (adjective)   (number)

days during a regular workweek, for _____

                                            (number)

hours a day. I work in <u>short/long</u> stretches during the

                                    (circle one)

workday because it allows me to _____ and

                                        (verb)

_____, which makes me feel _____.

    (verb)   (adjective)

The two most important priorities in my life that I

schedule work around are _____ and

                                  (noun)

_____. The pace of my workday would best be

    (noun)

described as _____ and _____.

              (adjective)   (adjective)

My workdays are primarily <u>weekdays/weekends</u>. I work an

                                  (circle one)

average of _____ weeks per month, but

               (number)

accounting for periods of vacation and other priori-

ties in my life over a twelve-month period, that totals

_____ weeks of work per year. That means I

   (number)

set aside personal and vacation time each year that

totals _____ <u>days/weeks/months</u>.

       (number)   (circle one)

Having that amount of time off makes me feel

_____! Living the ideal work year gives me
(adjective)

the freedom to _____ and _____.
(verb)   (verb)

This Lifestyle Design makes me feel _____ of
(adjective)

my career and _____ of myself.
(adjective)

Okay, you did the work; now take a moment to read through the way you described your ideal work year. Did you notice that the Mad Lib was written in the present tense? There is a reason. This Mad Lib provides a blueprint for what you want your ideal work year to feel like from the number of hours per day to the pace of the day, the week, the month, and ultimately the year. This template can serve as your script of how things *will* be instead of what they might be "if only." It's a starting point—good work! You're on your way.

Your Ideal Career

Think back to your senior year of high school. Was it an action-packed year? Traditionally that momentous year is brimming with excitement. There are homecoming games to win. Senior pictures to be taken. Prom dresses and tuxedos to be found. Yearbook committee members to be charmed. And, oh yes, career decisions to be made. For some, high school commencement means the end of formal education and the beginning of working life. For others, it is a milestone en route to vocational training. For yet others, graduation is a springboard into higher education.

No matter what avenue you chose, eventually you ended up in the work world for better or for worse. During your senior year, you likely made decisions that were defining moments in your life, decisions that affected the path your career took, either in big or small ways. Back then, looking at the sea of potential career paths and trying to make an educated decision was challenging on some level simply because you lacked life experience. That isn't the case anymore. Now you are a veteran of the work world and have a pretty good idea about which career fields you may or may not have an interest in. Likewise, you know which ones likely are the most demanding, which pay better than others, and so on.

Back then you had to blindly make career decisions based on the advice of books, guidance counselors, and family members. Today you can make these decisions for yourself based on life experience. Ask yourself the following questions:

- What do you really *want* to do?
- What would you do if money were not a concern?
- What is it that you like to do? Do you know?

Of course you do! Although I know so many people who don't think they do. Perhaps this is because so many people believe that they have to figure out how what they love will translate into money or a specific job title before they even consider it as a viable career choice, a classic example of putting the cart before the horse that limits our thinking. What is the solution? Simply think about what you enjoy doing; that's it. We'll talk about this in greater detail as we dive headlong into the fundamentals of the Patchwork Principle in Chapter 8, "A New Strategy—The Patchwork Principle."

Your Ideal Workplace

Location! Location! Location! In real estate and in the work world, your location matters; it can affect everything else in your life across the board, including how you feel about yourself, your lifestyle, and how others perceive you. It's time to think about *where* in the world you would like to work. Seriously, think about it: Where would you like to work?

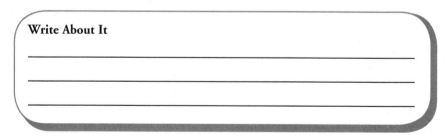

Write About It

_____

_____

_____

One of the fabulous features of working within the paradigm of the Patchwork Principle is that you and you alone determine where you work. And let's face it; everyone has a different idea of what the ideal location is. For the stay-at-home parent, reporting to an office sounds heavenly. To someone trapped in cubicle nation, working from a home office is the dream. What is your ideal location? Let's look at three sought-after location scenarios: working from home, working on-site, and working location independent.

Working from Home

For many people, working from home is the dream scenario. For others it is an imperative if they face a long commute from a rural location, unreasonably heavy traffic to and from the workplace, young children at home who are not suited for daycare due to emotional or physical challenges, an ailing spouse or parent who requires supervised care throughout the day, and so on. If one of these scenarios is true of your situation and you are eager to jump headlong into a work-at-home career paradigm, be sure to take a realistic look at yourself and your surroundings and determine if your lifestyle is well suited to this kind of arrangement. Some key questions to ask yourself include the following:

- Can I stay on task and meet important deadlines without getting distracted by the home telephone, television, refrigerator, friends, or family?

- Do I have the office equipment necessary to do the job? (Most employers will expect this.) Can I afford to purchase what I will need to get started?

- Can I handle the high-tech headaches that may occur or will these make me feel overwhelmed? Can I troubleshoot basic technical questions or learn to do so if necessary?

- Will I enjoy working alone, away from the social setting of the workplace? Will assuming a much more isolated, introverted way of working energize me or leave me feeling lonely and sad?

- If I have children or pets at home while I work, will they interfere with my work in any way, including noise pollution that could tarnish my professional image when communicating with my boss or co-workers?

- If family, friends, or neighbors stop by during the workday, will I have the nerve to turn them away in order to stay on task and meet important deadlines?

- Will I be tempted to work outside of my scheduled office hours because the work is there on the desk in the corner of my home office?

Working from home offers great freedom and cost savings, but it may or may not be a feasible option for you depending on your personality and circumstances. Look before you leap and make careful preparations to ensure your success.

> **Set Up Shop**
>
> Chapter 18, "Get Your Move On," walks you step by step through the business of setting up shop, including a practical discussion about determining which office location may best suit your professional needs.

Working On-Site

For anyone who has been stuck in the house for too long, the lure of getting up and out of the house every day can be irresistible. Just ask any stay-at-home parent or long-time unemployed worker how they feel about the idea of getting up and out of the house each day to work on-site at an office, construction site, or another workplace setting; they long for the opportunity! So, too, do those individuals who are extroverts by nature, for whom the opportunity to talk with other people in a workplace setting is stimulating and essential to their emotional well-being.

However, for most people, working on-site is the only choice they have ever known, and, as a result, it is the least interesting option to them because it is all too familiar. Is this true for you, too? If so, keep in mind that with the Patchwork Principle you can choose to seek out work that allows you to work off-site or on-site or a combination of the two. It's your choice; choose what best fits with your Lifestyle Design paradigm.

Working Location Independent

If you long for the open road, the high seas, or some other fantasy scenario, there is good news! Your dreams *can* become a reality, and for many they already are. People who work like this are known as *location independent.* This term can be generalized to those who value the ability to move from one geographic location to another at will without it compromising their work. However, working location independent is not necessarily tied to high-adventure travel; in fact, it may be applicable to you if you are interested in any of the following scenarios:

- **Being a snowbird:** This lifestyle means living "up North" (as they call it in the Midwest) during the spring and summer months and "down

South" during the rest of the year. This may be especially appealing if you are working well into your retirement but wish to enjoy spending your free time with family and friends of a similar age who live a snow-bird lifestyle.

- **Working while on the move:** If your spouse's or partner's career forces you to pack up and move to a new location regularly, working location independent may be an option. Spouses of military personnel, professional sports coaches and players, or high-profile positions that are traditionally short-lived (CEOs, for example) can make a good living by working location independent.

- **Caring for an elderly parent:** If you care for aging parents who live in another city, state, or country, it can be challenging to be true to them and hold on to your job, depending on the circumstances, the boss, and the corporate culture. Working location independent can offer you the ability to maintain your career and care for your loved one without concerns about requesting time off or catching up on work upon your return.

Although working location independent can be applied to any of the preceding scenarios, the term is most often associated with that fantasy scenario we all dream about. The one I'm referring to is nomadic in nature: Bermuda today and Australia tomorrow. Such a lifestyle may sound unfeasible, but more than 25,000 people are location independent right now![4] These individuals are driven by wanderlust and travel the globe to wherever the wind takes them, all while making a pretty good living. What type of work do these globetrotters do? A sampling includes coaching, consulting, copywriting, graphic design, IT work, reporting, market research, online teaching, and translation of technical documents.

If you think this career lifestyle is practical only for twenty-somethings, single people, or DINKS (double income no kids), then think again! The Location Independent Professionals (LIPs) network includes every lifestyle scenario, including a parenting network. Leaders in this lifestyle field are Lea and Jonathan Woodward, who were interviewed in 2009 by *The Guardian* about the location independent movement. When asked the question, "Why this lifestyle?" here was the response: "Basically, we just thought, 'Let's live life while we can!' We're running a professional business, not backpacking. But when we have downtime, why not be able to stroll along the beach and watch the sunset?"[5] If this sounds appealing to you, visit the LIP Web site (www.locationindependent.com) for more information.

So then, what is *your* ideal workplace location scenario? Is working from home what you dream about on the long commute home each night? Or is the thought of putting on a business suit and spending the day working downtown with other professionals what energizes you? Or is it simply kicking the dust off your shoes and heading out for the open road to work and live an adventure-filled life with no one location tying you down?

Whatever your dream may be, the first step is clearly defining what matters most to you and then seeking out work that meets those criteria. I'll talk about how to do that in the second half of the book, but for now let's take this vision of where you would like to work and expand upon it. Think about not only *where* you would like to work, but also *who* those people are that you would most enjoy spending time with in a workplace setting.

Your Ideal Work Mates

Former U.S. President Franklin D. Roosevelt once said, "I'm not the smartest fellow in the world, but I can sure pick smart colleagues." Roosevelt attributed his successes to his ability to assemble a great team. Other highly successful people also believe that their successes are a direct result of the people with whom they surround themselves. However, how many of us truly choose our boss and co-workers? Before accepting your last job, did you ask the boss if you could interview your potential co-workers to see if you enjoyed their company or agreed with their work ethic? Of course not. And yet how great was the impact those co-workers had on your everyday life once you were on the job? Very! They were the people who essentially could make or break the job for you, right?

Along these lines, your Lifestyle Design absolutely must take into consideration and clearly define the characteristics of an ideal co-worker, or whether the absence of co-workers is more suitable. Have you ever really thought about whom you would like to work with? The following sections include a few talking points to get a dialogue going in your head.

Identifying Key Characteristics of Your Co-workers

What are the most critical characteristics of a co-worker? What are those things that really matter to you? The list is different for each one of us. As you begin to design your ideal lifestyle, consider the fact that you can cultivate your team of ideal co-workers by surveying the territory during the interview process, listening and watching for cues that might indicate if those are the people with which you wish to spend your days, and perhaps being so bold as to ask a would-be employer for a brief introduction. As you begin to define the characteristics of your ideal co-workers, consider the following questions:

- Are they your professional equals or are they people you can learn from?

- Are they polished and measured or rough around the edges and boisterous?

- Are they in your age category? Older? Younger?

- Are they ultra conservative, ultra liberal, or somewhere in the middle?

- Are they the politically correct sort or do they speak frankly?

- Are they champions of human rights or fully unaware of the world around them?

- Are they advocates for diversity or prejudiced with no holds barred?

However you define your ideal co-workers in your mind's eye, know that you are more fully in control of whom you work with than you realize. In the second half of the book, a lengthy and practical discussion about the Patchwork Principle will describe how to choose your co-workers with ease.

Working as Part of a Team

Are you a team player? Some people are just meant to be part of a team; they thrive when they get to work and play well with others. Does this describe you? If it does, then working independently from home, for example, which is only one scenario among many, may be a little daunting at first glance because you do so much of the work in isolation. After all, a growing number of companies around the world farm out work to off-site locations.

Before you lose heart, remember that you can choose to seek out work that brings you inside, on-site, if that is a better match with your personality. The work that you choose to accept can be whatever you determine to be a good fit for your Lifestyle Design. So, if you are a team player, identify those jobs where you get to charge into the workplace and collaborate with a larger team. The great news is that the competition for on-site jobs will be considerably less than for off-site work because most people prefer to work from their home office or another location of their choosing, meaning that on-site work is plentiful.

Even if you choose to work off-site but still long to be part of a team, you're in luck. Today many individuals work collaboratively via the Internet using specialized software tools that allow team members to share data. In addition, hardware such as videophones and webcams allow employees to hold large team meetings in which they can speak with one another and in some cases even see one another despite the physical distances between them.

Teamwork in this day and age is no longer limited by geographic location. Videoconferencing, collaborative workspaces, instant messaging software, and other technologies allow team members scattered around the globe to feel like they're in the same room. If working with a team is important to you, take advantage of the opportunity by looking for mention of these collaborative technologies in the freelance ads or drum up your own leads by working with companies that you know use such technologies.

Going Off to Your Own Corner

Are you a loner? Some people prefer to work alone. They seek solace from the opportunity to go away from the world and focus on the task at hand with everything they have. Are you one of those people? Certain types of work, such as writing, graphic design, computer programming, and accounting, lend themselves more readily to working solo. However, in the world of freelance, most advertised work is meant to be done independently, away from the larger team. If you are a loner, this is great news.

Many freelance positions today have an underlying expectation that you complete the work and simply e-mail it to the boss once completed. Although there may be established benchmarks that allow the boss to make sure you are making steady progress, for the most part you work independently.

Your Money or Your Life

Let's talk for a moment about, as the O'Jays sing, "Money, money, money, money, *Mo-ney!*" When you think about money, does your mind typically race to the amount that you want to make? Of course it does! However, that number is usually some pie-in-the-sky amount that would afford you exotic luxuries, right? For example, $100 million or some other number with a great many zeros after it. Hey, there is nothing wrong with dreaming big; I am all for it. But let's begin this conversation about money by thinking not about how much you *want* but instead about how much you *need.*

How much money do you really need? You do need a certain amount of money in order to maintain those things that matter to you. Such items might include a place to live (a house, condo, or apartment), some form of transportation (a car, motorcycle, or bus), food, clothing, and other important necessities as well as some fun stuff, too. But how much does all of that really cost? Seriously? How much money would you need to make just to cover the basics? What is that magic number that holds you hostage at the present time?

Think about this from the perspective of "your money or your life," which is essentially what you are deciding between each day that you wake up and go through the daily grind. You are choosing your daily wage over a day of your life lived freely. I invite you to take a few minutes to calculate how much that number amounts to on a daily basis.

How Much Money Do You Make Each Day?

Figuring out the math is simple. Think about your annual income and then remove the three zeros after the comma ($30,000 becomes $30, for example). Now divide that number by 2 ($30/2). That number is a rough estimate of your hourly wage ($15). Now take that hourly wage and multiply it by the number of hours in your workday ($15 x 8). That total ($120) is the amount you earn each day that you go in to work—before taxes and other deductions. This amount is a rough estimate because taxes and deductions are not included, and as you may guess, the after-tax figure is usually a little more instructional. Write that number here: $_____.

If you want an all-out reality check, take a look at your end-of-month pay stub that shows actual take-home dollars and then divide that amount by the number of days worked to determine your actual daily rate. Depending on your tax bracket and other deductions for health insurance premiums and so on, the daily rate can drop by as much as 50 percent from the pretax amount. In this example, the daily rate would drop from $120 earned per day to $60 earned per day. In other words, each day of that person's working life could be purchased for only $60! That's a fire sale if I've ever seen one.

How Much Do You Need to Work?

Now that you know how much you earn each day, I want you to determine how much you would need to earn to cover the basic expenses you have at this time. Make a list: housing, transportation, food, and so on. For now, don't include the extras; just look at the necessities (but keep in mind that health insurance is a necessity that you need to account for, which we will discuss in Part VI, "Set Up Shop"). Once you total up your necessary expenses, what is the dollar amount? I encourage you not to guess; stick to the facts.

Write it here: $_____ per month. Circle the number so that you can easily refer back to it later on.

Are you already making less than you need to cover your costs? This is the most common scenario. And keep in mind that this is *before* you even factor in the fun stuff! So the bottom line is, you work a lot and make a little. Are you tired of that? Who wouldn't be?

Typically people look at the mandatory expenses in their lives and believe that the only solution is to keep working and in fact work even longer hours to make extra money in order to somehow "get ahead" of their bills. That is the trap that so many people fall into; there is a better way. Let go of your preconceived notions as you move to the next section, which asks you to think about something seemingly counterintuitive: limiting the number of hours that you work despite your expenses.

> **Scrutinize Your Expenses**
>
> Each of us defines "extras" differently. What can you really live without? Think about each expense carefully, because those are the very items that may stand between you and your dreams. How badly do you want to make a change? Delayed gratification can really pay off—literally and figuratively!

How Much Do You Want to Work?

Now that you know how much you need to earn to cover your bases, it's time to figure out how much you would *like* to work if money were no object and then reconcile the two. Set all of your immediate concerns about money aside for just this moment while you think things through. I'm not talking about working for zero hours and being a millionaire; instead I mean, realistically, how many hours each day or week would you like to work in order to feel productive and fulfilled? Good news! You already figured this out earlier in the book; flip back to the Mad Lib exercise you completed about your ideal work year earlier in this chapter. Is your ideal workweek a part-time venture or a full-time venture? Copy those numbers from the Mad Lib into the blanks below and do some quick math:

Number of hours you would work each day: _____

Number of days you would work each week: _____

Number of weeks you would work each year: _____

Now, do some simple math to figure out your base work year in hours and days:

1. Multiply the number of hours _____ x _____ days each week.

2. That total is _____. These are the total hours of work you would commit to each week on average.

3. Now, multiply the preceding total _____ x _____ number of weeks you would work each year.

4. That total is _____. This is the number of hours you would like to work each year. **Circle it;** this is the first part of a two-part goal.

That circled number represents how much you want to work. But how much do you think you *need* to work based on your expenses? This is your chance to figure it out, concretely. Take the dollar amount of your necessities (the number you circled in the previous section titled "How Much Do You Need to Work?") and divide that by the number of hours you circled in the preceding section.

$_____ (necessities cost) / _____ hours each year listed above

This number represents how much you actually *need* to work. **Circle it;** this represents your bottom line.

How does that bottom line dollar figure look to you? Is it more or less than you expected? However you feel about the number, it is the reality you must contend with at the present moment. Keep in mind that at any moment you can change this number by downsizing some of your primary expenses (such as a house or car) in exchange for additional freedom and peace of mind. Downsizing is not a requirement, by any means; it is simply a choice that you may wish to consider if exorbitant living expenses are holding you hostage and keeping you from thriving.

Your Ideal Attitude

Finally, let's examine your attitude about being employed. Think back to the last time you woke up on a workday. Did you bounce out of bed eager to get going, or did you hit the snooze button and think something to the effect of, "Ugh, it's only Tuesday!" This speaks to the level of or lack of passion you feel for your work, a pervasive force that can either feed or starve other areas of your life with consequences that can affect your personal and professional relationships, your health, and your income—your overall success and enjoyment of life.

Having passion for your work is like yeast; it is naturally occurring and can have an utterly transforming effect. Yeast permeates the dough, causing a chemical transformation, just as passion can have positive effects on the body such as better overall mental and physical health, faster recovery from major illnesses, and increased longevity. Passion is a powerful force that energizes and drives us forward, full throttle.

Passion Is Powerful

Have you ever met someone who is passionate about a hobby? His or her weeknights and certainly weekends revolve around it. Because I live in Milwaukee, which is the home of Harley-Davidson, I can tell you that there are many people in this city who "live to ride." They spend their weekdays polishing and fine-tuning their motorcycles, and they dedicate their weekends to road trips. They may have friends who also "ride" and with whom they socialize and network. They may read trade magazines about the bikes and perhaps take classes about safety, maintenance, and so on. So what's my point?

My point is that their passion leads them to naturally create a network of people, seek out learning opportunities in order to improve themselves, develop a dynamic schedule that allows them to get everything done that they need and want to, and put it all into action. Now imagine if this passion could be applied to a career—your career! Imagine if you could design a career that had you so excited that you found yourself thinking about it even on your "off hours," not because you had to but because you enjoyed it! Designing your career is a fundamental component of the 9-to-5 Cure; feeling passionate about your work is a must! Consider the following exercise.

EXERCISE: HOW WOULD YOUR IDEAL CAREER MAKE YOU FEEL?

If you designed the ideal career for yourself, what words would describe how it would make you feel? Circle any and all of them in the following list.[6]

accomplished	courteous	generous
admirable	dedicated	genuine
amazing	delightful	gifted
amusing	deserving	glorious
approachable	determined	gracious
articulate	disciplined	gregarious
attentive	earnest	gutsy
benevolent	ecstatic	helpful
blessed	effective	honorable
bold	eloquent	immaculate
bountiful	empathetic	immense
bright	energetic	impeccable
brilliant	engaging	incomparable
captivating	entertaining	incredible
caring	enthusiastic	ingenious
charismatic	equitable	inspiring
charming	expressive	intelligent
cheerful	exquisite	intuitive
comfortable	extraordinary	inventive
compassionate	fascinating	jazzed
congenial	fearless	kindhearted
conscious	flexible	loyal
constant	fortunate	magnanimous
courageous	friendly	majestic

(continued)

(continued)

marvelous	powerful	stable
motivating	quick-minded	steadfast
optimistic	remarkable	steady
original	resourceful	stunning
passionate	respectful	stupendous
peaceful	rousing	trustful
perceptive	selfless	understanding
persistent	sensational	unique
pleasing	sincere	venturous
poetic	spirited	

WHAT MATTERS MOST

Now look back at the words you circled. They are the leading indicators of your core needs and wants for your personalized 9-to-5 Cure. What do those words imply about what matters to you? Does being original matter? Or feeling intelligent? Or having stability? Or a combination of factors? What are those key components for you?

Write About It

_____

_____

_____

So many people wall off those things in their life that they are really passionate about when it comes to their career. Perhaps it is fear of failure that holds them back. Perhaps it is lack of confidence. Perhaps it is something else. Whatever the reason, the price they pay for denying themselves is steep: They pay with their lives, lives wasted doing something that is tolerable but not energizing. They survive instead of thrive. So many people spend their careers just going through the motions, learning to adapt to whatever comes their way over the course of their decades of work in order to remain employed until retirement age. This life is their one life to live, and yet they spend it so passively. They allow circumstances to design their career, and so it meanders haphazardly. What a sad journey it must be! Don't make this same mistake; instead be the exclusive designer of your career, tailored to fit your life. Play an active role in the life you live. If you aren't managing your career, nobody is!

The Shape of Your Ideal Career Outlook

Now let's look at the shape of your ideal career outlook. Sounds odd, right? Stay with me. Most people view their work life as either cyclical (a circle) or linear (a straight line), as shown in the following diagram. Which view best depicts your attitude? For example, do you view each year at your job the same old thing (cyclical), or is it a stepping-stone that is part of a larger plan (linear)?

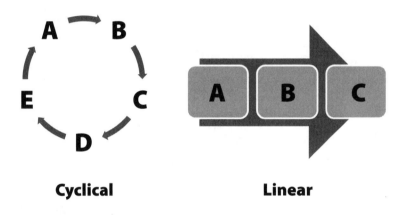

Cyclical   **Linear**

If you answered cyclical, then I might venture to say you are someone who talks about "surviving another year" at work. You may view work as an endurance test and be subject to a greater incidence of burnout. If your view of work is linear, then I might guess that you talk about work in terms of milestones such as "having two years of experience under your belt," implying that there is a next step on the horizon. Incidentally, working linearly is the better of the two options because it means that perhaps you are constantly aspiring to "become" whatever it is that you dream of for yourself. That's productive and positive.

However, let's take that thought one step further. Instead of thinking of a cyclical or linear model, consider a spiral such as a double helix or a circular staircase. The spiral reaches up and up, representing a striving to become better and better. With a spiral model, individuals strive to build upon the previous experiences and reach for even greater dreams and goals.

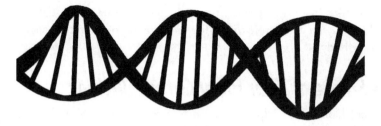

Double Helix

Cyclical Versus Spiral

So how do the cyclical and the spiral models compare? The spiral is the complete opposite of the cyclical model because whereas the cyclical is about routine and redundancy, the spiral is about constantly seeking out newness both for the sake of continued career growth and as a wellspring for creativity, continuous improvement, and energy. Although the cyclical can be comforting to those who crave routine, it is also a recipe for burnout because, among other things, there is nothing new to look forward to—it's boring!

With the spiral there is always something new on the horizon. There is a repeated return to the starting point (the beginning of a fiscal year, for example) and then a journey toward the same endpoint (the end of a fiscal year, for example). With the spiral model, something new is always on the horizon. Each day builds on the next, and in turn each year builds on the previous to create a unique experience at each juncture. This change does not have to imply constant chaos, not by any means. Developing an underlying foundation of routine (a predetermined schedule) with the overarching spirit of continuous improvement and innovation, the exploration of and experimentation with new ideas is the lifeblood of the spiral model.

Linear Versus Spiral

Okay, so how about the linear model—how does it compare with the spiral? Whereas the linear model sees Point A and Point B and moves away from one and toward the other, the spiral moves to and from multiple points simultaneously, seeking out many directions with each step: left, right, center. The spiral model also sees multiple goals simultaneously and extends forward in all directions, able to twist and turn in order to reach higher and higher.

Although the linear and spiral models share a plan for forward progress, the linear model has trouble adjusting to setbacks that may block the way in the same way that a mile-long domino lineup fails when interrupted by the misplacement of a single piece. Conversely, the spiral is reaching up and out in so many directions simultaneously that if one move fails, another can pave the way for progress despite a simple failure.

For example, imagine if your goal was to land an account in a certain industry. If you solicited a specific group of companies by e-mail with the hope of breaking into that industry but that failed, you would have to stop, rethink your approach, select a single new approach, and try again—that's the linear approach. However, if you solicited that same group through multiple media platforms such as in-person contact, networking, and so on all at the same time—that's the spiral approach.

Furthermore, if you used something we will call *momentum*, you would experience success that builds on itself, leading to results with ever-increasing ease. There is an entire section in Chapter 9, "Guiding Beliefs of the Patchwork Principle," dedicated to momentum in this context. For our purposes right now, imagine if you worked for a few hours a year in any capacity in a few of those sought-after companies or worked in complementary companies that interacted with those organizations. Somehow you could use those familiar contacts and that job history to work your way into those sought-after accounts. That's momentum! The more accounts you have, the more decision makers who know your work and like it, and the more likely they are to talk about you or enthusiastically provide a good reference for you as you branch out in the industry.

Identifying the Shape of Your Current Career Outlook

Write about how your current outlook serves you and how it detracts from what you are capable of becoming. What needs to change in order for your outlook to transform, or does your outlook need to change at all?

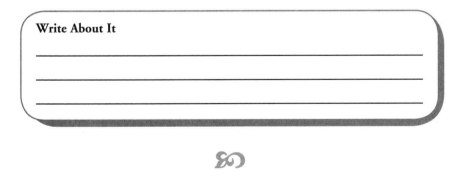

Write About It

_____

_____

_____

Congratulations! You have taken the time to consider some of the most important factors that make up your ideal Lifestyle Design. You now have a rough sketch in mind of what the lifestyle of your dreams consists of, which you will fine-tune as you work through this book. Now let's get to work on the business of making it an economic reality, an achievable goal. Let's talk about how to work on purpose, for a change.

Endnotes

[1] David Newlands and Mark Hooper, *The Global Business Handbook* (Burlington, VT: Gower Publishing Company, 2009), 83.

[2] Timothy Ferriss, *The 4-Hour Work Week* (New York: Crown Publishers, 2007), 7.

[3] The Sloan Consortium, "Staying the Course: Online Education in the United States," 2008, www.sloan-c.org/publications/survey/staying_course (accessed August 22, 2010).

[4] Lea Woodward, e-mail message to author, March 10, 2010.

[5] Oliver Burkeman, "This Column Will Change Your Life: 9-to-5 or Free and Easy?" *The Guardian*, September 12, 2009, www.guardian.co.uk/lifeandstyle/2009/sep/12/change-your-life-nine-to-five (accessed August 22, 2010).

[6] Michael Doraush, "101 Words That Feel Good," Chiropractic Blogs, http://blog.planetc1.com/2007/11/26/101-words-that-feel-good (accessed August 22, 2010).

PART III

Work on Purpose

CHAPTER 7

The Headlines—Survivalnomics

Okay, you're all charged up and ready to make your dreams come true. Great! But first, a dose of harsh reality: The headlines will tell you that a thriving lifestyle is impossible. The media want you to believe that your only option is to survive—and lucky if you can, at that! Welcome to the Age of Survivalnomics, where all of those dog-eat-dog adages are ever present and you get a regular dose of doom each time you turn on the television, read the newspaper, or scroll through the feed on Twitter or Facebook.

The Age of Survivalnomics

Survival has been part of the human experience since prehistoric times. Surviving is a primitive, inborn desire to carry on, and modern man is hard-wired to survive after eons of genetic code have favored the perpetuation of humans with this important trait. The adrenaline and cortisol our bodies release in preparation for a "fight or flight" experience serve us well if we, for example, find ourselves in a dangerous situation. But what if I told you that many people spend their work lives in "survival mode"? Would that surprise you? Sadly, I have a feeling it may not.

Surviving is a word commonly paired with work in modern-day conversation. Examples might include, "If I can only survive this work day," or "If I can only survive at this job long enough to see retirement." On a daily basis people work at jobs they do not enjoy for less pay than they are worth and with concerns about being fired, laid off, or downsized. They work for bosses who are unpleasant, ineffective, or even abusive in some cases, and yet they persist. Why do they choose to continue on this path? They do so because they must, or so they believe.

Survivalnomics is a term you may be unfamiliar with, but it's a concept that you know all too well. It is a desperate economic reality that we all readily accept as the norm, whereby both employers and employees struggle to survive in a seemingly zero sum game of business. Both parties are in a perpetual state of fight or flight where both the boss and the employees struggle to survive in the business world. They believe they must fight, attack, and constantly prove themselves in the workplace if they are to survive.

This belief triggers an automatic response that causes our hardwired selves to leave rational thinking behind. We numb ourselves in preparation for the next attack and the possible pain associated with it. We work in survival mode on some level, whether we are keenly aware of it in our conscious mind or not. The experience is hard on our body, mind, and spirit, demonstrated by ailments such as high blood pressure, depression, and heart attacks—and yet we persist.

We persist in the workplace for thirty or more years because we believe we must. After all, we all have to "earn a living" in order to survive. Or do we? We earn at the expense of living. We survive the experience, or we try to. However, now more than ever before, the concept of "work" is changing. We are dissecting it, and so are employers; there are serious consequences that are only beginning to show themselves. The implications for the future of work are dire if you ask the average 9-to-5er. However, I believe it is actually a new opportunity to work on your own terms and reinvent your life. But before we get too far, let's take a look at the changing face of work.

Taking Inventory of Our Work

As traditional thirty-year career positions are going the way of the dinosaur, the concept of career is rapidly transforming. Society is beginning to unpack the contents of traditional jobs and take a brutally honest look at them. What is a job, exactly? Is it a set of responsibilities we perform in a six-by-six-foot cubicle? Is it any set of tasks that provides us with health insurance and some paid time off? Do we need to reside stateside, or can we be location independent, commuting from a beach in Thailand this year and a mountainside in Switzerland the next? Which factors are the most meaningful to *us*? Which elements are the most important to *employers*?

We as a society are just beginning to dissect our jobs and take inventory of what those valuable pieces of the thirty-year career are to which we swear our loyalty to a company (or several) and surrender the best years of our lives. Employers are doing the same thing in many ways; company leaders are taking a look at our jobs and determining which responsibilities are the most valuable and relevant to the company's bottom line. This evaluation and other factors have led to a spike in outsourcing (American companies farming work out to third parties such as contract workers in the United States or overseas), reverse outsourcing (companies overseas hiring Americans as contract workers), and other configurations that allow companies to pay only for what they use and move on. As a result, our modern-day economy is "characterized by...declining employee benefits and job insecurity for all categories of wage earners..."[1]

As a result, this new trend has given rise to a growing workforce referred to by many different terms including *contingent workers, giggers, temps, consultants, independent contractors,* and *freelancers.* Whatever the label, these workers currently account for nearly one-third of the U.S. workforce, and that number is predicted to rise, due in part to the combination of a slow economic recovery and technological advances that make data sharing seamless and readily available to the masses.[2]

Crowdsourcing

Take for example the concept of *crowdsourcing,* which can be defined as "the act of outsourcing tasks, traditionally performed by an employee or contractor, to a large group of people or community (a crowd), through an open call [to work]."[3] In simple terms it is an arrangement whereby employers assign even the smallest tasks to a large number of individuals who have absolutely no knowledge of the larger project. Workers work when and if they choose, doing narrowly defined tasks in exchange for per-piece payment.

One example is Amazon's Mechanical Turk or MTurk (http://aws.amazon.com/mturk), which pays workers (known as *turkers*) pennies for tagging photos, transcribing data, or doing simple research.[4] Another example of crowdsourcing is Txteagle (www.txtagle.com), which is on track to become one of the largest employers in Africa.[5] Txteagle utilizes the crowdsourced manpower of Africa. African companies utilize Txteagle workers to complete what are called *micro tasks,* such as image sorting and tagging via cell phone (referred to as *mobile crowdsourcing*) for large corporate clients. Workers receive compensation either in airtime known as *mobile money* or, in select countries, in credits that, once accumulated, are paid out in local currency by cell phone kiosks. Txteagle workers and those who work for other companies like Txteagle amount to electronic day laborers, where unskilled workers complete mundane tasks in exchange for extremely low wages.

Perhaps it is a new version of the assembly line in which each person contributes to the development of a larger product, only in this case the product may be unknown to the workers. Crowdsourcing turns each worker into a human cog. It's not empowering or emotionally rewarding, but it pays the

Work as a Turker

The following list provides some basic data about Amazon's MTurk that you may find surprising:

- 57% of the workers (ahem, turkers) reside in the U.S.

- The average age of a turker is 31 years old.

- 66% of turkers have a college or advanced degree.

- 38% of turkers are full-time employees elsewhere.

- 14% of the turkers make more than $70,000 per year in combined income from MTurk and other employers.

Even though the average wage is only $1.25 per hour, 18% of workers report that they sometimes or always rely on MTurk to make ends meet.[6]

bills. Well, actually it likely doesn't even do that unless you live in, say, Kenya where the Txteagle home page states that the average person survives on less than $5 per day.[7]

But what does any of this have to do with you and your career? Well, crowdsourcing is a form of employment just like any other mentioned under the guise of Survivalnomics. Crowdsourcing certainly is at one extreme of the freelancing spectrum, with the opposite end being one that presumably pays high wages for skilled labor—and I'm guessing that's the end of the spectrum you are interested in. After all, you are looking for a reasonable amount of income and to apply skills that possibly took years of on-the-job training to acquire, not to mention the education you accumulated along the way. This brings us to the opposite end of the spectrum: gigging.

Gigonomics

Although the idea of freelancing is not a new concept to musicians, artists, journalists, and others across a wide array of occupations, what is new is that formerly well-positioned white-collar workers with impressive levels of education are entering the freelance world in droves. This increase caught the attention of the media in recent years and entered mainstream consciousness in early 2010 when a series of articles and television stories about the phenomenon hit the Internet and the airwaves.

This group of promising new upstarts who were in dire straits due to massive layoffs nationwide and stagnating unemployment defined a new economic movement referred to as *Gigonomics*, which is working an ongoing series of *gigs* defined as "a bunch of free-floating projects, consultancies, and part-time bits and pieces" that giggers "stitch together" in order to make ends meet.[8] It's the penny-ante slog of working three times as hard for the same amount of money (if you're lucky) or a lot less (if you're not). Gigging is a seemingly bleak portrait of what was once the upwardly mobile workforce that is now clawing at projects in order to survive. Can you see the parallels in the depiction of gigging in comparison to crowdsourcing?

So just how many of these giggers really exist? *ABC News* answered the question with a televised report by Diane Sawyer titled "Making Ends Meet." This report estimated that 21 million Americans "cobble together an income from a number of employers." In that same report, Betsy Stark said that instead of working one job, giggers work "one job after another." The report drew a dreary picture of the new norm and interviewed seemingly poised, well-spoken professionals who attested to the challenges associated with gigging, including "not much security" or how they must "juggle seven or eight jobs a day." Soon after the *ABC News* report aired, *Newsweek* joined the conversation citing reasons for the new *Gig Economy*. These reasons included the continued rise in unemployment numbers across all fifty states, lack of corporate loyalty from employees, and a willingness by corporate managers to outsource in order to "only pay for what they can use."

During the weeks and months that followed these reports, bloggers grabbed hold of the concept, and magazines and newspapers both online and in print analyzed and conjectured about the desperation faced by these professionals who were freelancing for lack of other options. They all painted a picture of a career archetype that I thought would be more aptly labeled *Survivalnomics* than Gigonomics.

The Gigaverse

This picture was a startling revelation to me, someone who had happily been living and working in the then-unlabeled *Gigaverse* for many years. In fact, I had deliberately chosen a freelancer's lifestyle many years prior in order to take charge of my time and escape the rat race of the 9-to-5 work world. And while the media feeds provided a steady diet of despair about the lifestyle, I was fully engaged and enjoying my life in a way better than I could have ever imagined.

For weeks I spent a great deal of time crawling the Internet for more information about my own Gigaverse and the people in it. I felt like this profession that I had dreamed up for myself many years ago suddenly had a name, and like a patient with an illness that is finally diagnosed, I found myself in a desperate search to learn more about Gigonomics.

After I completed an exhaustive search for new articles and blog entries available that first month that the buzzwords caught hold, I sat back. I began searching deep inside myself for answers. I began processing everything. I had been so happy with my career lifestyle for many years. Was I just in denial? Was I sugarcoating the experience in my mind? My heart and my bottom line told me otherwise. So why did I feel so happy with what countless articles equated to a career based on lack—lack of money, options, promotion, and more. What was wrong with me? Why was I so incredibly happy? Several weeks went by before I was able to answer that question.

One day a client called to offer me a new project. The assignment paid well and sounded interesting, but I needed to adjust the deadline in order to accommodate an upcoming family vacation. The client was pleased to make the necessary adjustments, and I verbally signed on. I hung up the phone, satisfied with the situation. My schedule was now officially filled to capacity once more, which always felt good. I was happy with the work I was doing and with the money I was making. I felt like the work I did was interesting and contributed to the lives of others in a meaningful way. Moreover, rare was the time when my work life interfered with my personal life. I felt happy.

And that's when it hit me: I felt happy!

I was a so-called gigger, and yet I felt happy. But according to the media's version of Gigonomics, the two didn't go hand in hand. In that moment I came to the realization that I simply am *not* a gigger. I am *not* living in that Gigaverse predominated by lack. In fact, I am not living anywhere *near* it!

Instead, my career lifestyle is one that I chose deliberately because it brings happiness to my life, not one that I chose out of desperation. It is filled with an abundance of employment opportunities, not a desperate search for the next gig. I live life on my own terms, by choice. I own my time. I call the shots. I am home for my family when I want to be and for any special events that come along. I vacation often and enjoy long periods of leisure time. My life feels balanced. I feel whole. It is a career lifestyle that is none like I have ever heard of or known before. I love it, truly. At the very core of my being, I am happy.

✃

I write this book because my greatest wish is to share the secret of this career lifestyle with you and the 21 million Americans who are currently "cobbling together" work. There is a better way, I promise you! The name for this counterculture employment strategy that throws misery out the window and gives happiness a front-row seat is what I call the Patchwork Principle. This principle is a proven strategy for finding work that you love in abundance, and it organically pairs with the lifestyle by design that you have in mind. Reject the premise of Survivalnomics and never look back.

Endnotes

[1] Mike Stathis, *America's Financial Apocalypse* (Dallas: Apex Venture Advisors, 2006), 292.

[2] Drake Bennett, "The End of the Office... and the Future of Work," *The Boston Globe*, January 17, 2010, www.boston.com/bostonglobe/ideas/articles/2010/01/17/the_end_of_the_office_and_the_future_of_work (accessed August 22, 2010).

[3] *Wikipedia*, s.v. "Crowdsourcing," http://en.m.wikipedia.org/wiki/Crowdsourcing?wasRedirected=true (accessed July 16, 2010).

[4] Joel Ross and others, "Who Are the Turkers? Worker Demographics in Amazon Mechanical Turk," ACM CHI Conference paper, 2010, www.ics.uci.edu/~jwross/pubs/SocialCode-2009-01.pdf (accessed September 1, 2010).

[5] Txteagle, "About Txteagle," http://txteagle.com/about.html (accessed July 16, 2010).

[6] Joel Ross.

[7] Txteagle.

[8] Tina Brown, "The Gig Economy," *The Daily Beast*, January 12, 2010, www.thedailybeast.com/blogs-and-stories/2009-01-12/the-gig-economy/full (accessed August 22, 2010).

CHAPTER 8

A New Strategy—The Patchwork Principle

So maybe you're thinking that this big pie-in-the-sky concept is all well and good, but you need a concrete action plan. I agree.

The remaining chapters of this book focus on outlining the specifics of the Patchwork Principle. This principle is the business model that organically pairs with Lifestyle Design; in combination they *are* the 9-to-5 Cure. In this chapter we'll take a look at the second half of this familiar equation, which is dedicated to discovering enjoyable work in abundance:

THE 9-TO-5 CURE EQUATION

Lifestyle Design + The Patchwork Principle = The 9-to-5 Cure

or

Quality of Life + Enjoyable Work in Abundance = The 9-to-5 Cure

---

Allow me to give a big-picture explanation of how it all works in this chapter; then I'll talk about the guiding beliefs in Chapter 9, "Guiding Beliefs of the Patchwork Principle," and the mindset in Chapter 10, "The Mindset of the Successful Patchworker." Ultimately I'll help you get moving with the tactical information you need to get started.

Right now, it's time for Patchwork Principle 101!

The Big Picture in a Nutshell

The Patchwork Principle is a freelance career strategy based on the simple idea that working for a number of employers simultaneously presents unique business opportunities and insulates you from sudden and total job loss. By working for multiple businesses at any given time, you not only hedge your bets, but also increase your visibility across a wide array of organizations and have access to a rich network of people at all levels of many organizations whom you can tap for leads to spark future opportunities. These levels of heightened visibility, dynamic network, and unique access to the organizations are the precious resources that serve as building blocks for this career strategy. Working at many organizations simultaneously multiplies your visibility and network exponentially.

The Power of Momentum

As multiple organizations become accustomed to working with you and as word begins to spread about your stellar work ethic, you will discover momentum building, whereby new leads generate themselves and you are able to pitch new ideas and land new work with ever-increasing ease. Ultimately, the goal is to convince the decision makers at select organizations to bring you back for work at regular intervals (weekly, monthly, or quarterly) to stabilize your income and make it predictable. These regular accounts form the brick and mortar of your Patchwork career; they are the foundation upon which you build your success. These accounts are the ones around which you schedule other sporadic projects.

The Guiding Belief that Access Is Power

Although you may be—and should be—actively working with many businesses over the course of a calendar year, these sporadic projects are not income you can count on. That said, each of these accounts is still important in the overall scheme of things because each represents an opportunity to earn income, be present in a new networking environment, become familiar with a new organizational culture and climate, and maintain access to the decision makers who know you by name. Access is power.

The Fish and Pitch Strategy

Your Patchwork career, then, is a small business. It is a business where you are the owner and you supervise the performance of one employee: yourself. The sole focus of your business is to identify gaps in organizations, which you can fill, of course, and then pitch new ideas to decision makers either in person or by some other method. Essentially you fish for new leads and then pitch ideas to the decision maker, setting yourself up for a successful catch. The odds of success are much greater than when searching for a traditional career position because you offer a short-term, no-strings-attached, immediate solution to a known problem.

The Rationale Behind Your Premium Rate of Pay

As a Patchworker you charge a premium for your services due to the nature of the employment arrangement. The employer essentially pays a higher rate for the convenience of hiring you in a no-risk, at-will employment arrangement whereby either party can end the relationship at any time with no liability. This structure is similar to the temporary employment agency model whereby businesses pay a premium to the agency in order to have a prescreened employee report for work for a limited period of time to complete a task; the relationship can end at any time for any reason. However, in the Patchwork model employers know *exactly* who they are hiring—you!—and you collect the premium in the form of a higher rate of pay. Incidentally, you are not just a candidate walking in the door; you have a clearly defined action plan and are ready to begin implementing it on day one. The premium rate that you charge is a good investment, and the employer knows it because you make sure of it as soon as possible during those first days on the job.

> **Work on Contract**
>
> You can choose to enter into a contractual relationship with an employer and still be a full-fledged Patchworker. However, keep in mind that employers will often pay a premium for a no-strings-attached relationship that cannot be justified in a more traditional employment arrangement.

The Unlimited Power of Momentum

As a Patchworker, you are the star employee who does exceptional work, self manages, and gets along with *everybody* in the organization. You are the dream hire. You are memorable and leave a lasting impression on as many people as possible. The employer keeps you in mind for future projects because you bring credible solutions without strings or drama. You perform like a dream employee every time you take on a project. The decision makers keep you in mind, call with additional offers over time, and tell colleagues at other businesses about you, who in turn also call you with unsolicited offers. This dynamic form of client building is called *momentum;* it moves your business forward, making it profitable and abundant with offers.

> **Get Along with Everybody**
>
> Getting along with "everybody" is a choice. Choose to practice your best people skills for the sake of your business. If the interpersonal issues facing you on the job are unbearable, complete the project as promised and decline future offers to work for that employer again.

The 9-to-5 Cure

Your list of employers is dynamic and ever changing. Over time you become highly selective and work only where, with whom, and on what projects are most attractive based on criteria that matter most to you. And finally one day you arrive at the realization that you have designed a unique career that fits your lifestyle. You successfully reclaim your career and your life! You escape the 9-to-5 work world—and are cured!

Today's Patchworker

A *Patchworker* is a freelancer with a successful mental attitude. Let's start by defining it in this chapter and address the attitude in Chapter 9. According to Wikipedia, the term freelance "was first used by Sir Walter Scott in *Ivanhoe* to describe a 'medieval mercenary warrior' or 'free-lance.'...It changed to a figurative noun around the 1860s and was recognized as a verb in 1903.... Only in modern times has the term morphed from a noun (a freelance) into an adjective (a freelance journalist), a verb (a journalist who freelances), and an adverb (she worked freelance), and then the noun 'freelancer.'"[1]

Today's freelancers are entrepreneurs in the purest sense; the wares they sell are their skills. Freelancers are usually hired to perform a specific task; however, this is a general rule and not an absolute. In most cases, freelancers are expected to possess the equipment needed to do the work, and as a result they operate from wherever the tools are located, which is often a home office. However, the freelancer may also work on-site or out in the community.

The freelancer operates as an independent contractor in a no-strings-attached employment arrangement that is absent of legal liability; however, adherence to deadlines and other forms of workplace responsibility apply. The freelancer is understood to work for multiple organizations at any one time and may negotiate a unique rate of pay with each one. Pay can be hourly, project based, or some other agreed-upon formulation. Freelancers invoice employers and then calculate their own tax deductions and pay the appropriate agencies. Freelancers are small business owners who manage one employee—themselves.

The Patchworker Agenda

The Patchworker carries all of the standard responsibilities of the freelancer but has an agenda beyond earning money: life. The lifestyle factors that Patchworkers identify as mission critical are at the forefront of decisions they make related to which freelance projects they accept. Patchworkers are not interested in scrounging for work of any kind; they are selective because they have the big picture in mind. These Patchworkers have an attitude of purpose going into the negotiation, thankful for the opportunity to be considered for the job but also mindful of priorities—in other words, their lifestyle by design.

If the terms of the job are not a good fit with the lifestyle the Patchworker has in mind, the Patchworker declines the offer knowing that an unhappy work life means a return to the unfulfilling lifestyle encountered in the 9-to-5 work world. Does this mean that Patchworkers are chronically unemployed because they are hyper-selective? Not at all. Patchworkers simply go into any negotiation with more in mind than the money. And in most cases employers are flexible in negotiating nonmonetary terms because they anticipate competing with other employers for the Patchworker's time. The greater the competition, the greater the employer's flexibility in some cases.

Now that we have clearly defined what a freelancer is and how that is different from a Patchworker, let's take a look at the outlook for this type of work in the immediate future and beyond.

The Forecast for Patchworkers

The number of freelance opportunities available to a potential Patchworker at any one time is tremendous. As manufacturing jobs disappear from within its borders, the United States is moving toward an economy that is fueled by consultancy. Some of these consultancy projects are more highly valued within this new service-centric economy and include jobs related to strategy, technology, sales, and marketing. Although this shift began in the 1980s, it is accelerating due to federal free trade policies[2] and is expected to generate approximately 4.5 million new wage and salary jobs.[3] These positions are the tip of the iceberg and represent some of the many fields that abound with opportunity. Some of these fields include traditional freelance fields such as writing, photography, and graphic design as well as some nontraditional fields such as administration, waste management, and environmental remediation. In fact, these three nontraditional fields are expected to grow by 18 percent by 2018.

If you are still unconvinced that the field of freelance work has growth potential, consider this statement from the U.S. Department of Labor:

> The largest growth will occur in employment services, an industry that is anticipated to account for 42 percent of all new jobs in

the…services sector. The employment services industry ranks fifth among industries with the most new employment opportunities in the nation over the 2008–2018 period and is expected to grow faster than the average for all industries. Projected growth stems from the strong need for seasonal and temporary workers and for specialized human resources services.[4]

Although these jobs that are formally routed through a temporary agency may or may not be of interest to you, what the jobs represent is stunning: the need for millions of short-term workers by companies nationwide. This represents vacancies that *do* and *will* exist in large numbers for potential Patchworkers. Although this shift toward short-term or seasonal work, consultancy, and freelance work is a disturbing trend for 9-to-5 employees, it is a windfall of opportunity for the Patchworker. Short-term, no-strings-attached employment agreements are approaching like a tidal wave, so grab a surfboard and get ready to ride!

The Patchwork Principle is not only relevant in today's world; it's critical. Literally millions of freelance positions are available at any given time in the United States and around the world. As we will discuss in Chapter 12, "Go Fish," some of these positions are advertised widely whereas others are not. In some cases, industry-specific sites advertise to their select group, such as freelance work for chemists; however, most work is advertised widely on job search engine sites such as Elance.com that cater to the freelance masses.

Making sense of it all begins by understanding the five fundamental types of advertised positions, weighing each opportunity carefully against your Lifestyle Design, and then choosing the right Patchwork position (or positions!) for you.

The Five Patchwork Position Types

There are five standard Patchwork position types: the stand-in, the walk-on, the plug, the quick fix, and the star. Each of these types represents the structure of the position itself as opposed to the personal attributes of the Patchworker. The types are not industry-specific but instead represent the parameters and history of the position from the employer's point of view. Patchworkers have the opportunity to seek employment opportunities that represent a variety of these position types, or they can specialize in one type in particular. The configuration is a personal choice that reflects the customized Lifestyle Design of the individual Patchworker.

The Stand-In

The *stand-in* position is a previously full-time position that was simply eliminated on one side of the books and added back in on the other side but without benefits and other costly perks. The responsibilities are critical to the organization, but due to costs or other factors, the company is no longer willing to commit to the more expensive configuration of this position.

Consider some of the pros and cons of the stand-in position type:

Pro: The stand-in position can be a wonderful opportunity if you derive health insurance benefits through a spouse's employer and prefer steady work concentrated at only a few locations.

Pro: This position likely pays a premium for skilled work that previously paid a much lower wage when benefits were attached to it. This is an easy way to generate large amounts of income with very little or no marketing effort if you negotiate well. Employers need a skilled worker to step in and they know it.

Con: The number of hours concentrated on this one assignment can render your schedule completely inflexible in the face of new opportunities with other companies.

Con: Little time is available to network and grow your list of potential employers, which can prove a liability too costly should the stand-in position suddenly be eliminated.

Con: The position likely requires regular office hours. The rigidity of this schedule may make you feel as if you are back in the 9-to-5 world; be sure to negotiate aggressively for terms that are critical to your lifestyle before accepting the position.

The significant benefit of this position type is the opportunity to enjoy what is likely to be a stable, long-term employment arrangement. Because the company has a history of being committed to the ongoing necessity of the duties associated with the position, this arrangement would likely continue into the foreseeable future. A company that finds a quality worker willing to forego the costly benefits can reap the rewards of enjoying a long-lasting, high-paying employment arrangement.

The Walk-On

The *walk-on* position is a part-time or full-time position that a company creates on a trial basis in order to test it. The employer is attempting to determine whether the set of responsibilities justifies an entirely new position, whether it is fiscally feasible, and so on. These positions are typically found at organizations poised for growth or at least within a department of the organization that is forward thinking.

Consider some of the pros and cons of the walk-on position type:

Pro: The decision maker typically is trying to convince the organization of the need for the new position. Therefore, hiring an extraordinary employee to fill the position during this trial period is of utmost importance to the success of the experiment.

Pro: The decision maker will likely pay a premium and agree to additional lifestyle-minded concessions during the negotiation process in order to recruit the best candidate.

Con: The walk-on position is likely to be stressful because the nature and scope of responsibilities is constructed organically and with high expectations. A great percentage of the assignment is likely to be "duties as assigned" with the boss perhaps expecting too much of the employee, at least initially.

Con: If this is a full-time position, consider the cons previously listed for the stand-in, which are even more relevant because the walk-on position is expected to be a short-lived opportunity. If your schedule is dominated by this one short-term position, when it ends you could be scrambling to fill the empty spaces on your calendar. Be sure to get a firm end date so that you can prepare yourself for a successful transition.

This position appears to be a gamble in some respects because if the company ultimately determines that this trial run has proven the position to be unwarranted, the employment arrangement could end suddenly. However, if the position proves to be one to which the company wants to commit, you are likely to receive a long-term employment commitment. Regardless of the outcome, performing well on the job allows you to become familiar with the organization (and the organization with you) in the event that future opportunities arise—and they will. From that perspective, this position type has a payoff regardless of the outcome.

The Plug

The *plug* is a temporary, full-time, or part-time position born of a recent change within the organization because of a staff member's sudden departure, an employee's maternity leave, and so on. These are well-defined positions with fixed responsibilities and are implicitly temporary.

Consider some of the pros and cons of the plug position type:

Pro: These positions can absolutely open the doors of opportunity for you at a new organization or within a new department at a familiar organization. Because organizations are, by nature, constantly in flux, the Patchworker who performs well can be called upon repeatedly by the same organization. Larger organizations present a greater opportunity for repeat business.

Pro: The employer has experience managing the employee who previously occupied the slot, so the stressors associated with filling the walk-on position do not apply.

Con: The employer may have unrealistic expectations about how quickly you can perform at the same level that the long-time veteran of the position did.

Con: The employee who is simply absent but has intentions to return may feel threatened by you and withhold information that you need to work effectively.

Con: If the vacancy resulted from a sudden departure, you may be challenged by a backlog of items that need immediate attention.

Con: Be wary of full-time configurations of this position; see the cons listed for the stand-in position.

This position type is fantastic for the Patchworker who craves constant variety and change in duties and responsibilities. On each "assignment" you will encounter new people within the organization in a new location of the building or workplace, and you may experience a change in the pace of the workday as a result. The disadvantage of this position type is that the work isn't necessarily steady, but the opportunity to meet a variety of decision makers within the organization can lead to future opportunities for longer-term employment, if that is of interest to you. A Patchworker with a schedule comprised solely of plug positions will likely encounter great fluctuation in income, based on the on-demand nature of the work. Therefore, it is best to pair this position type with one or more of the other types in order to stabilize your income.

The Quick Fix

The *quick fix* is an ad hoc position created with a well-defined purpose in mind. The position tends to include project-based work that is generally founded on immediacy. The task likely requires the skills of a specialist. This is the position type most commonly found on freelance job sites, which cast out the net to the widest audience possible.

Consider the pros and cons of the quick-fix position type:

Pro: The organization pays a premium for skillful, immediate service.

Pro: The position is short-term and, therefore, does not detract from your ability to maintain contact with multiple organizations simultaneously. These positions are the most readily available on freelance job sites and are available in great numbers, thereby increasing your opportunity for work.

Pro: If the company regularly hires freelancers for project-based work, doing a good job means you could become one of the go-to people whenever a project pops up. These companies can be wonderful clients who readily share your name with colleagues that need immediate, skillful help with a project.

Con: The quick-fix position likely requires you to drop everything and make time available on your schedule within a few days. If you cannot respond readily due to an inflexible scheduling circumstance, you will likely be passed over.

Con: The environment *may* be fast and furious, a real pressure cooker. If you perform well under pressure, this is most certainly the job for you; if not, run for the door.

The quick fix is my favorite position type because the work is well defined, is short term, and pays well. The work readily accommodates your prescribed Lifestyle Design in that you can accept the work when it fits into your schedule and decline it when you have other priorities. This position type is a true departure from the rigid 9-to-5 job; in fact, this employment arrangement is enviable to a 9-to-5er. Numerous employment opportunities are available both at brick-and-mortar companies in your local area as well as online through employment sites such as Elance.com. What's not to love?

The Star

Being the *star* is the holy grail of freelance opportunities. It is the opportunity to perform a specialized task on an ongoing basis, for which you charge a premium. The work is steady and predictable, and you have an opportunity to settle in and get to know the norms and expectations of both the decision maker and the organization at large.

Consider the pros and cons of the star position type:

Pro: Many! These are the bread-and-butter positions that you come to count on and around which you schedule everything else. They allow your schedule and your income to develop normalcy, however you define it within your lifestyle framework.

Con: With these types of projects, you can quickly become too comfortable with your circumstances and lose sight of the need to keep fishing for new leads and refreshing old ones.

Con: Others in the organization may become resentful of your circumstances over time, wishing they enjoyed the same freedom and recognition that you do, especially if your rate of pay is made public. As a result, the workplace environment can become hostile, but such antagonistic behavior is less applicable if you do the work off-site in your home office.

Being the star is fabulous. You are considered a talented asset within the organization, and there is a hint of celebrity status that accompanies it. The organization expects top-notch performance from you, so be prepared. However, if you can perform well, your bottom line will reap the rewards. I know a man who paid off his entire mortgage working as the star at a company as a specialized computer operator for a single year, which is an extreme example, but what a great one!

As a Patchworker, you may hold several of these position types simultaneously at any given time. As offers surface over time, you have the opportunity to test each type and determine which are a good fit for your lifestyle. Ultimately, you create a work schedule that is a veritable patchwork, where you work for multiple employers and likely in multiple position types.

The Freelance Dance

Creating a schedule comprised of work performed for multiple organizations takes some fancy footwork both on your calendar and in practice, a skill I refer to as the *freelance dance*. The amount of time you spend working for each company each day determines how much dancing around you have to do to earn the amount of money you have in mind. Projects can range in frequency and include any of the following timeframes:

- Daily
- Weekly
- Monthly
- Seasonally
- Quarterly
- Project-based (one time)
- Project-based (recurring)
- Sporadic

The type of position you choose ultimately determines the pace and predictability of your schedule, which ultimately translates into a lifestyle choice. For example, if you were paid the same hourly rate for working one 30-hour project or two 15-hour projects, which would you choose? The answer depends on your personality, your interests, and the anticipated duties, which is the beauty of being free to customize your career. You can do the work that is most interesting to you and in the configuration that is most attractive based on your preferences.

Here are a few examples to get you thinking along those lines:

- If an action-packed day inspires you, perhaps you schedule yourself to be on-site at several organizations in a single day.
- If variety energizes you, perhaps you work on several different projects from your home office each and every day.
- If you value being able to focus on one project for concentrated periods of time, perhaps you work a full day for a single employer.

Keep your ideal Lifestyle Design in mind and then negotiate the circumstances that add energy to your workdays.

Practical Considerations

Keep in mind that the more employers you work for in a single day, week, or month, the greater the paperwork that awaits you as a business owner. For example, if you must invoice each employer to receive payment, this adds a new layer of work to the process that you must factor into your overall workload when planning your schedule.

Also worthy of note is the fact that for every organization you work with, there will be multiple e-mail messages and other communications that you must contend with, including innocuous office updates that simply require time to sift through. The first year that I became a Patchworker, I was employed by more than a dozen organizations simultaneously and thought that the combined invoicing and e-mailing alone should have counted as an additional job. And because I was the boss, I decided to treat it like it was. I created time on my calendar twice a day to sift through e-mail, open the snail mail, and return phone calls, which provided a sense of order and calm.

Rest assured that you don't have to figure everything out all at once. Being a Patchworker is a learn-as-you-go proposition in many ways. Seek out advice from seasoned freelancers in person, through books and blogs, and via dynamic communication networks such as Twitter and specialty Internet mailing lists. It's a good idea to begin accepting positions slowly to allow yourself time to iron out wrinkles that appear in your scheduling, bookkeeping, and other systems. However, if you have a personality like mine, then you may not be able to resist just jumping in with both feet and figuring it out along the way. Choose the style that is the best fit for you and enjoy the freelance dance on your own terms.

Endnotes

[1] *Wikipedia*, s.v. "Freelancer," http://en.wikipedia.org/wiki/Freelancer (accessed August 22, 2010).

[2] Mike Stathis, *America's Financial Apocalypse* (Dallas: Apex Venture Advisors, 2006), 244.

[3] United States Bureau of Labor Statistics, "Career Guide to Industries, 2010–11 Edition," United States Department of Labor, www.bls.gov/oco/oco2003.htm#Labor%20Force (accessed August 22, 2010).

[4] United States Bureau of Labor Statistics.

CHAPTER 9

Guiding Beliefs of the Patchwork Principle

Every successful company has a credo; it's a set of fundamental beliefs or guiding principles. *Credo* is a Latin word that literally translates to mean "I believe." For example, if you visit the corporate Web sites of either Johnson & Johnson or Walmart, you'll see that they devote a page to spelling out what they proclaim to believe. These simple statements are meant to guide the daily operations of the business, shape policies, and so on; they spell out the guiding beliefs of the business.

Along those same lines, this chapter is devoted to spelling out the eleven guiding beliefs of the Patchwork Principle.

The 11 Guiding Beliefs of the Patchwork Principle

The following guiding beliefs of the Patchwork Principle are designed to inspire, guide, and motivate you as you go forth to create your own business:

P   is for Purpose. Life matters; work on purpose.

A   is for Access. Access is power.

T   is for Time. Own your time, own your life.

C   is for Choice. Choose your company wisely.

H   is for Happiness. Happiness is the key to success.

W   is for Work. You will always have more work than you need.

O   is for Originality. Be an original; separate yourself from the pack.

R   is for Revenue. Small jobs can yield big payoffs.

K   is for Knowledge. Know that you can be anything you want to be.

E   is for Energy. Momentum equals money.

R   is for Reward. A life lived well is the best reward of all.

Each of these guiding beliefs plays an important role in the success of your business and your Lifestyle Design. Let's take a look at them in detail.

P *Is for Purpose: Work on Purpose*

Work on purpose—I love this phrase. It can have so many different meanings, each with its own redeeming message. It has depth and complexity, and yet it is just three simple words. I liken it to the way we see ourselves: We each have depth and complexity, and yet we are all just simple human beings. We often stifle the deepest desires of our hearts in the name of work, but what if we didn't? What if *you* were to *work on purpose*?

After reading the book to this point, think about what you have determined to be *the* most important personal and professional priorities on the list you are formulating. What is it that really matters to you? Is it your career? Is it your family? Is it having complete autonomy at work? Or is it being able to attend all of your daughter's soccer games this season? Is it having the biggest boat at the yacht club or the most expensive car in the office parking lot? Is it spending time with loved ones or a circle of close friends? What really matters to you? Seriously, take a minute to think about it and fill in the blanks below.

Write About It

_____

_____

_____

_____

There are four basic categories that generally account for what matters to us in life, with the priority order of each determined by our own personal values and goals:

- Time
- Money
- Relationships (family, friends, dating)
- Work

Now, depending on who you are and what you value, your priorities may tend toward one category more than others. Go ahead, take a minute to write the priorities you just listed next to the appropriate category in the following pie chart:

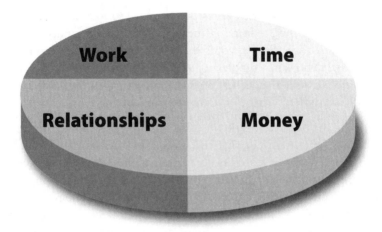

Now, take a minute to look at what matters *most* to you in life: time, money, relationships, or work. Although each of the categories is important, one may be paramount in your life depending on a number of factors, including your age, marital status, or value system. This exercise makes no judgments; instead it is about identifying what matters most to you.

So, based on how your priorities fit into each of the categories, which category matters *most* to you? Write it here:

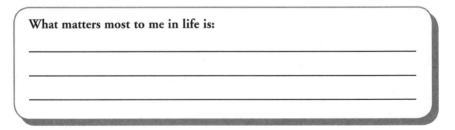

What matters most to me in life is:

Now that you have sorted out what matters to you most in life, you have a focal point going forward. What matters most to you is what this book is really all about, right? It's about creating a thriving career that matches your lifestyle, which is a reflection of what matters most to you. So, if what matters most to you is

Time, then you might be interested in using the Patchwork Principle to create a career that allows you to work shorter days, take the summer off for travel, or work only nights and weekends to complement your spouse's schedule in order to avoid putting the kids in day care. In survey after survey, people in the United States report that free time, even more than money, is what they most value and long to have more of. Are you one of those people? If so, applying the Patchwork Principle is your opportunity to take control of your time and take back your life.

Money, then you are interested in leveraging your many accounts against one another and you also have an interest in strategic scheduling to allow you to fit as many hours in as you can each week for your most lucrative accounts. Maximizing your profits is simply a matter of mastering a freelance dance that suits the goals that you have for your business's bottom line. Unlike a salaried 9-to-5 employee, a Patchworker has limitless earning potential with the only boundaries being those determined by the priorities of your Lifestyle Design.

Relationships, then the Patchwork Principle interests you because it allows you to be there for the special occasions in the lives of your family and friends. It also allows you to easily plan your work schedule around your family or friends' sporting events, medical appointments, or vacation periods. If you are single and dating, it means that you can plan romantic getaways well in advance without worrying about having to cancel at the last minute because of an unforeseen meeting at work.

Work, then the Patchwork Principle can provide you with a unique and interesting career that has the potential to be both a wellspring of employment and a source of status because it is what many of your friends and colleagues so desperately want: freedom from the 9-to-5 grind. There is a certain amount of self-satisfaction and feeling of superiority that comes from knowing that you figured out how to earn a living that is recession-proof and completely on your own terms. If being ahead of the curve is important to your identity and your identity primarily is derived from your work, then you are in luck because this strategy is way out in front in comparison to the 9-to-5 approach!

The fact that you are taking time to reflect on what your priorities are and how to create a career that fits into your lifestyle puts you at a distinct advantage compared to the general population. Most people go about their daily lives in a trance. They stop dreaming and just exist. You can see it in their eyes. Take a look at a bus or subway car full of people during the morning commute to work. Most people are on autopilot, but you can always find a few people who are fully awake and ready to take on the day because they have purpose. Now you might think that it's simply the difference between being a "morning person" or not, but I'm here to tell you it's bigger than that. People who live with purpose wake up energized and ready for a new day of possibilities. They know that there is much to be done that day that is worthwhile, and they look forward to getting started.

A Is for Access: Access Is Power

You have heard the phrase "access is power" more times than you can count, right? The story goes that if you knew Oprah or Ellen personally, they might give you a chance to be on the show and feature your product or service, which in turn could catapult your career overnight. That would be fabulous, and if you do know either one of them, then by all means pick up the phone! Now for a reality check. How many of us actually know a national celebrity? Not many. So now what?

If you take a lesson from the Patchwork Principle playbook, you cultivate access to people who have the ability to help you achieve greatness, albeit on a smaller scale. Consider this example related to the advertising of this book:

> As I write this book, I have twenty-eight active accounts. That means that I am either on the payroll or am working as an independent contractor for each of the twenty-eight organizations. This does not mention my inactive accounts, with which I have ongoing relationships but am not actively working for at the present time. Okay, now let's consider the "access-is-power principle," which is where those accounts and this book intersect.

> The week I learned this book was being picked up by a publisher, I mentioned it, one by one, to the decision makers at each of my active accounts. When I shared the news with them, I also asked if they would allow me to promote the book in their corporate publications (many of which are distributed quarterly to every single household in their respective cities). Thankfully, each of them quickly gave me a supportive nod, and I pitched a few rough ideas right there on the spot.

There are surely another seventy or so accounts that are "inactive," which means simply that although I am not currently working for them, I have in the past and could possibly again in the future. What it absolutely means is that I can (and will!) contact all of them and ask if they would be willing to help advertise my book. This is also a fabulous opportunity to remind them about my skills and abilities and refresh their image of me.

Now, if you step back and look at this real-life scenario, you'll notice that because I had *immediate* and *familiar* access to the decision makers, I was able to approach them with ease, and they felt the same way. They knew and liked the quality of my work from past experience and, therefore, felt comfortable trusting that my future work, this book, would yield something similar. They also knew something about my character and reliability and how others reacted to me in the workplace. This previous experience with me gave the decision makers added confidence that blindly agreeing to help promote this book was a risk they were willing to take. After all, when an organization helps advertise someone, it is an endorsement of sorts and they have to be selective in order to maintain their credibility.

Cultivating your access to key decision makers in your business or industry is critical to the success of your Patchwork business. These relationships take time to develop and need to be nurtured on an ongoing basis in order to remain current and for you to continue to be relevant to them. It takes effort, but it is an investment that is well worth your time.

T *Is for Time: Own Your Time*

Life matters too much to a Patchworker to spend it any way other than living on their own terms. They are willing to work full throttle when it's appropriate, but they have the choice to design a more reasonably paced schedule if that suits them better during a certain part of the week or year—or they can make it a lifestyle. The key word in that last sentence is *choice*. That one word is the most powerful noun in the world. If you don't believe me, then ask any administrative assistant if they envy the freedom with which their boss chooses to come in late, leave early, take a long lunch, or jet off to a conference at some resort location; they are envious, believe me! The power to choose a life lived with purpose is yours; know what matters most to you and then keep that at the forefront as you design your Patchwork schedule.

Owning your time—true freedom—begins with accepting the fact that your time is priceless and finite. It means rejecting the 9-to-5 thinking in terms of "Five days are theirs, two days are mine." The bias-free reality is that "seven days are yours, ZERO days are theirs"—unless you choose otherwise. Choose otherwise! Choose! Otherwise, you will continue to be stuck in that cycle of captivity where the employer owns your time forty-plus hours each week for the thirty prime years of your life. Choose freedom!

RESULTS-ONLY WORK ENVIRONMENT (ROWE)

Freedom from that 9-to-5 mindset requires a shift in your outlook relative to time, and it is directly in line with an innovative idea called the Results-Only Work Environment (ROWE). In the book *Work Sucks,* Cali Ressler and Jody Thompson outline the basic premise that, when given the opportunity, employees can work in a schedule-free environment and still produce great results. Where you work, how you work, and when you work is up to you; there is no judgment as long as you produce. Ressler and Thompson say that it's just like TiVo for work! Who doesn't love that kind of freedom and flexibility?

Now let's take a slice out of the ROWE model designed for corporate America's employees and put it into context for the Patchworker. When you are a Patchworker, getting results is all you care about. You have no interest in scheduling meetings or shuffling paper just to pass the time. The Patchworker enjoys a life of ROWE, if you will. Freedom is paramount, but the focal point isn't on time off; it's simply a sharp focus on getting in, getting results, and then going about your day. The day isn't about work. Instead, work is only one small component of the overall activities of the day. For example, here is what my day looked like one recent Wednesday:

Had breakfast with my family	8 a.m.–9 a.m.
Taught a class for two hours	9 a.m.–11 a.m.
Went to the gym	11 a.m.–12 p.m.
Shopped for groceries and ran errands	2 p.m.–4 p.m.
Read a book	4 p.m.–5 p.m.
Made dinner	5 p.m.–6 p.m.
Spent the night with family	6 p.m.–8 p.m.
Worked on a proposal	8 p.m.–10 p.m.

As you can see from this example, my day was really my own. I taught a class and worked on a proposal (both activities were billable hours, by the way), but I lived my life that day, too. I fit work into my life instead of the other way around. In other words, where work was concerned, I got in, got out, and got on with my life. I chose to save working on the proposal until the evening after the sun had set, when I typically feel more creative. It was my idea of a perfect day.

Before this section ends, please note that owning your time requires some advanced planning and commitment. When you work in a Patchwork Principle environment, you may choose to accept work that requires you to set appointment times and be there, in which case you had sure better be there! For example, if a client asks me to teach a class, it is up to me to determine the date and time the class will meet, but then I had better get it onto my calendar and show up as planned. Being reliable and honoring your commitments is an inherent ingredient of success for successful Patchworkers. On the other hand, if you choose to do strictly project-based work, you can practically throw the calendar out the window and revert to a customized ROWE forever! I've done this, and it's fantastic for many reasons, but alas I'm an educator at heart and so I commit to being in the face-to-face classroom regularly simply because it is a source of happiness for me. That's the beauty of the Patchwork Principle: You choose what work makes you happy, and you choose when you do it—and we haven't even gotten to the part about being paid a premium for it! "Smash the clock!" as they say, and never look back.

C Is for Choice: Choose Your Company Wisely

How many people do you know who like the actual work they do but not the organization they work for or the people they work with? I think we all know a few people in that situation. A client of mine, "Lynn," worked as a full-time child psychologist and absolutely loved her job so much that she didn't mind a bit about being underpaid and sitting in a run-down office space for more than twenty years. All of those things were irrelevant to her. When she thought about her career, only the faces of the children whom she helped came to mind.

However, a few years ago a new director was hired, and in Lynn's estimation he was heartless. Children were now referred to as "cases," and quotas were put in place to be sure that a maximum number of children were cycled through the office in order to maximize profits. These quotas meant that sometimes children were hurried out the door after a grueling counseling session at the expense of rushing the next child in. The director changed the entire office culture, and not for the better in Lynn's estimation. Ultimately, she made the decision to retire early—from work that she dearly loved—because the organization was no longer in alignment with her values. How sad. One lousy boss and suddenly her career was history.

This story repeats itself over and other for so many people in today's work world. However, bosses have virtually no influence on the Patchworker's overall career satisfaction. In fact, the boss is an extremely small factor in the overall scheme of things. For example, if you have a dozen accounts and one of them goes sour because the boss is a dud, you can choose to simply finish up the assignment and then never work with that person again. It's that simple. How many people spend the better part of their careers complaining about a terrible boss at one company after another? Many! Are you one of them? Life is too short; take control of the reigns and determine which organizations are the best fit for you.

As you entertain offers from different potential employers, keep in mind that choosing your company wisely is, in my estimation, even more important than the work you actually do for the following reasons:

- **It can affect future opportunities.** Consider that working for a top company in your field can encourage other lesser companies to hire you because you have the credential of working for one of the industry leaders on your resume. Likewise, consider that working for a morally offensive company can preclude you from working for a company that holds its values in high esteem (such as a religious organization).

- **It can affect your earning potential.** Where you work can affect your earning potential with future organizations. For example, if you work at Company X for $45 per hour, then Company Y may receive a referral, call you up, and offer the same rate of pay that you received at Company X. This has happened to me more times than I can count, and it is difficult to negotiate up without Company Y feeling like they are getting ripped off. It is a sound reason for not accepting work that is at a rate of pay far below your asking price.

- **It can affect your outlook.** Working for a company that treats its employees, its customers, or the environment poorly can rub off on you. Although it will likely not cause you to suddenly start behaving badly as well, it can affect you in other subtle ways such as making you feel lousy about going in to work or being affiliated with the organization, or angry about how the organization is harming or exploiting the environment. Sometimes it is hard to spot a bad organization during the interview process, so if you unexpectedly find yourself working for this type of organization, finish the work you committed to and get out as quickly as possible. If the company is unethical, you may also want to consider striking them from your resume or list of past clients that potential clients may use to size up your experience.

- **It can affect your pace.** Working for a company that is fueled by stress and chaos on a regular basis can leave you feeling stressed out. Long assignments with organizations such as these can create a sense of being back in the 9-to-5 world, where you are on edge and think about work after hours. On the other hand, if stress and chaos energize you, then these companies might be the ones you gravitate toward. Remember, the choice is yours and yours alone.

- **It can affect your health.** Working for companies that treat people or the environment poorly can take a toll on some people. I'm one of them. For example, if I know that the product Company X is making contributes to the exploitation of the rain forest or child labor overseas, then I feel a sense of responsibility for the injustices that are being carried out; it weighs on me. If you react in a similar way, avoid aligning yourself with these companies for your own peace of mind.

For the sake of your integrity, your income, and even your health, choose the company you keep with great care. After all, you are a product of the company you keep.

H *Is for Happiness: Happiness Is the Key to Success*

Happiness is at the heart of a thriving Patchwork career, and that seeps into the fabric of every corner of your life. Happiness also drives your business forward and, in my experience, is the magic that gives you a competitive advantage over someone else delivering the same product or service, because you radiate an image that makes people want to seek you out. You inspire, and that draws people to you. But what makes Patchworkers really happy about the work that they do? Let's take a look at it from a scientific standpoint; this is the not-so-secret recipe!

The Recipe for Happiness

Malcom Gladwell, the author of *Outliers*, studied the extraordinary careers of people who rose from obscurity to great acclaim and came to the conclusion that "…autonomy, complexity and a connection between effort and reward—are, most people agree, the three qualities that work has to have if it is to be satisfying. It's not how much money we make that ultimately makes us happy between nine and five. It's whether our work fulfills us."[1] This statement speaks directly to the heart of the Patchwork Principle, which incorporates each of these three critical components; let's look at each one relative to the framework.

Autonomy

Autonomy is defined as the quality or state of being self-governing, according to Merriam-Webster.[2] In a career context, it is the ability to make your own decisions instead of the boss making them for you. When the Patchwork Principle guides your career, you are in complete control of everything that takes place in your career. Where you work, whom you work with, when you work, what wage you are willing to accept, how you market your business, where you locate your business, and more—everything is up to you.

Now this scenario is both good and bad. What I mean by this is that when you are in a 9-to-5 career, there often are opportunities to hide behind a committee and blame bad decisions or lack of decisions on the group process. However, when you are a thriving Patchworker, the buck stops with you. If you make a great decision, then you reap the rewards. If you make a poor decision, then you pay the price. However, according to Gladwell and others who have studied happiness and success, it's not the results that determine how autonomy makes us feel; instead it is the *opportunity* to make our own decisions and call the shots that is satisfying. This sense of independence is certainly one of the well-known, age-old attractions to becoming an entrepreneur. Working for yourself is quite simply the opposite of working for "The Man," with autonomy being a key differentiator. This independence is also perhaps the greatest gift that you give to yourself on a daily basis.

For a thriving Patchworker, change can happen in an instant. There are no layers of decision making; you're it! You can easily try out new ideas and take them for a spin without asking for permission. No one knows your business better than you do, and although it is valuable to seek feedback from trusted colleagues about key decisions, the number of people you do or do not involve in the process is your choice. In other words, if you have an idea tonight and want to try it out tomorrow, autonomy affords you the freedom to take action when, where, and how you choose. Let me give you an example:

> When I set up shop for my business, I needed to name it and develop a logo. In a single day, I brainstormed a long list of names, checked the state and federal trademark records to see if a business with the name already existed, and came up with a short list and some corresponding logo designs that I pitched to a trusted inner circle. By 10 p.m. that same night, I had a name and logo design for my business. Now that's autonomy!

It is no surprise then that one of the keys to having a fulfilling career is being autonomous. After all, you are a capable human being with the intelligence to make logical decisions. Why would you want to defer all of the most important choices about your work life to someone else? Autonomy counts for a lot in my book.

Complexity

Gladwell defines complexity in this context as "work that engages your mind and your imagination"—in other words, work that is both interesting and appealing. It's the opposite of work where the tasks are redundant, predictable, or "canned," none of which allows for engagement of any kind because the outcomes are already predetermined. Examples of work lacking in complexity, based on this definition, include cashiering, stuffing envelopes, sorting packages, assembling products, and the like. These jobs that lack in complexity are often described by another word, in colloquial terms—boring!

Boring jobs abound in the 9-to-5 world to such an extent that entire Web sites are dedicated to passing the time, complete with "goof-off games" and other time wasters. Is this really how you want to spend the prime of your life? Just staring at the clock and doodling or playing online? I ran across an article on eHow.com, titled "How to Survive a Boring Job," that suggested ways to pass time at work. The article included such ideas as getting up and going to the supply closet for a chance to get away from your desk, even if you already have a stockpile of supplies on hand.[3] If this describes your current workday, please, for the sake of your mental health, find something different to do!

And it's not just mental health that suffers when you work in a boring job. Your physical health deteriorates as well. A study at the University of Texas School of Public Health found that "workers who spend their lives in undemanding jobs with little control over their work are 35 percent more likely to die during a 10-year period than workers in challenging jobs with lots of options and decision-making [opportunities]."[4] If boredom is dangerous to your mental and physical health, then what's the solution?

The solution is seeking out work that engages your mind and your imagination. When you work within the framework of the Patchwork Principle, you fully engage your mind at every turn. For example, on a regular basis you seek new opportunities by doing research to identify gaps in organizations, crafting your pitch, negotiating your rate, and so on. Your mind is fully engaged throughout the process—even before you are on the job. Within the Patchwork Principle framework, your career can be anywhere and doing anything you want from day to day. If you want to spend today working indoors and tomorrow working outdoors, schedule your work accordingly. If you want to work three days of the week this month doing work you are familiar with and two days of the week experimenting with a new area of interest, then make it happen. With the Patchwork Principle, the only limits to engaging your mind are the boundaries of your imagination.

Connection Between Effort and Reward

The concept of "connection between effort and reward" is a simple but powerful premise. Take, for example, someone who works at a job on an hourly basis. They know that for every additional hour they work, the larger their paycheck will be. This is the opposite of a salaried employee, who may be required to work additional hours for no additional pay in order to "get the job done." According to Gladwell's theory, the hourly work would be rewarding and tied closely with happiness, and a recent study at Stanford University arrived at the very same conclusion: "Workers who get paid by the hour are happier than salaried employees because they see a clear link between output and reward."[5]

This is good news for Patchworkers, who know that the more leads they generate, the greater number of accounts they are likely to land. The greater the number of accounts, the more income they are likely to generate. Thus, for every effort there is a direct connection tied to a reward. Working smarter instead of working longer hours counts, too. The goal isn't doing more necessarily, but instead knowing that your efforts will be rewarded. This connection is at the heart of every entrepreneurial endeavor and is directly linked to job satisfaction and career happiness.

A certain amount of optimism goes hand in hand with this approach to work, including the belief that there is work to be found and that effort will be rewarded. To be a Patchworker, you have to muster up some level of optimism in order to be successful. Believing that you can re-create both your work and your life is the driving force that keeps you pressing forward even in the face of temporary setbacks. Cultivating optimism is an inside job, and it has its benefits beyond work. In his book *The Pursuit of Happiness*, David Myers reports that optimists are healthier and "are less bothered by various illnesses and recover better from coronary bypass surgery and cancer. Blood tests…link optimism with stronger immune defenses."[6] Myers goes on to say that optimists enjoy greater success, due in part to how they process setbacks in a positive way.

This idea circles back to what many people refer to as "visualization," as discussed in Rhonda Byrne's blockbuster *The Secret*, which details the Law of Attraction, or in Norman Vincent Peale's groundbreaking book *The Power of Positive Thinking*. If you want to be successful at this shift to a new career lifestyle, you must come at it with a sincere belief that you can be successful. In other words, if you believe that there is work out there just waiting to be found, then the work is more likely to show up. It is the Law of Attraction, which according to Byrnes is "a law of nature" that predates biblical times. The belief is that everything you think, speak, or act upon attracts that which you focus on into your life. Therefore, if you broadcast positive thoughts, words, and actions about landing new accounts, the Law of Attraction will bring opportunities to you or you to them.

A statement by Jack Canfield, author of *Chicken Soup for the Soul* and contributor to *The Secret*, makes a statement that I truly believe is what keeps so many people from living as Patchworkers: "Most of us have never allowed ourselves to want what we truly want, because we can't see how it's going to manifest." Making the transition from the traditional 9-to-5 world to Patchworking requires a certain amount of optimism about the fact that your efforts at creating a career on your own terms with a lifestyle to match can come to fruition. If you believe, not only is the Law of Attraction at work in your life, but also you feel better, are more motivated, and, as a result, are more creative and likely to find work. Positive begets positive; negative begets negative. You have a choice, so why not choose to be positive?

Being Happy Pays Dividends

Happiness is a must for the successful Patchworker. However, if you still suffer from burnout or disappointments from your 9-to-5 career, don't despair. You can cultivate happiness over time. The more closely you align your everyday life with your core values, the faster you will race toward a better outlook. And happiness has a payoff that can translate into tangible benefits for your business. Alexander Kjerulf, a work happiness speaker and author, believes that happy people[7]

- Work better with others

- Are more creative

- Fix problems instead of complaining about them

- Have more energy

- Are more optimistic

- Are way more motivated

- Get sick less often

- Learn faster

- Worry less about making mistakes—and consequently make fewer mistakes

- Make better decisions

This list could also describe the fundamental characteristics of a successful Patchworker. Being happy pays, literally and figuratively! Cultivate happiness, why not?

W Is for Work: You Will Always Have More Work Than You Need

Will I be able to find enough work on a consistent basis? Is this the question that is at the forefront of your mind as you read through the pages of this book? In my experience the answer to the question is, "Yes, if you are willing to do the footwork and stick with it." Are you a skeptic? If so, I'm sure you are not alone. The media and our society in general spend so much energy spreading and reinforcing fear-based sound bytes that the message is impossible to ignore. However, the job data and the general perceptions out there among the media's talking heads and at workplace water coolers is often just plain wrong.

Although current unemployment reports may show an increase of job losses nationwide, I want you to change how you view those numbers and the beliefs deeply held by so many about available jobs. Those numbers that all of the news networks drone on and on about regularly represent traditional job openings. Those jobs absolutely do go up and down in availability over time depending on any number of economic factors and indicators. However, those jobs are not the "work" I'm describing in this book. The work I'm describing can be for a posted part-time position, but it is more likely one that you seek out; it's identifying a need (known or unknown to the would-be employer) and then finding a solution. If you can pitch an immediate, no-brainer solution, an abundance of employers will always stand at the ready to hire you. (If you're reading this book at a job fair while you are in a line that is two hours long, I suggest you leave the line, walk out the door, and go home to rethink your career strategy. Go do something more productive and where your odds are better. Start looking for needs

> **Note the Official Disclaimer**
>
> This is the official legal disclaimer where the author states that securing work is not guaranteed. Success is a combination of persistence, talent, and some old-fashioned good luck along the way.

and coming up with solutions for businesses in your area; start brainstorming about it. Right now!)

The belief that no one is hiring at certain times of the year or certain times in the economy's history is false. For example, in the middle of the U.S. financial crisis of 2008 and the biggest spike in unemployment in decades, my business was booming. In fact, my business was performing at the highest levels to date during the worst part of the stock market crash. My job was inverse to the economy; the worse things got out there, the better they got over here. Why? The simple fact is that no matter what is going on in the economy, every business that plans to stay in business must keep moving forward. To do that, they often need to hire additional workers for specialized projects or to fill in gaps that do not justify hiring a full-time employee. Employers, especially in a bad economy, want to hire people who are brought in on the following terms: short term, project specific, and at will with no liabilities to account for. They want to hire YOU!

When the economy is in great shape, you will have work just like everyone else. When the economy is tanking and 9-to-5ers are clutching their ID swipe cards for dear life hoping they can hold onto their job for another week, your career will be in high gear. I lived through it; I still am, as the economy is slow to recover. Believe me when I say that there is more work out there than you will ever want or need. I'm currently employed to the point of overflow. It's not that I possess some never-before-seen skill set; it's simply that I apply the Patchwork Principle, and it results in more work than I can handle. It's fabulous, and it's something that you can do, too. Join me in enjoying ultimate job security!

ULTIMATE JOB SECURITY

Forget about the ups and downs of working for a set employer where if they have a bad year, so do you. Instead, ride the prosperity wave. You can choose to affiliate with companies that are doing well, so long as they do well. If the company begins to lose ground or nosedive, simply move on or come back when things turn around.

Does this sound like an attractive way of life, but you still worry about job security? I get this a lot. Allow me a moment to provide an alternative perspective from the traditional pitch that we hear throughout adulthood. Here it goes:

(continued)

(continued)

Full-time career employment is the antithesis of the Patchwork Principle approach. Full-time career employment provides a false sense of security because at any moment, loss of that job renders the person fully unemployed and without any income—in an instant everything can change. However, if you are happily employed as a Patchworker, the loss of one job simply reduces your workload by one account, which you can gradually (or immediately) fill in with a little effort. Also, keep in mind that when cutbacks occur, often the high-paying positions are the ones that are cut; the "small potatoes" jobs that only account for five to ten hours per week of earnings are usually spared because human resources believes, sometimes erroneously, that their impact on the company's bottom line is insignificant.

Being a Patchworker affords a true sense of job security because there is not an ongoing dependence on a single employer for livelihood. If budget cuts result in layoffs at an organization, that change does not have a devastating consequence because no single job is of great consequence. It is the sum of the parts that is powerful; the collective employment of the Patchworker determines the income for that year. And in the event that funding is cut for a project or position, the Patchworker has the know-how and networks all over town to drum up additional work. This scenario brings to mind that famous phrase "The sun never sets on the British Empire" because the goal of the Patchworker is to develop a vast network of contacts and assignments, which you can think of as "territories" in a variety of locations and industries. If you develop accounts in South Carolina and South Africa, then your career "empire" would be like the British Empire after all!

For the Patchworker who operates locally, don't be fooled into believing that your accounts will be small in number due to geographic limitations; that is how I operate, by choice, and business is booming! Your empire isn't a place; it's a dynamic whereby you apply your skills and your newfound power. It's the Kingdom of You! Isn't that exciting to think about? I mean, c'mon, in practical terms you are the ruler of your territory; you are in charge of your career destiny. It's a little corny, but it's completely true, just like this popular George Crane quote: "There is no future in any job. The future lies in the man who holds the job."

O *Is for Originality: Separate Yourself from the Pack*

Let's face it. As a Patchworker you are not like the typical prospective employee who walks in the door for an interview with a decision maker. For one thing, you are more interesting right from the get-go. You have a unique career paradigm and are self-employed. That implies a certain amount of self-discipline, tenacity, and confidence that makes people want to learn more about you. Also, there is nothing about you that raises those standard red flags in the mind of a potential employer that might get flagged if you were a 9-to-5er walking in the door (for example, why are you currently unemployed?). Instead of going to the decision maker in a desperate attempt at locating full-time career employment and all of the costs and rigmarole that go along with it, you are a delightfully trouble-free answer to the organization's needs. When you meet the potential employer during that first meeting, please know that this person is wondering if this is all too good to be true. He or she wonders if hiring a high-quality worker without all of the proverbial "strings" is really as simple as saying, "You're hired!"

Sometimes you can spot that "is-it-too-good-to-be-true" look in their eyes. I remember seeing this look in the eyes of a potential employer many years ago. She called me in to serve as an immigration compliance officer for a college in my area. The job required years of specialized knowledge in order to navigate the complicated trappings of the federal paperwork and computerized reporting system. Remember my "dream job" and the years of training leading up to it? It was all of that stuff. So, here I sat across the desk from a seemingly nice woman who called me out of the blue to pitch an offer, based on a recommendation from an employee from within the organization. Their current full-time employee had fallen ill suddenly, and they were in desperate need of an interim solution. I knew that finding another available, local, part-time employee with my depth and breadth of training and experience was next to impossible; I knew this was going to cost them: BIG. I offered to forward my CV (curriculum vitae) to her for review, because I knew that my long history of specialized experience would prepare her for the dollar figure I would pitch. We agreed to meet and discuss the job further.

During that first meeting, I learned about the organization's expectations and I responded with mine; I could do whatever was necessary to make this situation one that she didn't have to think about again. That was exactly what she wanted to hear—I was a solution staring her right in the face.

When it came time to discuss salary, I knew that pitching my highest hourly rate was the only logical thing to do. However, I also knew that everyone likes to think they got a bargain, so I doubled it. With a straight face I named double my hourly rate and sat there smiling, composed, and silent. She looked like a freight train just rolled into her office. Then she glanced at my CV sitting on her desk, the stack of problem files beneath it that she was hoping to hand off to me, and she took a deep breath and began negotiating. Ultimately, she got a bargain, and I landed an amazing deal! We both walked away happy. She would go on to shuffle me around the organization for various specialized tasks for the next six years. Good thing I negotiated well back on day one, right?

Okay, so what's my point? The point is that whatever your skill set, the Patchworker is an original. You're not the standard temporary employee sent over by an agency, and you're not the 9-to-5er desperately trying to land any job available. You don't fit neatly into any of the typical employee scenarios. Instead, you are a conveniently available, high-quality worker who is ready to bring the needed solutions where and when the employer needs you. You are agile, able to start working immediately, short or long term. Hiring a typical full-time employee costs the employer an average of 42 percent more than it would cost to hire you due to benefits; you come without those pesky strings.[8] In turn, employers are happy to pay an inflated rate for the duration of your short-term appointment, which you can use to earn a higher wage.

FIND YOUR NICHE AND EXPLOIT IT

When you are searching in the vast sea of opportunity for Patchwork positions that are a good fit with your experience and Lifestyle Design, you may find it overwhelming at first and you can quickly box yourself into a salary corner if you select a popular field (such as graphic design) and work only within the boundaries of that job description.

Therefore, a great strategy that is also the secret to my success is carving out a niche and, if at all possible, discovering one for which there is a need that no one else in your geographic location is exploiting. If this sounds daunting or nearly impossible, ask yourself if you have heard someone say or recently thought to yourself something along these lines:

- I wish I knew who to call for help with this.

- Someone should offer this product/service; it would be a hit!

I realize that this may sound like a simple-minded approach, but it works! This is exactly how I discovered my niche in the computer field. You might think that I came into the field with amazing credentials, but let me set the record straight:

- Do I have ultra-advanced IT training? No.

- Is there a real demand for the services that I provide? Yes.

- Do I change the lives of others for the good every single day? Yes.

- Can I earn a good wage? Yes, in fact I earn twice the amount I ever could have earned at my "dream job" with more than a decade of higher education and real-world preparation.

Do you know how I stumbled upon this niche? Simply by helping several neighbors in my area and realizing there was a real-world need for this computer service. That's it. There was no elaborate search process that helped me uncover an unfulfilled niche. I just thought it up one day while sitting on the couch and helping a neighbor solve a computer problem over the phone. Then I did a ton of follow-up market research in my area to be sure that my hunch was right, and voilà! So, while this might take some of the razzle-dazzle away from your image of me, know that the Patchwork Principle is an everyman's approach and the science of identifying your niche doesn't require anything more than keen observation and perhaps some creative thinking. You can do this!

R *Is for Revenue: Small Jobs Can Yield Big Payoffs*

American architect Julia Morgan once said, "Never turn down a job because you think it's too small; you don't know where it can lead!" This statement encapsulates this core belief of the Patchwork Principle nicely. However, the concept of a career that is comprised of many small jobs can be challenging for some people to wrap their minds around. After all, in American culture, small is undervalued. Small is small, big is big, and that's that. However, realistically we all know on some level that small can be powerful, and at the very least it can be a building block for something else. We know this at our core, however much we fight the notion. Let's face it; SMALL IS BIG!

Creating a big career out of small opportunities has definite advantages. For example, although a company may lack the political will to hire new full-time employees at any given time, they are generally eager and willing to hire someone pitching an immediate solution that requires only something like five hours of pay per week to accomplish. In fact, they might even hire you on the spot without any HR rigmarole or budget-approval process. (Now *that* is an advantage!) When you seek out small opportunities, as opposed to a full-time career position, you have a greater rate of success than the 9-to-5 guy. Your success will be due, in part, to the likelihood that the decision maker will agree to take a chance on a no-risk, part-time worker with a tangible solution in mind, as opposed to an expensive, permanent employee who cannot be hired (or fired) without due process. The choice is easy!

If you are concerned about whether or not businesses are willing to hire temporary workers in great numbers, it may be reassuring to learn that the U.S. Bureau of Labor Statistics (BLS) reported that employment agencies placed

3.1 million workers into temporary jobs in 2008.[9] And in late 2009 the *New York Times* reported that in a single *month* 52,000 temporary jobs were added to the labor force, which was "greater than the number of new workers in any other category. Not even health care and government, stalwarts through the long recession, did better."[10] And

> **Inspire Opportunity**
>
> Remember that visibility inspires opportunity. The more often a potential employer sees you, the more likely they are to think of you when a new project opens up that needs to be filled.

most impressive was the guiding outlook by the BLS in a recent publication that stated temporary employment "is expected to grow 19 percent over the 2008 to 2018 projection period, compared to the 11 percent growth projected for all industries combined. The industry is expected to gain about 599,700 new jobs over the period." The BLS went on to indicate that one reason for businesses to hire temporary workers is to allow for expansion, "incurring the additional costs associated with permanent employees."[11]

All of these are or will be advertised position openings that you can surely inquire about, but just imagine the unpublished work that people are being hired to complete on an everyday basis. I can attest to it; that work is 100 percent of my business most of the year. No matter what the economy is doing, for good or for bad, the work is there. And as you look at the projections for growth in advertised temporary positions between now and 2018, it seems like a boom time for Patchworking. Whether the future brings a downturn or an uptick in the economy, an excess of small employment opportunities will be waiting for you! In bad times businesses hire temporary and part-time workers. In good times they hire—period. Small jobs can yield big payoffs.

K Is for Knowledge: Know That You Can Be Anything You Want to Be

What if I told you that you could try out a new career field every few years? How about *every* year? How about *several times* a year? Well, I am here to tell you that you can be anything you want to be and change your mind regularly if you choose to do so. If you ask me what my favorite part of living the Patchwork Principle is, I would have trouble narrowing it down to just one specific component. However, I can tell you that this be-anything-you-want-to-be piece would be near the top of the list.

When you have a career that is comprised of, say, twenty-eight part-time jobs, you can easily try out new career interests from year to year. To experiment with a new area of interest, simply "fish" for work in that area and see whether your pitch can land you the position. I do it all the time! For example, I started out being a Patchworker by selling my skills as an immigration specialist.

After I felt confident about how my business was progressing, I indulged myself by fishing for work in Web site development, which had always been an interest of mine. Making this seemingly monumental shift from one profession to another was a piece of cake. One day I simply pitched an idea about developing a Web site to an organization for which I already worked. The client liked the idea, and later that year I worked (and learned) and had a lot of fun developing a great product for them. I also added a new skill to my career tool belt.

During another year, I thought about how I had also always wanted to write a newspaper column and experience that lifestyle. So, one day I wrote to the editor of a regional newspaper and asked if I could write a technology column for the paper; she agreed. Now I write a monthly piece and enjoy a nice response from readers who send in ideas and comments. It's creative and fun, and it also gives me a new credential to hang my hat on that helps me qualify for other positions that are in that same line of work. What more could you ask for?

Okay, I'll try to dial down the enthusiasm, but it's not easy! When you can sample new career fields at will and be paid for it, your energy level goes through the roof. I'm not saying that I have lots of odd jobs at any given time; I don't. What I do have is a core career field, education, which I use to anchor my income. Then I allow myself to explore other avenues. When I find something that I like, I put it on my mental list of "things I want to try out again," and the next time my calendar opens up, I pursue work that allows me to explore that interest a little more. That's it. There is no complicated career change formula. It can be an organic process whereby you allow new opportunities to present themselves over time, or it can be one where you seek out specific experiences in order to build your credentials or fulfill a lifelong dream.

If you find yourself trapped in a "job" or "career" but long to pursue your "calling," then Patchworking can lead you away from one and toward the other with ease. Taking a page from Jonathan Haidt's book *The Happiness Hypothesis*, we see that work falls into one of three categories:[12]

1. **Job:** The purpose is to make money. Work is simply necessary for survival. Clock-watching is central to the day.

2. **Career:** The focus is on advancement and prestige. This is the epitome of the rat race where everyone is competing for limited resources.

3. **Calling:** The work is done for its own sake; it is intrinsically fulfilling. You believe it contributes to a greater good or a larger worthwhile cause.

When you look at this list of choices, where does your most recent job fall along this spectrum of work? Are you at a "job"? Are you pursuing a "career"? Or are you engaged in your life's work, a "calling"? As a Patchworker you can transition to at least beginning to sample work that is in alignment with your calling rather quickly.

> **Track Market Trends**
>
> Follow the news about emerging markets or trends in specific fields that are growing or are predicted to grow over time. Cultivate small jobs in those fields or within those organizations to get a head start. After all, you are agile and able to shift and turn as the market changes and grows.

Some people are skeptical because they believe, erroneously, that their current skill set determines which of these three work categories they will be able to enjoy over their lifetime. However, Haidt addresses this, saying that people typically think of a blue-collar worker as having a "job," a white-collar worker as having a "career," and a minister as having a "calling." But he goes on to cite an example of a hospital janitor who believed that his work was a calling because he contributed to the larger mission of the organization, healing people. And even more interesting to me was Haidt's citation of a study that found that, contrary to popular belief, all three categories of work were represented in nearly every profession.[13]

Therefore, it's important to fully grasp the fact that no matter what your skill set, you can pursue a calling. Your limits are not determined by your work history, education, or lack thereof. Your limits are determined by your ability to stretch and grow, to open your mind to new ways of thinking about your work and your life. The work you do as a Patchworker is not meant to be a method of mere survival but instead a conscious decision to choose a fulfilling vocation that fits into the lifestyle framework you customized. "The most important question to ask on the job is not, 'What am I getting?' The most important question to ask is, 'What am I becoming?'" as motivational speaker Jim Rohn once said. Each time you accept new work, it is either solidifying the direction of your current career or taking you in a new direction; choose wisely.

In the beginning you may simply look for work that fits into your lifestyle framework. That is a starting point, and a fine place to begin at that.

However, know that by being a Patchworker you have the freedom to sample a variety of career interests. Think of your own career potential like an iceberg. Your area of specialization or the set of skills that you bring to the table during an interview are your visible, known skills—the visible part of the iceberg. The rest of your interests, talents, skills, and abilities are below the surface just waiting for you to, if you'll forgive me, "test out the waters" and see where they lead you.

However you feel about your work and your life when you begin this process, the goal is to move toward a career lifestyle that is engaging and energizing. Whatever shape that takes for you today or in the future is yours to design. You can be anything you want to be.

E *Is for Energy: Momentum Is Energy That Generates Income*

One of the many payoffs of the Patchwork Principle is that it builds momentum. Momentum is the muscle of your career that keeps your business moving forward. In the beginning, generating new leads takes effort. However, once you are in the door and have established relationships with decision makers and co-workers alike, producing new leads within that organization is a snap. And if you do a fantastic job (which you must!) and word gets around (which it will!), departments may trade you like playing cards (they do!) and even "fight" over who gets to have you (it's fabulous!)!

Now, multiply that experience by the one hundred accounts that you may land in the course of, say, two years. If 10 percent of them have you on the payroll in some capacity at any one time, that translates into having ten jobs simultaneously. As one project draws to a close or funding is cut in a department for which you work, you simply drop back to having *only* nine jobs. If you want to fill that empty job slot in your schedule, you just contact any of the other ninety accounts and start fishing. The more you work within your network of active or dormant accounts, the easier landing new projects gets because you already have a relationship with the decision makers, which makes the inquiry process nothing more than a series of casual conversations (or perhaps e-mail messages).

Ahead of a project ending, I typically begin networking with new or existing accounts to fill the anticipated opening. Commonly, however, other accounts have already asked me to "fit them in" when my schedule opens up; this momentum allows me to remain happily employed, to the max! The number of offers also allows me to be highly selective about where I am willing to work based on my level of enjoyment on the job, exposure for future projects, rate of pay, and other relevant factors. You may think to yourself, "Well, good for you, but I'm starting at square one!" No worries. Building momentum can happen quickly; it took me six months from formulating the initial idea of starting a Patchwork business to having my calendar reach a level of maximum saturation. Six months from zero to hero, as they say. It's all about persistence, timing, and a little luck.

Momentum equals money! It allows you to easily maintain a consistent standard of living. Your income doesn't ebb and flow with great variation. Instead it remains steady, even as the work you do changes. As one project ends, the next begins. When you enjoy the momentum that develops from the Patchwork Principle, you can bask in the glow of knowing that you are layoff-proof. Say goodbye to the career rollercoaster everyone else is used to riding based on the economy, office politics, and the like. Say hello to consistent career employment in a new format—and on your own terms!

> **Limit Your Availability**
>
> Once your calendar reaches maximum saturation for the first time, it may be a struggle to say no to accounts that come calling when you just don't have any free time available. I remember being afraid of losing the account if I couldn't "jump" when the client called. However, in time I came to realize that there was some element of fascination with my limited availability that made me seem more interesting, and many of those organizations were willing to wait until I could get on board. (People want what they can't have. Why is that?) Also worthy of note is the fact that organizations will pay more for your services when they know you are in demand.

R *Is for Reward: A Life Lived Well Is Its Own Reward*

As we wrap up this section on the guiding principles of Patchworking, excerpts from this poem by Elizabeth-Anne "Bessie" Anderson Stanley seem to appropriately summarize the true intent of the paradigm:

> He has achieved success
>
> Who has lived well, laughed often, and loved much…
>
> Who has filled his niche and accomplished his task…
>
> Who has left the world better than he found it…
>
> Who has always looked for the best in others and given them the best he had;
>
> Whose life was an inspiration; whose memory a benediction.[14]

Aligning yourself with work that speaks to your soul is powerful, bringing joy to your own life as well as to the lives of those around you, including family, friends, and clients. Having the time to really live your life and give a reasonable amount of attention to those things in your Lifestyle Design that matter most to you is empowering, calming, and ultimately highly lucrative because your enthusiasm for your career lifestyle attracts people (potential clients, for example) to you. Here is what Ralph Waldo Emerson had to say about the very same topic:

> Enthusiasm is one of the most powerful engines of success. When you do a thing, do it with your might. Put your whole soul into it. Stamp it with your own personality. Be active, be energetic, be enthusiastic and faithful, and you will accomplish your objective. Nothing great was ever achieved without enthusiasm.[15]

Living life on your own terms allows you to shape how you spend your days and with whom. It means living the dream you have for yourself, whatever that may be, instead of stifling it in the name of the almighty dollar. Patchworkers are self-made successes who live life on their own terms and live the dream 9-to-5ers only imagine. Patchworkers live a life that is truly gratifying. A life lived well is its own reward!

Endnotes

[1] Malcom Gladwell, *Outliers* (New York: Little, Brown, and Company, 2008), 149–150.

[2] *Merriam-Webster Online*, s.v. "Autonomy," www.merriam-webster.com/dictionary/autonomy (accessed January 2, 2010).

[3] Angela DeFini, "How to Survive a Boring Job," Ehow.com, www.ehow.com/how_2168855_survive-boring-job.html (accessed August 21, 2010).

[4] "Boring Jobs Kill," National Recreation and Park Association, August 2002, http://findarticles.com/p/articles/mi_m1145/is_8_37/ai_91398918 (accessed August 21, 2010).

[5] Sydney Morning Herald, "Being Paid by the Hour Makes Us Happier," *Sydney Morning Herald*, February 26, 2010, www.smh.com.au/executive-style/management/being-paid-by-the-hour-makes-us-happier-20100226-p7yi.html (access August 21, 2010).

[6] David Myers, *The Pursuit of Happiness* (New York: Avon Books, 1992), 117.

[7] Alexander Kjerulf, "Top Ten Reasons Why Happiness Is the Ultimate Productivity Booster," http://positivesharing.com/2007/03/top-10-reasons-why-happiness-at-work-is-the-ultimate-productivity-booster (accessed August 21, 2010).

[8] Mike Stathis, *America's Financial Apocalypse* (Dallas: Apex Venture Advisors, 2006), 259.

[9] United States Bureau of Labor Statistics, "Career Guide to Industries, 2010–11 Edition," United States Department of Labor, www.bls.gov/oco/cg/cgs039.htm#emply (accessed August 21, 2010).

[10] Louis Uchitelle, "Labor Data Show Surge in Hiring of Temp Workers," *New York Times*, December 20, 2009, www.nytimes.com/2009/12/21/business/economy/21temps.html (accessed August 21, 2010).

[11] United States Bureau of Labor Statistics.

[12] Jonathan Haidt, *The Happiness Hypothesis* (Cambridge: Basic Books, 2006), 221.

[13] Haidt, 222.

[14] *Wikipedia*, s.v. "Bessie Anderson Stanley," http://en.wikipedia.org/wiki/Bessie_Anderson_Stanley (accessed July 20, 2010).

[15] *Wikibooks*, "The Practice of Learning Theories/Motivation," http://en.wikibooks.org/wiki/The_Practice_of_Learning_Theories/Motivation#KNOWLEDGE_OF_LEARNING_MOTIVATION (accessed July 20, 2010).

CHAPTER 10

The Mindset of the Successful Patchworker

It's time to get your game face on! It's time to get that motivational chant going in your head that will propel you forward. You are a team of one. You are playing all the positions and calling all the shots. You have to be mentally prepared for what may come and be able to stay focused on what matters throughout it all. Get your mind ready to take on the world, Patchwork-style.

Being successful is a mindset, a mental attitude. Your mindset as a Patchworker is *key*. Just like an athlete, you have to condition so that you can perform at the top of your game. Like Arthur Ashe, the famous tennis pro, once said, "You are never really playing an opponent. You are playing yourself, your own highest standards, and when you reach your limits, that is real joy." Are you ready to get in the mindset necessary to find joy in the career lifestyle that you have in mind? Then let's get to work!

Know Your Patchworker Personality Type

Let's take a look at the Patchworker personality. Simply put, the Patchworker is someone who is known for doing stellar work, being consistently motivated, and always being on task. You can always spot a potential recruit in a large organization. It's the person in the office who is constantly overachieving and innovating. They are driven from within, period.

Do you know someone like this? I do. In my former 9-to-5 life, I managed an employee who was a classic case. Amy evaluated admissions materials to help the university determine if the applicant seemed qualified for acceptance into their program of choice. In the twenty hours she worked each week, she could evaluate ten times the number of files that her full-time counterparts could review. Adding to that, she provided a much more thorough evaluation than her co-workers and brought great enthusiasm to the job. In her spare time she managed the other evaluators' files by organizing them, setting up a filing system for the entire office, and maintaining it. She never overstepped her bounds and had the admiration of all of the others in the office. As her manager I had no choice but to thank my lucky stars that she worked in my office and increase her pay and position as much as possible throughout her tenure. Amy had all the makings of an independent, self-motivated Patchworker: She produced stellar work and she self-managed.

Self-management is critical. Managing yourself can be the easiest or the most difficult challenge of your professional life, depending on your personality—not the personality that a clinical test identifies for you, but the one that you know deep down best describes you. Traditionally, people tend to categorize themselves as Type A or Type B. Although additional types such as Type C or hybrids like Type A/B exist, this discussion will stick to the basics. Looking at the two major personality poles, take a moment to identify your own personality type based on the following descriptions:[1]

- **Type A personality traits:** Impatient, time-conscious, concerned about their status, highly competitive, ambitious, business-like, aggressive, and constantly striving toward a new goal. Type A people are often high-achieving workaholics who multitask, drive themselves with deadlines, and are unhappy about delays. They are often described as "stress junkies."

- **Type B personality traits:** Patient, relaxed, and easygoing; generally lacking a sense of urgency. Type B people are often described as apathetic and disengaged.

Each type has pros and cons and is riddled with values and judgments, which is why I probably shouldn't tell you which type I am, but then again I have a feeling you can guess.

If You Are Type A

If you are a Type A personality, then developing a plan for yourself or for your business and staying on task is a piece of cake. The challenge for Type A people is expecting more from themselves than is possible. A Patchworker example of this might be constantly trying to rearrange a schedule in order to free up additional time to fit in a new client and take profits to the next level. There is no good reason for raising the bar to new heights necessarily, especially if your current level of income is satisfactory. For the Type A personality, money may not be motivating the inner drive; instead it's just a need from within to push themselves to the limits. However, this kind of "pedal to the metal" mentality can lead to burnout in no time and doesn't truly honor the Lifestyle Design in spirit.

The key is to "stick to the plan" (i.e., your set hours dedicated to earning) and be ever mindful not to set yourself up for pacing that would rival a NASCAR race. For the Type A personality, however, sticking to the plan is not easy; scoring the next assignment and closing the deal is addicting for the ambitious. Despite this incessant drive that you may feel if you're a Type A, I urge you to establish a manageable tempo for your work life and honor it as much as possible. Failure to do so can lead to burnout and negatively affect your quality of life, which is the primary motivator for Lifestyle Design in the first place! In fact, this ability to keep the big picture in mind is one of the most salient factors that differentiates you from an experience reminiscent of your 9-to-5, rat-race-paced lifestyle. Yuck. Guard your time like gold!

If You Are Type B

If you are the relaxed and easygoing Type B personality, then the preceding paragraph may have sounded completely foreign and perhaps ridiculous. The challenges for Type B personality Patchworkers are not in slowing down the pace but instead on staying focused. You may have to devote more energy to coaching yourself in order to stay on task and energized by your daily routine. Patchworkers with Type B personalities can benefit from developing a meaningful "must-do" list at the end of each day, which they can use as a "go to" list at the start of the next day. Keeping the must-do items realistic and concrete is critical, or else it will simply become an ongoing laundry list instead of a motivational tool. Type B people also do well when they sketch out the big picture, such as setting goals for the year, and then chunk those goals down into monthly and weekly goals that they must accomplish in order to reach the ultimate goal(s) for the year. This structure allows Type B Patchworkers to maintain proper pacing over the course of the year in order to accomplish those goals that are most important to them.

Your Type Does Not Set the Limits

While most entrepreneurs tend toward the characteristics of a Type A personality, it is only one of many factors that must be considered when determining whether you have what it takes to be a successful Patchworker. If you self-identify as Type B and think that walking away from this idea of being a Patchworker is the only way, I urge you to instead take the useful bits of information that you can learn from the construct, reject all the rest, and keep going forward. That is how you really carve out success for yourself—

by learning wherever possible and charging ahead no matter what. After all, work isn't a competition when you are a Patchworker. You're not competing with a co-worker for a raise or promotion. Instead, you are competing only with yourself and the goal you set out in front to chase after. The most effective competition is one where you challenge yourself—and you are on your way!

Use your personality strengths to your benefit and take an honest look at those that do not serve you well within an entrepreneurial framework. Your personality does not set the limits; on the contrary, it sets the stage for personal and professional success. Ultimately, success all comes down to working hard, staying on task, and following through. Thomas Jefferson knew this, for he once famously said, "I find that the harder I work, the more luck I seem to have." Find some of that "luck" for yourself—it's within reach!

Master Your Approach

Being a superstar gets a bad rap when you're a kid. Early on in life, kids who enjoy learning or who excel in the elementary school classroom are often the target of teasing from their classmates. Terms such as *brownnoser* and *teacher's pet* frequent the commentary made to the star performers who are eager to please their teachers. Then these superstars go on to high school and either conform under pressure or rise above it. Those who have the courage to stand strong capture the attention of teachers and, as a result, are more likely to earn higher marks, win scholarships, and have greater educational opportunities, generally speaking. Then later in life they enter the work force only to find that a similar system is also in play. Why wouldn't it be? The workforce is just a bunch of grown-up kids, and so the same cycle repeats. Those who are superstars advance; they climb the professional ladder and leave everyone else clinging to the lower rungs. The "climbers" are those who know who they are and keep advancing because they hold strong to their goals. Outside pressures and circumstances have no bearing on their progress.

The successful Patchworker thinks and acts like one of these superstars, someone who has both the enthusiasm and the knowledge base that wow an employer. All of this and nimble, too, with the ability to work short-term, long-term, once a week, once a month…you name it!

A veteran Patchworker is the first person whom the boss thinks of when a new project surfaces that needs to be outsourced. The Patchworker is the person ready to bring dynamic solutions at a moment's notice, and *the boss knows it!* This means repeat business for the Patchworker, with absolutely no cold calling! In fact, even if a highly qualified person *did* call the boss, that boss would likely still give their superstar Patchworker the right of first refusal because they are familiar, have a proven track record, and are easy to plug back in to the organizational culture (as opposed to orienting a brand-new, unknown worker).

Because being a superstar is a key to repeat business (a.k.a. momentum), the Patchworker is selling their skills to the boss and the organization at large throughout the year and especially while they are on the job. Repeat business and referrals are the rewards they reap, and those rewards come in the form of dollars.

SUCCESSFUL BY DESIGN

Be observant of yourself and how others react to you. Know your limitations and play up your strengths. For example, if working in a bustling workplace environment energizes you, then seek out those surroundings. If you know that on the telephone you are not a very effective salesperson, then avoid positions that require you to interact on the phone. If you tend toward gossip or drama, then perhaps working from home is a more ideal situation for you.

Whatever your strengths or weaknesses might be, know them and play to your strengths, which is critical because in the coming pages you will be asked to consider creating a niche and working within it. We will look at how word about you can spread like wildfire within a niche industry. If you fail to know yourself and accept assignments that are ill-suited for your personality and talents, word will get around. Inversely, if you know yourself well and build a reputation for excellence, new leads will generate based on word of mouth within the industry. It is true what they say: Word of mouth is the best form of advertising!

Adopt a Healthy State of Paranoia

Now, the word *paranoia* is a bit of an exaggeration, of course. However, both during the interview stage and even after having been hired, being keenly observant of how others perceive your performance continues to be of great importance. The ability to sense any tension or other factors that may threaten your ability to continue working in the existing position requires keen observation. For example, if your relationship with your supervisor changes for any reason, inquire. If your co-workers are suddenly unfriendly, bring a sweet treat to the office and get them talking. Quiet tension is a threat to all Patchworkers because the positions that they occupy on the organizational chart are easily added to or removed; they are not the lifeblood of the operation, with rare exception, although they would like to think otherwise. Therefore, if there is tension, seek to resolve it immediately.

I most definitely live in a state of healthy paranoia, where my proverbial antennas are always up. If there is one thing that I have learned from my experience, it is this: Being a social butterfly has its benefits. If there is any "underground" news, people will share it more readily with a workplace friend than with anyone else in the building. Each day upon my arrival to any workplace, I immediately switch on my computer, check my e-mail inbox for any news, and make "the rounds," saying hello to co-workers and asking how they are and if anything newsworthy has happened since last we spoke.

Please note, I am not asking for gossip but rather information that is relevant to the workplace environment. Sometimes there is a fine line distinguishing one from the other; therefore, my goal is to never be the purveyor of gossip but simply to collect information that may be relevant to my job. Along these lines, I must mention that the fastest way to be "shown the door" is to be perceived as a gossip monger. As the saying goes, "perception is everything," so be sure to manage your interactions with others carefully. Each person has their own style in a workplace environment; mine is to be sugar-sweet and disinterested in gossip, which means that the gossipers will still tell you the important tidbits, but they have no expectation that you will respond to their remarks. It works!

Your co-workers are the social network that delivers messages to you, from you, and about you throughout the organization. Just as a computer network requires careful maintenance to ward off viruses that can harm it or cause it to behave unpredictably, so too does your social network require careful attention.

The American writer Logan Pearsall Smith once said, "Style is a magic wand and turns everything to gold that it touches." Your workplace style, in person or online, is a powerful force that can draw people in an organization to you. Compelling people are memorable. Memorable people are at the top of the employer's mind when it's time to hire for an upcoming project. Great style makes good cents…ahem, sense!

THE SPRINTER'S ADVANTAGE

Your workplace style as a Patchworker may need to be significantly different from your former full-time employee self. Full-time, career-minded employees see themselves as a relatively permanent fixture within an organization, which affords them some room for bad behavior. However, Patchworkers must hold themselves to a higher standard, keeping in mind that they are in fact entrepreneurs with a reputation to maintain.

Full-time employees often settle into a workplace environment and think of it as a home of sorts. Given this, they can become too informal with co-workers and forget about important boundaries and etiquette standards. Think about your own internal standards of behavior at a guest's house versus at your own home; your behavior at a place that you do not consider your own turf is more measured, as it should be. This awareness gives Patchworkers a distinct advantage over their co-workers because they approach the task at hand as a sprint instead of a marathon, allowing their performance to be more noticeable and memorable within the organization.

These are the choices that lie before you. What is your choice? Are you ready to *make it happen*? Are you ready to finally S.T.O.P. (See The Outrageous Possibilities) and begin living on your own terms? If you are, then this last section of the book is a "boots on the ground" blueprint for leaping out into a brave, new world full of unlimited possibilities and making the life of your dreams a reality.

Endnotes

[1] *Wikipedia*, s.v. "Type A and Type B Personality Theory," http://en.wikipedia.org/wiki/Type_A_and_Type_B_personality_theory (accessed August 31, 2010).

PART IV

Make It Happen

CHAPTER 11

Take Inventory and Build Your Brand

This chapter isn't a what-do-you-want-to-do-with-your-life kind of discussion but instead is an honest look at the tools in your career toolbox. Once we take a good inventory of what you have to work with, then we'll talk about molding those into an overall brand that you can communicate to potential customers.

What Do You Have to Offer?

Your toolbox contains a number of skills and experiences that you have collected over the course of your career and your life. These tools are all worth accounting for, and we will. But first let's take a look at what *expert skills* you possess and then build on those.

The 10,000-Hour Rule

You may think that you really aren't an expert at much of anything, but perhaps you are if you think about it like Malcom Gladwell, author of the riveting book *Outliers*. He makes a case for what he calls "The 10,000-Hour Rule," which is a guiding belief that professional success in any field is due in large part to dedicating 10,000 hours to practicing a specific task in order to become an "expert."

Let's break that huge number into something more manageable so that you can determine what you may, in fact, be able to market as an expert skill to potential clients:

10,0000 hours / typical 8-hour day =
1,250 days of dedicated skill-based learning

1,250 days / 5 days per week =
250 weeks

250 weeks / 4 weeks per month =
62 months

62 months / 12 months per year =
approximately 5 years

Five years. That is the approximate amount of time that it takes to become an expert at something if you work at it five days a week for a typical 8-hour workday. If you work at it less frequently or more intensively, then the calculations must be adjusted accordingly. Given all of that, what are you an expert *of?* You are absolutely an expert of something!

Your Expert Skills

To jump in and get started, simply become what you already are. In other words, take the expertise that you already possess and use those skills to get you out there in the marketplace, at least initially. But remember, this time you will use your expertise to find work on your own terms so you may need to apply familiar skills differently. But for now,

let's focus on identifying your areas of expertise. What areas have you dedicated 10,000 hours to either in concentrated amounts or in small chunks over the course of your lifetime?

Although your expert skills in a specific area may not appear obviously marketable, the goal here is just to create a laundry list. So after each of the following sections, write down any skill that meets the 10,000-hour rule and let's see what turns up (you will think about how to package and assemble this information later in this book):

> **Explore the *Occupational Outlook Handbook***
>
> Take a look at the *Occupational Outlook Handbook* (www.bls.gov/oco), which provides an overview of typical skills and duties associated with standardized job titles. Keep in mind, however, that only you know what your previous work history entails and what your true areas of expertise are. The *Occupational Outlook Handbook* is meant only to jog your memory as you look back over your work history.

- **Do you have previous work experience?** This area is the most obvious place to begin the inventory of your expert skills. The trick is thinking back on the skills that may have previously been very sharp and could be once again with a quick dusting off. The best way to take that walk down memory lane is to locate a copy of your resume or curriculum vitae (CV), grab a highlighter, and start circling any expert skills that you can pluck out of that chronology. Use this official document to jog your memory, but don't rely on the text that appears on the page exclusively because those words are, of course, only a mere snapshot of the work you actually did in those previous positions. Your resume or CV is merely an edited, brief summary of those experiences. In this moment try to think about all facets of the work you did previously in order to conduct a full inventory of your skills. Use your resume or CV as a jumping off point.

Write About It

_____

_____

_____

- **Do you have a history of military service?** In my civilian estimation, military service is a combination of work experience (the previous category) and technical training (the next category). Most people enlist for a period of several years and train for a specific position that is, with rare exception, highly technical and specialized. The hands-on skills gained during your military service are only the obvious takeaways that may render you an expert about one or more technical topics, such as handling a weapon, driving a Humvee, or repairing a jet engine. Put all of those skills on your list and include the credentials associated with each that you can tout when the time is right. Also, remember to list any "soft skills" you learned that may be worth mentioning as you interact with potential clients. An example of a soft skill is having a wealth of experience with active learning while in high-pressure situations.

> **Translate Military Experience into Civilian Expertise**
>
> If you have trouble translating your military experience into relevant civilian work, visit the O*NET Web site (http://online.onetcenter.org/crosswalk) and enter your Military Occupational Classification (MOC) in the corresponding box. The results are exhaustive and impressive, and they may just give you some fabulous new areas of expertise to add to your list that you have not thought about since your discharge. Hooah!

Write About It

_____

_____

_____

- **Do you have academic or technical training?** The obvious expert skills here might be, for example, having attempted or completed an associate's degree in some specific technical field, such as welding, or a bachelor's degree that emphasizes specialized knowledge in some area such as biology. Aside from professional training for medical doctors or other similarly lengthy programs, your academic program may not meet the 10,000-hour threshold, but remember to include on-the-job experience where you put those skills to work and deepened your understanding of the concepts learned on campus.

Write About It

_____

_____

_____

- **Do you have any unique and noteworthy life experiences?** I'll tell you right now, if you have a unique life experience to bring with you to the pitch, *that* is going to be your conversational hook! People love a good story, and a unique story is even better. "Unique life experience" can be defined in many ways, but here are a few examples to get you thinking along those lines:

  - Have you lived in another country? On an Indian reservation? On a military base?

  - Have you ever worked for a wealthy millionaire? For an absolute genius? For a starving artist?

  - Have you biked across the country? Hiked the full length of the Appalachian Trail? Competed in an Ironman competition?

  - Or have you done something else?

  Think! One person's unique experience is another person's humdrum life. Someone I know has lived in five countries and has had to run for her life on several occasions due to political uprisings in the region where she lives. However, when I asked her to list her unique life experiences during a career-related exercise, she believed that she didn't have any to offer. Are you kidding me? Compared to her friends in the region, she was living an average life, but to me she was living a life filled with drama, intrigue, and adventure. The point is, never underestimate how interesting your life may sound to someone else.

Write About It

_____

_____

_____

- **Do you have a gift?** Are you gifted in some area of your life that may not commonly be considered a work-related skill? For example, I am gifted when it comes to interacting with people whose native language is something other than English. I come to life, and so do they. There is an instant rapport whether we meet on the city bus, in line at the grocery store, or by phone during a customer service call. That is an intangible gift that I've had since childhood. A woman I know has this same gift when working with the disabled. Someone else may be gifted in working with the elderly. Do you have a gift—or perhaps several? Consider not only the gift(s), but the actual skills associated with each. Do you have any formal or informal work or volunteer history where you put those gifts to work in specific ways?

Write About It

_____

_____

_____

- **Do you have a hobby?** Deconstruct your hobby and think about the many individual skills that you have honed in pursuit of an activity you enjoy. For example, if you are a shutterbug, think about how much time you have dedicated to learning about mechanics, lighting, composition, cropping, and printing. Those are technical skills that can make you some money. I'm not saying that you will be a professional photographer out of the gate, or perhaps ever, but I am saying that you may be able to package those expert skills alongside other skills for a winning pitch. We'll get to that. For now, think about your hobbies and the specific, expert skills associated with them.

Write About It

_____

_____

_____

- **Do you have a record of volunteer service?** Although unpaid, volunteer service can sometimes result in the development of specialized skills. For example, if you volunteer at a botanical garden, perhaps you have training in how to care for orchids, which may, in turn, give you an edge when applying for a job with a national gardening outlet.

Write About It

_____

_____

_____

- **Do you have a child?** If you do, you know very well that children require a wide array of specialized skills and knowledge and a great deal of concentrated time to care for. Some people pay a great deal of money for this experience. Take, for example, a first-time mother who pays for post-partum assistance. Another example is a friend of mine who has two children diagnosed with severe autism; she has undoubtedly acquired some level of expertise with regard to raising autistic children and may be regarded as an expert about some facets of the parenting experience that may be of relevance to a potential client. Someone else that I know struggled with infertility for many years and could easily be categorized as an expert about coping with and overcoming infertility from an emotional standpoint. She would also be a wealth of information regarding local doctors, available local and national resources, support groups, educational outlets, and more. If you have a child, think about any skills you may have acquired over the years and add them to the list.

Write About It

_____

_____

_____

Finally, list any *soft skills* that could be applicable in your work life as a Patchworker. These soft skills are the interpersonal abilities that enable you to effectively interact with other people. Common examples of these abilities are coaching, teaching, motivating, negotiating, leading, and socializing.

Write About It

_____

_____

_____

What do you think? Are you an expert at anything? Or perhaps at many things? What did your self-inventory reveal? Continue adding to your list of the traditional and nontraditional skills and abilities that you possess, and then begin brainstorming about the many ways that you could apply those skills. Capitalize on your natural gifts and talents; then couple them with your area(s) of expertise for a winning combination.

What Do You See Out There?

Okay, so now that you have some of your expert skills and abilities at the front of your mind, what do you see in the marketplace? Observe your surroundings—only this time, look at the marketplace like a business owner, not like an employee. Think about where and how you could potentially insert yourself into an organization as a Patchworker. Here are three great shortcuts to get you started:

1. **Utilize communication tools.** Such tools allow you to have quick access to news or events taking place within organizations or industries you would like to tap for work. Examples include electronic mailing lists, blog posts, and social networking media such as Twitter and Facebook.

2. **Scan the appropriate trade publications.** You can use these publications (both online and in print) to learn about trends that you could be part of. Then you can approach the trendsetters with a pitch about how your product or service is a good fit with the organization's new initiatives.

3. **Get some boots-on-the-ground experience.** Actually comb your hair and jump into a plane, train, or automobile and visit the location of potential clients to have a look around. I have a trick for learning about the pulse and culture of a workplace, and it has worked well on several occasions: Pack a bag lunch and find a place to sit in the atrium or some other bustling public space in the potential client's building. Enjoy a leisurely lunch while making seemingly idle conversation with anyone who sits nearby—essentially, interview them about the company in an innocent manner and learn fabulous insider information that would never be available otherwise. Surprisingly, people rarely ask what I am doing there, and when they do, I have a prepared answer that is appropriate to the situation. Generally speaking, however, it's best not to mention your interest in working for the company because people tend to censor what they say to potential co-workers. My advice is, be truthful but be vague.

> **Assess the Organization**
>
> Determine whether your vision and the reality at these places ring true. In other words, do these businesses that you envision as wonderful places to work meet your expectations when you walk in the front door? For example, do people generally seem happy to be there? Are the working conditions pleasant? Is the attire formal or informal? Is parking too costly? Is the commute problematic? Getting a view of the environment first-hand can help you determine whether the organization might be a good fit.

Surveying your territory for existing opportunities that you could plug yourself into is an important step in this phase of the process, but let's take it one step farther. In this next section, consider any niche products or services in your territory that are not currently being met by existing businesses. Explore the possibility of defining a niche for yourself and reaping the financial rewards.

What Do You Not See Out There?

I have said it before, but I'll say it again: Finding a niche is how I hit it big as a Patchworker. I don't mean to say that it turned me into a millionaire; it hasn't. However, what it did do was immediately take me from flailing to fully booked in less than one month. It sounds impossible, I know, but that is my story. Having said that, I feel compelled to flash one of those ads that you often see on weight-loss commercials: Results not typical.

However, in all honesty I think that the results of this find-your-niche strat-egy *could* very well be the norm for just about *anyone*. If you remember my story from earlier in the book, I found my niche by asking myself simple questions. It wasn't rocket science; in fact, the idea was so simple minded that I hesitated to tell you the real story. The way I found my niche was simply realizing that a group of friends all needed the same basic computer services, and they all kept calling me, hence my business idea. It was a niche. It set me on the path to becoming a Patchworker. It set me on the path to this moment in time, when I could share this book with you. It's true—or as they say in Washington, D.C., it's a "true fact."

Identifying a niche seems impossible, right? All of those pessimists out there believe that anything worth doing has already been done. However, for good or for bad, I'm an eternal optimist and so I believe in possibility, always. When it comes to putting your finger on a niche, try thinking about it from this optimistic vantage point of unknown origin: Instead of thinking about what you're missing, try thinking about what you have that everyone else is missing.

Look around; see what everyone else is already doing successfully and think about how you could put a unique twist on an already-existing product or service. This originality affords you a "first-mover advantage" that can cata-pult you right into a thriving business.

Even if a limited number of people already provide the very product or service that you want to offer, survey the territory and see if there is enough business available to insert yourself into the marketplace. The only sure way to find out is to pitch your product or service to potential customers and see if you get any bites. Remember, just because someone else is already doing what you would like to be doing doesn't preclude you from joining in. It just means enjoying a little friendly competition. The world is a big place. Find a way to carve out your own territory where you can operate independently of your competition, if you have any. It's an alternative that's worth pursuing.

How to Pitch Your Niche

Having a niche means that others will be intrigued by your unique spin on things, which can get you some coveted media attention if you play your cards right. Pitch your niche in the form of a press release or an e-mail message to newspapers, radio stations, and television programs, both local and national. Getting a press release out there is as easy as navigating to the company's Web site and looking for the Contact Us link, which typically

Safeguard Your Niche

Protecting your niche from would-be competitors is a tricky endeavor. On the one hand, you want to get the word out about your business to as wide an audience as possible. On the other hand, you don't want anyone stealing your idea if it is truly original. A good way to balance this is to market your niche idea only in specialized media outlets, at least until you build momentum and have a stable client base. Then you can widen your marketing reach. Protecting your niche is something you want to always keep in mind when marketing in person, online, or in print.

allows you to submit a press release either by filling out a Web form or sending an e-mail message. Writing directly to media personalities who report on products or services in line with what you offer is also a great way to get some positive attention for your business. Alternatively, use the company's Web site to look for the e-mail address of the reporter you wish to contact.

Receiving attention from the media will not only help to get your message out there, but also will give your business some added credibility if picked up for a newspaper article, radio mention, or television bit. It's the same principle as the As Seen on TV logo that appears on product packaging. People figure that if the media have found the product worthy of time and attention, then maybe they should, too. This is exactly what you want for your business: attention! Being awarded time and attention by the media in any small way is a form of recognition and a way to reach new audiences all rolled into one!

Collecting credentials for your business and for yourself in every way possible is a great way to build a case for your niche's credibility. Cultivate new titles and awards for yourself and your business in every way possible. Apply for every major and minor award out there in your city and state, and nominate yourself for awards. Better yet, ask colleagues to nominate you. Awards tend to build on themselves with one award causing others to believe that you must be award worthy, which results in them crowning you yet again. Apply! Apply! Just like the lottery, "you can't win if you don't play."

$$\mathcal{SO}$$

Now that you have identified which expert skills you could pitch to a potential employer, it's time to discuss how to identify opportunities to apply those skills in a workplace setting. In other words, it's time to talk about how to "fish" for leads that utilize your skills *and* fit into the Lifestyle Design you have in mind.

CHAPTER 12

Go Fish

I grew up on a lake in the Midwest, and fishing is a big deal in that part of the world. Before dawn the fishermen rise and pack their coolers, secure their tackle boxes, grab a few fishing poles and a net, and then set out on their boats to get in position on the lake before daybreak. Each fisherman has his theories about which lure works best, as well as corresponding stories about the size of the fish he caught with each kind. Each fisherman has a different opinion, a different strategy. The thing is, no one is wrong. Although fishing is, in fact, partially about how you approach the task at hand, it's also about just casting out the line over and over to see what you get at different times and in different locations.

Fishing for clients works in much the same way. There are theories, and none of them is wrong (well, except for a few lunatic ideas). But ultimately it comes down to casting the line out and reeling it in to see if you get any bites. It's about the combination of technique and persistence. Let's talk about what fishing is within the context of the Patchwork Principle and how to go about it and then review a few pointers from an experienced fisher… fisher*woman*, that is!

What Is Fishing?

To get started, let's define the term *fishing* in the way it works within the framework of the Patchwork Principle:

Fishing
To cast out inquiries in search of job leads.

Simple enough, right? In other words, fishing is looking around for work. However, you are not looking for just anything that happens to surface; you are looking for

> **Fishing vs. Phishing**
>
> Let's be clear that the term *fishing* used in this book refers to the legitimate pursuit of employment. This term is not related in any way to a computer term pronounced the same way but spelled differently, *phishing*, which is criminal mischief associated with stealing sensitive information via the Internet from people without their knowledge.

work that is enjoyable and that ultimately will fit into your Lifestyle Design. Keep that in mind because as Henry David Thoreau once famously said, "Many men go fishing all of their lives without knowing it is not fish they are after."

Within the context of the Patchwork Principle, there are two fundamental fishing techniques:

- The Eagle Eye
- The Seagull Scavenge

Let's talk about each one and what each has to offer as you set off on your journey to score the first of many new clients for your business.

The Eagle Eye

The eagle is a magnificent creature, well known for its keen eyesight and masterful ability to swoop in and spot an opportunity from great distances. Perhaps this is why, as Wikipedia notes, "the Albanian word for eagle is 'shqiponje' deriving from the root 'shq,' which is the same for the word 'shquaj' ('distinguish') and could be explained with the outstanding ability of the bird to distinguish clearly objects from long distances."[1] This quiet bird with a stealth approach can look out on the vast landscape and clearly *distinguish* an opportunity available in the vicinity.

The Patchworker who operates like an Eagle Eye enjoys carefully analyzing his or her territory (brick-and-mortar businesses, online organizations, and so on). The analysis results in the identification of key opportunities, which are gaps that signal a need the Patchworker can propose to fill. The Patchworker performs methodical research to learn more about these organizations to craft a pitch that will strike the right tone and make it clear to the decision maker that the Patchworker understands the organization's needs and is proposing a customized solution. This Patchworker takes pleasure in a great deal of concentrated effort focused on accomplishing a single goal instead of dividing attention across several goals. The Patchworker carefully selects opportunities that appear to warrant special preparation, does the necessary research, and then carefully pitches solutions to the decision maker before making an approach.

There is an old African proverb to this effect:

Be present where you are.

But I would like to put an American spin on that old saying:

Life is like a sweepstakes, and you must be present to win!

Observation is the key to success for the Eagle. Being observant serves anyone well in life; however, for a Patchworker, observation is critical to livelihood. If you can observe a need within an organization before anyone else does, you can pitch a proposal to the decision makers, identifying yourself as *the* solution to the problem.

Here is a perfect example: I worked at a large technical college where the filing system in the office in which I was working as a consultant contained countless reams of confidential documents; the office was in utter chaos. This bedlam caused ongoing problems for administrators at all levels of the organization. Although I was hired to perform a very technical legal function for the college, I sensed that pitching a solution to the filing system issues would be well received. I pitched the idea and was instantly hired to put my plan into action. The college could easily have delegated this job to a salaried administrative assistant at *no* additional cost to the organization; however, they instead chose to pay my highest consulting rate simply because I observed a need, pitched the solution, and was willing to take action immediately.

Being eagle-like can be a rewarding approach for a number of reasons, including the following:

- **You have an opportunity to do in-depth research about one specific organization, which allows you to gain some level of expertise about a business in your industry.** This informal process of educating yourself about the major and minor players in the field builds your knowledge base, which allows you to speak intelligently to prospective clients.

- **You have an opportunity to really "wow" the decision maker with detailed, customized solutions for the organization.** Your pitch will likely leave a lasting impression on the decision maker who may keep your contact information on file for future reference.

- **The odds of getting a meaningful response from the decision maker are very high.** The level of effort you demonstrate in your communication will be obvious and will likely spark some interest—or at least intrigue—about you and/or your proposal.

- **The approach requires more mental exercise than repetitive effort, which can feel more rewarding at times.** Instead of racing around pitching ideas to a number of organizations, you are able to concentrate on a select few. However, this extra effort can make you feel more invested in the outcome, and it can be unsettling if the pitch falls flat.

Although you may think that existing employees within an organization have the upper hand, I have found the opposite to be true. Being an Eagle is distinctly *easier* for a Patchworker than an existing employee because you are not so entrenched. In other words, you are able to spot an opportunity on the landscape instead of trying to separate yourself from the people, the politics, and the systems that are in place in the work environment.

Think about how you feel after being away from home for a long time and then returning. Does the landscape look different to you? Do you see things, both good and bad, that you never noticed before? Perhaps you were in the military and returned home from a tour of duty only to find that the people or the places seemed to have changed. Perhaps you went away to college only to return at the semester break to find that your childhood home and neighborhood looked smaller. This phenomenon is often referred to as *re-entry shock* or *reverse culture shock*. The "shock" occurs from distancing yourself from the familiar environment and then coming back to it with new experiences that give you a unique perspective on familiar surroundings. This distance is what's missing for the existing employees within an organization; when they look around, they see only the familiar systems instead of the gaping holes. That's where you come in!

As a Patchworker, whether you sporadically work for the organization in question or have never worked there at all, you are viewing an organization as a visitor. You are not "part of the machine" in any way. This gives you the ability to see how existing systems work (or fail to do so), identify missing systems, and see the "big picture" instead of getting caught up in the office politics at a micro level.

The Eagle quietly observes the landscape, identifies opportunities, and swoops in to pitch an idea to an immediate need. If you remember the 1987 movie *Wall Street*, Michael Douglas played an ultra-rich stock speculator named Gordon Gekko. He taught his young protégé the secret to his success, which describes the Eagle approach in plain and simple terms: "I look at a hundred deals a day. I pick one."

The Seagull Scavenge

Seagulls are noisy birds that squawk loudly as they scavenge for food on the landscape. They are opportunistic and well known for being resourceful and intelligent, adaptable and resilient.[2] And are they gutsy—whoa! They dive into seemingly perilous situations regularly in order to check out opportunities, and they aggressively protect that which becomes theirs. In fact, The Royal Society for the Protection of Birds says, "No other family of bird divides opinion as much as the gulls."[3] Let's face it; they are noisy, persistent birds who rummage around a vast area and make contact with a multitude of possible opportunities in a single day of flight.

The Patchworker who operates like a Seagull Scavenger enjoys a fast-paced, exhilarating day searching for opportunities among a wide array of businesses. They have a rough strategy in mind about which direction to head, but are not against going off course when a new opportunity appears. They expend a great deal of energy getting the word out about themselves to a large number of decision makers, essentially squawking out their marketing pitch with the hope that an opportunity will present itself in response. The pitches are relevant to the organization but are not necessarily *highly* customized solutions. The Seagull approach is simply playing the numbers and hoping that a percentage of the pitches will spark inquiries from decision makers interested in learning more about the Patchworker.

Being seagull-like can be a rewarding approach for a number of reasons, including the following:

- **You have the opportunity to present yourself to a large number of potential employers.** Be sure the lasting impression you make is a positive one that portrays you in the best possible light.

- **The approach requires more repetitive effort than mental exercise.** This can allow you to still be productive during periods when you are not in the mood for deep, analytical processing due to time of day, location, and so on.

- **It is more spontaneous in nature, allowing you to test out a new approach, angle, or pitch at a moment's notice.** This approach is markedly more creative than the Eagle's measured manner, which can be fun and energizing. It also allows you the opportunity to learn which pitches seem most effective; these experiences help you to work "smarter" instead of "harder" over time and eventually render you an expert pitcher.

The Seagull approach is a high-energy approach. Playing the numbers is key, and the resulting quantity of incoming interest can be tremendous. The Seagull uses a wait-and-see approach—whereby a show of interest is thrust out into the marketplace—and then follows up on the responses systematically.

Comparison: The Eagle vs. the Seagull

The approaches of the Eagle and the Seagull are quite different, but each has an important role to play in the overall success of your Patchwork business, as shown here:

Eagle	Seagull
Specialist	Generalist
Highly selective	Less selective
Stealth	Purposefully noticeable
Few communications	Many communications
Carefully crafted proposals	E-mail messages or missives

You may find that you utilize one approach more than the other for any number of reasons, but generally speaking you will utilize both in combination. Keep in mind that one approach may be better suited for your industry or a specific company, which only you will be able to determine based on your experience and observations. There is no magic formula for determining which approach will always work for you; however, there are two generalizations that can be made:

- **The Eagle approach may be more appropriate for decision makers at organizations that are conservative in nature and adhere to a stricter protocol.** Examples of these businesses include law firms, accounting firms, medical practices, educational institutions, and religious organizations.

- **The Seagull approach may be more appropriate, and in fact well received, at organizations that appreciate feisty initiative.** Examples of these businesses include factories; retail establishments; community organizations; and businesses that recruit creative talent, such as design studios.

Likewise, one approach may be a better fit with your personality type (but again this is an oversimplification):

- **Type A personality types are more likely Eagles,** willing to do the sometimes-tedious work of researching an organization, drawing up a customized proposal, presenting it, and following up with the decision maker. They anticipate specific results, respond categorically, and strategize about future communications. The possibility of landing specific accounts they have in mind energizes them.

- **Type B personality types are more likely Seagulls,** enjoying the opportunity to work at their own pace with only a loosely defined sequence of events in mind. Communications may be in the form of e-mail or brief social networking missives that are applicable to any number of recipients. They do not have definite outcomes in mind, preferring instead to see what turns up and be energized by the surprise factor.

Whichever approach you choose, there are definite advantages to fishing for work, including the following:

- **The odds of being hired are in your favor.** You are not competing against others in a resume stack.

- **The boss will be impressed with your insight and initiative** and will consider you a star performer from day one, which may lead to future opportunities within the organization.

- **The boss may have the authority to hire you on the spot** because the work will be short term and perhaps project based.

- **Funding will be more easily approved** for an immediate, well-defined need than a standard position. This is an understatement!

- **You will likely be paid at a higher rate** than you would be if the position were formally advertised. The decision maker is paying, in part, for immediacy and expertise.

Both the Seagull and the Eagle approaches offer opportunities for success. Now, take this fundamental information about the tactics of each approach and apply it constructively as you learn how to fish for leads, described in the next section.

How to Fish

To begin, let me say that fishing for leads is not rocket science. In fact, you have probably done some fishing in the past within the context of searching for a 9-to-5 job. This is good news. It means that no matter where you start from, you *can* do this! You can jump in and get started *right now*. The process consists of the following four basic steps, each of which is described in detail in the next sections:

1. Reflection

2. Observation

3. Identification

4. Evaluation

You will notice that "procrastination" is not on the list—so let's get going. Let's discuss each step in a way that teaches you to fully understand how to fish for your own leads, on your own terms.

Reflection

This entire section on reflection could be summed up by a single quote from the well-known actor, lawyer, and writer Ben Stein:

> The indispensable first step to getting the things you want out of life is this:
>
> Decide what you want.

Decide what you want *before* you start fishing! In the first half of this book, you figured out what kind of lifestyle you are after, and in this second half of the book, you figured out what kind of work you are after. In other words, you *have* decided what you want. Now it's time to go look for it. Go fish!

Stay on Track

As you fish around, you can easily get distracted and veer off course when a big opportunity presents itself. The promise of money or prestige can lure people back to living life on someone else's terms instead of their own. Don't let this happen to you. Stick to your guns, as they say, and don't settle for less than the life you have always dreamed of.

Observation

Observation is strategic looking around. Take Thomas Edison, for example, He was especially good at fishing for new ideas and leads related to his inventions. When asked how he did it, he said, "I find out what the world needs, then I proceed to invent." This is the same mindset that you must have when you set out to fish for clients. Although you don't have to have the know-how of Thomas Edison, you do need to invest some time in the process. When you're first starting out, you may spend a disproportionate amount of time fishing for leads, but rest assured that you will be able to scale back as you build momentum.

For the most part, the work you are looking for is the unadvertised and perhaps unrecognized opportunities in business and industry. Observation means looking at the landscape with your Eagle eye and seeing how you can insert yourself into various organizations in a meaningful way. This form of job searching is nontraditional, and that is partially why it is so effective. You are not competing with others in a huge resume stack on the decision maker's desk. Here is an example of how this strategy works from my early days as a Patchworker; in fact, this is how it all got started:

> When I made the conscious decision to leave my so-called university "dream job" years ago, it seemed that the only thing left to do was search for college or university decision makers that had a potential use for my skill set and solicit them. However, I soon discovered that none of them was hiring—not officially anyway! I felt stuck. "What am I going to do?" I thought to myself. So what did I do? Well, the only thing I could do: find a way to make myself useful to these organizations. (This was my first credible attempt at fishing for leads in nontraditional ways. At the time I had no idea that it would become one of the most important exercises of my professional life.)
>
> I spent every evening after work scouring the Internet for colleges or universities within a one-hour radius of my house. Then, I searched each institution's Web site in order to learn about the organizational structure and culture of each one in order to identify potential gaps in the various offices on campus.
>
> I began a letter-writing campaign to college and university presidents and described the gaps that I believed I could fill for them, including detailed plans full of statistical analyses that cited respected industry resources they would surely recognize. One day, I received a call from a college just five blocks from my house. The president requested a private meeting and hired me on the spot, a new position created just for me. I was thrilled!

Also, during my fishing expedition several consultant opportunities surfaced. This was not my first experience with consulting; I had been hired as a consultant many times in prior years. However, this was the first time that I was able to negotiate what I considered to be extremely high hourly rates for my services, because I was pitching immediate solutions to known problems. Usually it was the organization seeking me out, but with the tables turned, they were both impressed and excited, which translated into dollars. It was also the first time that I was hired on retainer, which meant being paid a regular stipend in order to make myself immediately available for consultation upon request. This was a brave new world! In a matter of months, I had left my old job, gone fishing with great results, and landed several new consulting clients. It was my introduction to being a Patchworker, and I was hooked!

That is my story, but it could easily be yours. Think about your own area of specialization, such as nursing, welding, accounting, teaching, or programming. Each area of specialization has core business types to which it caters. For example, the core business types for nurses include hospitals, medical practices, nursing homes, and home health care. If you are a nurse, you could select the business type that most appeals to you and begin searching for ways that you could insert yourself into the organization in a meaningful way.

Keep in mind that, generally speaking, the larger the organization is, the greater the likelihood that the organization has existing gaps in services waiting to be filled. However, the advantage of approaching smaller organizations is that the decision makers are often more accessible. Select one business type and begin fishing around; see what happens. If you find that one approach (Eagle or Seagull) is not getting you the response you had hoped for, then simply switch the approach, the level of decision makers you are contacting, or your pitch (which we will talk about in the next chapter). The key to success is to keep fishing.

> **Put Your Imagination to Work**
>
> Consider applying your skills in nontraditional settings or in nontraditional ways. For example, if you are a nurse, you could inquire at corporations that have on-site medical facilities or teach health-related classes in the community.

The most effective and information-filled place to begin your first fishing expedition is online. The following sections describe three ways to get started on your first online fishing expedition: Visit the Web sites, social media outlets, and blogs of potential clients.

Visit the Web Sites of Potential Clients

When you visit the Web site of a potential client, take time to learn about the organization's mission, vision, and current initiatives. Do they align with your own values and your new lifestyle framework? Because time is precious and the Internet provides a wealth of information, visit company Web sites by the hundreds!

> **Virtually All My Leads Are Virtual**
>
> I use this method to find about 90 percent of my clients, so I can tell you from experience that it definitely does work!

As you visit the Web sites of potential clients, keep in mind the following:

- **Learn about the organizational structure and culture** by viewing the posted images and studying word choice. I always take a moment to read the president's or CEO's welcome statement to look for clues about their priorities, both those that are written and those that are omitted.

  Omission counts for a lot in my book; it speaks volumes. For example, most organizations traditionally include a statement about a commitment to diversity. However, one organization that I visited online did not include a statement or mere mention of diversity anywhere on the Web site that I could locate. Then, when I looked through the staff directory, which included a photo of each employee, I discovered that the only people of color on staff were unskilled workers. Because I have a strong commitment to diversity in the workplace, I crossed that organization off of my list. One of the benefits of Patchwork is the choice to work with organizations that match your priorities and values.

- **Scan the staff directory** to identify the powerhouse decision makers. If you have an idea to pitch, begin by pitching it to those individuals who appear to be a good fit. Be sure to pitch your idea to the appropriate decision maker instead of just the person closest to the top. Pitching low and then working your way up is a better strategy than the reverse. The top dogs are often not directly involved in the hiring processes at their organization; they are more often in charge of steering the ship and fundraising. Know your audience and, if you need help figuring it out, take a look at the job postings to see if you should direct submissions to a specific person. Keep in mind that human resources personnel do not qualify as potential contacts for fishing purposes because they are in the business of carrying out the wishes of the decision makers, not making decisions independent of them.

- **Study the organizational chart** to determine who the key decision makers are for your purposes. Is there an obvious position missing from the chart that is calling your name? For example, a college in my area desperately needs a social media coordinator on their organizational chart—they just don't know it yet!

- **Scan the job postings** to see if any specific departments seem to be hiring in great numbers; this can be either a warning flag or an indication of a department flush with cash. Perhaps there has been a change of leadership and everyone jumped ship; then again, perhaps the organization just received a large grant. Find out which one it is. Organizations experiencing big shifts are ripe for welcoming new talent—like you!

Nearly every business in the world now has a Web site, so take advantage of these free, comprehensive, and image-rich resources as you fish online for leads. A wealth of information is available at your fingertips.

Visit the Social Media Outlets

Social media outlets, such as Twitter (www.twitter.com) and Facebook (www.facebook.com), provide a wealth of information that may provide (or at least imply) information about a company that the official Web site will never tell you. Why? Several reasons, including the following:

- These missives are more informal by nature.

- These postings are often maintained by a single person, unlike Web site content that is generally vetted by several people or even a committee.

- Company personnel generally do not traffic their company's social media outlets as much as they might the official Web site, which means content that might otherwise draw objections for being too forthcoming, for example, may go unnoticed for long periods of time.

This informality can work to your advantage, giving you the inside scoop in some cases. To get started in the world of social media, do the following:

1. **Sign up.** Opening an account is free and easy! In a matter of minutes, you can be part of an online community and listen to the real-time conversations of any one of the millions of individuals and organizations. Although the nature of your intended work may or may not require that you send out newsworthy announcements to the online community, your fishing expeditions could surely benefit from being someone who listens to the stream of news and other important announcements posted by individuals and organizations that could potentially utilize your services.

2. **Become a follower.** Opening an account is necessary in order to become a "follower" of those companies and individuals that matter to you. This membership allows you immediate access to their stream of posts in real time.

3. **Become worth following.** If your business would benefit from becoming a source of news and information about a specific topic, develop a regular feed that you send out to the people who will follow you in the form of an electronic newsletter or blog. This can position you as an expert in the field by regularly displaying your expertise about cutting-edge information, answering questions from your followers, and more. As word about you spreads throughout the social network (Twitter, for example), your list of followers will grow in number. The larger your list of followers, the greater your potential for sparking interest from someone looking to hire a person with your expertise. Your social media account has the potential to open new doors of opportunity; interested individuals and organizations may seek *you* out based on their interactions with you within this social media framework.

4. **Change with the times.** Social media is an ever-changing arena, so you need to be prepared to change with the times. For example, for several years my clients simply maintained a Facebook account because it was the outlet most often used by their clients. However, recently there has been a dramatic shift among many of my customers. They have abandoned their Facebook accounts and have instead built a presence on Twitter. This switch means that their posts now appear on Twitter instead of Facebook. As a result, I now have accounts on Facebook, where some clients still reside, and on Twitter, where the majority migrated. Those substantive posts are what I'm after, so I will follow them wherever my active clients and potential clients decide the announcements will appear.

> **Go Fishing via Twitter**
>
> If you are not sure where to get started, my advice is to begin by opening a Twitter account and search for organizations that are relevant to your fishing expeditions.
>
> While you are out there, search around for like-minded people for networking, brainstorming, and job search purposes. Keyword searches are the best way to find people who are discussing topics that are of interest to you. Then, once you find a few leaders in the field, check out their list of followers, who are usually like minded.

Social media sites offer access to free, immediate, and relevant information about a great number of corporations. These online resources can provide useful news about an organization as you research potential leads. Also available online are other information-rich resources such as corporate and employee blogs; let's take a look at them in this next section.

Visit Company and Employee Blogs

A *blog* is simply a modern-day diary. The word derives from the blending of the words *Web* (as in online) and *log* (as in diary) to mean an online diary. Corporate blogs offer a treasure trove of information about company activities. Some blogs are a series of announcements in a press release format whereas others are informal accounts of important happenings or simply the rant of a disgruntled employee. To get started, keep these points in mind when viewing a prospective client's blog:

- **Read through the current and archived** posts of company and employee blogs. Links to blogs commonly appear on Web sites on the home page, About Us page, or individual employee pages listed in the staff directory. Recent blog entries can give you information about new initiatives, comings and goings, and anticipated projects. However, remember to look through the archives to learn about organizational trends, such as the typical timeframe when new projects appear to be rolled out, when new batches of employees seem to be hired on or let go, and so on. History often repeats itself, in business and in life.

- **Sign up for the RSS feed at each relevant blog (and Web site) that offers this feature.** RSS stands for *really simple syndication,* which essentially means a plain-looking, no-frills format for viewing online text and image content. By using an RSS reader, such as Google Reader, you can view myriad updates to blog and Web site content simultaneously in one browser window instead of visiting each site separately and looking for pertinent updates. RSS will definitely save you time and make your fishing expeditions more productive and, let's face it, more enjoyable.

- **Look for links to the blog's social media accounts.** Such links will help you scout out other places where the organization might post relevant information. Generally speaking, blog managers post small icons that link directly to their accounts, which represent other social media outlets where similar information is posted.

Observation comes naturally to some people. For others it requires cultivation. Wherever you are starting from, whatever your natural inclinations, know that success comes from observation that is strategic, dedicated, and consistent. It's the same way that you get to Carnegie Hall: Practice, practice, practice!

Identification

This step involves looking at known, advertised gaps that organizations are actively seeking to fill. The identification process is the traditional job search, with a twist (a big one!). Previously, you were searching for full-time 9-to-5 work that fell within certain parameters, such as geographic location or health insurance benefits. However, now you are seeking Patchwork opportunities, giving you a completely different focus as you scout around for work. Now, your focus is work that is both enjoyable and a good fit with your lifestyle framework. Although the advertisements appear the same, the way you view them needs to change in order for you to see the plethora of new opportunities that await you. Let's look at some traditional search techniques and work through what matters and why in each instance.

Job Search Engines Aimed at the Masses

Thanks to million-dollar investments by leading job search engines, companies such as Monster.com and CareerBuilder.com are household names. These job search engines serve up a wide array of available jobs in every occupational field including legitimate positions posted by legitimate businesses and spiraling downward toward pyramid schemes looking for new contacts.

> **Google "jobs"**
>
> Google the word "jobs" for a list of results containing links to the major job search engines.

Some of these ads are actually seeking applicants, whereas others are posted merely to comply with standardized advertising requirements before the position can be filled, rendering the posting useless for the job seeker. Some ads reveal the name of the company that is hiring, whereas others indicate the name of the industry only. This lack of identification may indicate that the ad is either protecting the identity of a position that is currently filled (the person currently occupying the position is about to be fired, for example) or that the business of prescreening qualified and promising applicants was delegated to a temporary agency, known as a *direct hire*. So, after you sift through all of the listings, what is the take away for the Patchworker? Plenty!

- **Scan the ads.** You can search jobs based on location, industry, level of education, years of experience, and more. Use these postings to research a company for information about vision, mission, cues about organizational culture and names of decision makers. You may wish to apply for part-time positions that are a good fit with your career lifestyle or use them as a jumping-off point for a customized nontraditional pitch.

  For example, if a company advertises for a graphic designer, then you may want to pitch your skills to them as an independent contractor that can come in with a customized plan on day one. The pitch must be compelling, be tailored, and offer your skills as an immediate solution to their needs. Does your pitch need to mention having seen the advertised posting? Not necessarily—hold your cards close whenever possible.

- **Create a profile.** Although you are not seeking the traditional employment, it never hurts to create a profile that allows companies to find you, and it's free! If you have a Web site, blog, or social networking profile(s), be sure to include that information in your bio section.

- **Monitor the trends.** When you work independently, you can easily fall out of touch with trends in your field(s) of specialization or interest. In addition to subscribing to RSS feeds from leading organizations in the industry, following trendsetters and trendspotters in social networking communities, you may also want to watch as changes occur "on the ground" by watching the search engines. New job titles may appear, or the qualifications for existing jobs may be lowered or raised across the board.

Job search engines like these provide an excellent overview of the changing marketplace in real time. They present a big-picture look at known opportunities locally, regionally, and nationally. What a resource!

Specialized Job Search Engines

These search engines are a boon for Patchworkers! I just can't say enough about how much specialized job search engines have to offer, but I'll do my best to pack it all into the explanation in the sections that follow. These search engines are repositories of specialized job postings for work that is directly in line with your no-strings-attached, make-my-own-hours, set-my-own-schedule, work-from-home (or elsewhere) career aspirations. If your skill set qualifies you for work at any of these sites, which is likely due to the great variety of jobs available, you could very well earn a good portion of your income via these sites! There are three basic categories that are of greatest interest: freelance engines, specialty skill sites, and location-specific sites. Let's look at each category in detail.

Freelance Job Search Engines

Freelance job search engine sites are your best bet for finding short-term, part-time, or project-based work *in volume*. It's out there just waiting for you to click and bid. The sites contain ads placed by either individuals or businesses seeking help from skilled workers, or as one site phrases it, "online talent." Freelance job search engine sites specialize in matching employers with talent (that's you!). Quality sites manage the progress of and payment for the work in a virtual workspace online. After the project ends and payment is secured by the freelancer via the site's escrow-like system, parties on both sides leave feedback about one another, which is publicly visible going forward. This feedback is powerful, based on the same premise used on eBay, but in this case the feedback relates to services instead of products.

> **Familiarize Yourself with Freelance Web Sites**
>
> The major freelance Web sites featuring job ads aimed at a wide variety of freelancers include the following:
>
> - Elance.com
> - Guru.com
> - Jobshouts.com
> - Odesk.com
> - Snagajob.com
> - Sologig.com

Now, before you rush off and begin madly fishing around, let me mention a few important points:

- **If you have a specialized skill that is in high demand on these sites, you could very well find 100 percent of your Patchwork here.** The leading site currently is Elance.com, but there are literally dozens of sites to choose from, and you could register at each one and have a look around to determine which is the best fit. To scout out the many freelance sites available online, simply do a Google search for "freelance work."

- **Volume is the name of the game.** Each freelancer who applies for work on these sites submits a proposal that includes a proposed price for the work, which is either hourly or project based. Many qualified and talented people bid on nearly every reasonable project that is posted it seems, which drives the cost of the project down. This bidding war means that you would likely earn significantly less than if you were fishing for this same work independently (that is, doing the research, identifying gaps, and pitching your ideas to decision makers). However, there is a lot to be said for the ease of simply logging in to a freelance job site and scanning the ads. The *Boston Globe* reported that many workers find a healthy volume of work on sites like Elance, citing that workers often have nine or ten projects going at any one time.[4]

- **Momentum happens, sometimes.** Employers use these sites as a way to find talented workers, test them out, and then work with them on an ongoing basis and sometimes even make them long-term offers after completion of the initial project. When they provide feedback about your work on Elance, it builds your reputation and helps you find more interesting jobs. This process can lead to an ongoing relationship with multiple employers over time in true Patchwork style—in other words, momentum.

These freelance sites offer a fantastic volume of opportunity for you to peruse from employers located in the United States and beyond. Spend time reviewing these sites carefully to see if the jobs are a match with your skill set and Lifestyle Design. There is work available for practically every skill set imaginable; take a look around.

Specialty Skill Sites

Separating themselves from the pack, specialty skill sites offer work that focuses on the recruitment of talent with a specific skill set, such as graphic designers, writers, or photographers. To locate a freelance site that caters to professionals like you, simply do a Google search for the word "freelance" followed by the name of your specialty (freelance transcription, for example).

Virtual Assistants

The International Virtual Assistant Organization (www.ivaa.org) defines a *Virtual Assistant (VA)* as "an independent entrepreneur providing administrative, creative and/or technical services." A VA may provide general office support, such as reception (called "live phone answering"), executive assistance, word processing, and typing; or specialized support, such as bookkeeping, advertising, or paralegal services. VAs typically perform all work from their home office or some other space that they independently maintain. VAs who own the latest and greatest software and equipment are often at a distinct advantage over their colleagues, depending on the nature of the work.

Some VAs band together and create groups in order to offer a greater array of skills and services or to provide seamless service to clients in the wake of illness or injury. Approaching a VA group to inquire about opportunities to serve as a backup during busy periods of time is another angle for finding Patchwork in this VA environment. I made such an inquiry myself, and many groups were quite interested in vetting potential talent to join their group on a regular basis or to serve as a second string. You can find a list of VA groups on the IVAA Web site.

Telecommuters

Another specialty sector worth mentioning caters to *telecommuters*. This area may be of great interest to the Patchworker who is excited at the prospect of working in pajamas, being home with young children or aging parents, or simply working at home in order to escape the typical 9-to-5 work environment. Finding credible telecommuter work can be a challenge, so consider this a warning.

The key is working with a reputable site that specializes in telecommuter work and then vet the company for legitimacy. Take a look at FlexJobs (www.flexjobs.com) to get started. The greatest numbers of available jobs are in the following fields, in rank order: sales (think telemarketing), computer and IT, writing, Internet and e-commerce, Web and software development, education and training, customer service, business development, medical, and marketing.[5]

TELECOMMUTER EMPLOYMENT SITES

The following Web sites provide additional specialized employment opportunities for telecommuters:

- **Alpine Access (call center):** Provides call center services using home-based, virtual customer service agents. (www.alpineaccess.com)

- **Convergys (call center):** Provides customer care, human resources, and billing services. (www.convergys.com)

- **LiveOps (support):** Provides representatives for sales, licensed insurance, and food services. (www.liveops.com)

- **Spheris (support):** Provides support to medical professionals, including transcription and clinical documentation. (www.spheris.com)

- **VIPDesk (call center):** Provides call center support, concierge, and VIP services. (www.vipdesk.com)

Reverse Outsourcing

Finally, you may wish to consider working in a *reverse outsourcing* arrangement. If you are unfamiliar with this term, you are not alone. Although it is not a new concept, reverse outsourcing has been brought to the attention of the general public only quite recently as media outlets have cited it as a source of employment in a tough job market. What is it? Simply put, it is when companies overseas hire American workers.

While traditional outsourcing is when American companies hire mostly overseas workers to fill position vacancies, reverse outsourcing is when overseas companies hire American-based workers to fill position vacancies. In other words, it's the reverse. *ABC News* reported that in 2009 U.S.-based freelancers earned a combined total of $15 million from overseas employers within this reverse outsourcing framework and anticipates this figure to more than double in 2010.[6]

If you are scratching your head wondering why countries like China and India might hire Americans at a price much greater than hiring local labor, the reason is this: No one knows how an American thinks better than a fellow American. Companies that want to attract and retain customers in America hire Americans to deliver some of the front-end services such as Web content, public relations, marketing, branding, and customer sales. Sites that offer these opportunities include Elance (www.elance.com) and Odesk (www.odesk.com).

Location-Specific Job Sites

Location-specific sites are those that offer job postings for the masses but within specific geographic locations. These sites can be a fabulous way for you to penetrate a local business and get to know the decision makers, learn about organizational culture and quirks, and more. Although companies will advertise full-time positions that are not of interest to a Patchworker, the part-time and temporary listings may be just what you are looking for.

Generally speaking, all of the same sentiments mentioned in the previous section regarding job search sites for the masses apply to location-specific jobs. However, there are unique advantages to landing work with nearby organizations, including the possibility of building an ongoing relationship for on-site work, networking opportunities with local business people, or creating a niche in your hometown (this is the foundation of my own success). Many sites choose to specialize in advertising work in specific cities, regions, or states depending on their location, with midsize and large cities providing enough volume for sites such as www.milwaukeejobs.com.

Employment Agencies

I grew up hearing the everyday minutia about employment agencies from my family, which owns and operates a small staffing office in the Midwest. I always felt like I really understood what their office and others just like it all across the country had to offer to a prospective employee—until I became a Patchworker. When I initially embraced the Patchwork Principle, it seemed to me that employment agencies were not applicable. After all, they typically place prospective workers in one of these general categories: day labor, temporary light industrial, temporary clerical, or highly skilled permanent positions. Because it seemed that none of those categories was relevant to me, I scratched employment agencies off of my list of possible sources for leads.

Over the years I have come to see how much value there would have been in connecting with a few high-quality services in my area, especially as a new Patchworker eagerly seeking a great volume of leads. These agencies are in the very business of serving up leads that fit your skills and lifestyle preferences—free of charge! You don't have to figure out how and where you fit into the mix of jobs that comes across the employment agency's desk. You simply show up and let the agency do the rest. In exchange for filling out an application form, taking a few basic aptitude tests—perhaps a skill-based test, such as typing—and submitting to a ten-minute interview with an office staffing agent, you enjoy the benefit of receiving customized leads on a regular basis. The notifications continue as long as you agree to accept an assignment once in a while and prove to be reliable. Fair enough, right? Did I mention that this service is *free?* Okay, I did. So check out employment agencies in your area, which by the way, are now referred to in our politically correct culture as *staffing agencies.*

Face-to-Face Networking Groups

If the statistics are right, the majority of 9-to-5 jobs are found through networking efforts. However, you might wonder if this same truth (if it is one) applies when it comes to work that is of interest to the Patchworker. In my experience, it can. As the old saying goes, "People hire people," and so the more people you make contact with, the better it is for you.

Although there are, of course, those standard networking groups that we all know and frequent, there is one tool that I find particularly useful in identifying location-specific networking groups or other interest-specific groups: MeetUp (www.meetup.com). I love this site and have a lot of experience organizing groups and joining existing groups as a regular member. My advice is, scan the Meetup groups in your area and look for a freelancer's meetup, a specialty meetup (such as Web designers), or a group that may be seeking your services that would allow you to come in and offer a presentation and pass out business cards. Take a look at the Meetup groups in your area and consider the possibilities. Networking with both like-minded people and potential clients can be a lucrative and rewarding combination!

Evaluation

Evaluation is all about sizing up the opportunities that appear on the horizon and determining how closely they align with the priorities that matter most to you. You may wish to be highly selective right from the beginning or to work slowly toward that goal. Your approach will be determined in part by your finances, your emotional state, your personality, and other salient factors. Keep in mind the guiding principle discussed in Chapter 9, "Guiding Beliefs of the Patchwork Principle": Small jobs may lead to big opportunities, so consider the hidden potential of every opportunity.

If an opportunity appears to have potential, don't rule it out until after you get a chance to speak with the decision maker about the details of the would-be position. Sometimes the work you initially inquire about can be put on the back burner as the decision maker presents some more-pressing need within the organization for which you are qualified. In some cases, these secondary opportunities are even more attractive and potentially higher paying based on their priority at that moment in time.

Ultimately, only you can determine whether a potential opportunity for work is a good fit with your Lifestyle Design. Survey the possibilities, identify promising leads, and charge ahead; stand and deliver!

The Cardinal Rules of Fishing

As we wrap up this chapter, let's take a look at the cardinal rules of fishing to guide you as you set out to cast your line into the sea of opportunity:

1. **Create a strategy.** It may take some time to settle into a routine, knowing where, when, and how to fish for leads. That's completely normal; everything new takes time to perfect. However, with each passing day your tactics should improve. This progress will be affirmation that you are refining your search techniques and becoming more efficient in the process. Efficiency, or lack thereof, will determine how many leads you can identify and pursue in a given timeframe. Those leads translate into dollars, so efficient fishing is tied directly to your income. Create

an initial strategy and then keep refining it; it's that old "work smarter, not harder" speech.

2. **Toe the line.** There is a famous line in the movie *Wall Street:* "Life all comes down to a few moments. This is one of them." You are striking out on a new path to seek enjoyable work on your own terms. This is your moment. Make it one you can be proud of. Don't tarnish your reputation by resorting to spamming people or any other form of unsavory behavior. Your reputation is all you have, so protect it like gold. Unlike the unsavory characters in *Wall Street,* remember who you are and what you stand for.

3. **Keep your eyes open.** Use this time not only to research opportunities in your own area(s) of specialty, but also to learn about changes in the industry, including emerging trends. Let those trends be your guide as you look ahead to the future.

4. **Have fun!** Fishing is an integral part of the Patchwork Principle, especially when you are first getting started, so learn how to make it fun! Bring your laptop to a coffee shop or do whatever it is that inspires you.

Cast your net wide, enjoy the experience, and reap the rewards of fishing for leads. The more you fish, the better your technique will become. So, get started—go fish!

Endnotes

[1] *Wikipedia,* s.v. "Eagle," http://en.wikipedia.org/wiki/Eagle#The_word (accessed August 20, 2010).

[2] The Royal Society for the Protection of Birds, "Gulls and man," www.rspb.org.uk/wildlife/features/gulls.aspx (accessed August, 24 2010).

[3] The Royal Society for the Protection of Birds.

[4] Drake Benett, "The End of the Office and the Future of Work," *The Boston Globe,* January 17, 2009, www.boston.com/bostonglobe/ideas/articles/2010/01/17/the_end_of_the_office_and_the_future_of_work/?page=3 (accessed August 20, 2010).

[5] "Finding a 'Flexible' Job," Cable News Network, television interview, www.flexjobs.com/cnnvideo.htm (accessed March 5, 2010).

[6] "Working from Home: Reverse Outsourcing," *ABC News,* February 15, 2010, television interview, http://abcnews.go.com/GMA/JobClub/video/working-home-reverse-outsource-9840138 (accessed August 20, 2010).

CHAPTER 13

Stand and Deliver

It's time! It's time to stand up and proudly proclaim to the client who you are, what you have to offer, and how much it will cost to recruit you. The trick is getting the decision maker to extend an offer *and* pay the price that you have in mind. Making this happen is all about perception—in other words, delivering your marketing pitch in such a way that the decision maker feels like he or she absolutely must have the product or service that you are selling.

Perception Is Everything

Sometimes, igniting that gotta-have-it feeling in a prospective employer requires "tinkering with perception," according to Rory Sutherland, advertising guru. During a recent TED Talk, Sutherland told a story that illustrated just how powerful perception can be to the success of your product or service. Here's the story in a nutshell:

> Frederick the Great of Prussia wanted to introduce the potato to the Germans in order to both stabilize the price of bread and lower the risk of famine in the land by bringing this second source of carbohydrate to market. However, the German people found the potato disgusting, and a few farmers even refused to plant it. But Frederick was determined to make the potato a staple in his country and knew that he would have to tinker with the people's perception of the potato if they were going to embrace this ugly, tasteless vegetable.
>
> In an effort to do so, he declared the potato a royal vegetable that only the royals were allowed to consume. Then, he publicly ordered the royal potato crop guarded day and night. Secretly, however, he directed the guards to do a poor job of keeping watch. Quickly the German people's perceptions about the potato changed; they believed that if the potato crop was worth

guarding, it must be worth stealing. Before long a massive underground potato-growing operation was underway.[1]

What a great illustration of how tinkering with perception can cause people to rush toward a product instead of run away from it. Let's talk about some key elements of making an effective proposition and how you can effectively tinker with perception in the selling of your own royal potato.

Key Elements of a Good Pitch

The proposition is what we will refer to as the *pitch*—fish-and-pitch is the name of the game. This is the stage where you become a salesperson and sell the product—yourself! This stage is where you hook the potential client and dazzle him or her with your skills and personality.

Good pitches have a few key elements, as any salesman can tell you. However, when you are a Patchworker, there are some unique dynamics at play that you can use to your advantage and make your pitch distinctive, as discussed in the following sections.

> **Check Your Personal Life at the Door**
>
> Deliver a successful pitch by leaving the following at home:
>
> - Your ego
> - Complaints about your personal life
> - Body piercings (if not standard attire at the workplace)
> - Your temper
> - Jokes in poor taste

Do the Research

Before you make your pitch, be sure you know as much as possible about the person interviewing you, the decision maker (if that person is not the person interviewing you), the organization itself, and the work you will be discussing. This advice is right out of the standard pre-interview playbook that 9-to-5ers use. As a Patchworker, however, you are coming at the pitch from a slightly different angle. You are, of course, interested in learning about this opportunity but perhaps silently collecting information about the organizational culture, systems, or personnel in order to evaluate whether this one small job is a good match with your Lifestyle Design and also could perhaps lead to other opportunities for work, training, or both.

Presumably, you have already done some preliminary research, which lead you to this juncture. This phase of the process is meant for collecting information that you might not otherwise find in print, online, or elsewhere. Even if you do not land the job, the time you spend inside the organization can still be fruitful in other ways, such as introducing you to key decision makers, the organizational culture, and interpersonal dynamics that would otherwise prove elusive. Collect all of the information you can, and if you like the people and the place, you may want to jot down a few notes to use for future reference.

Know Who You Are and Sell It!

When you walk up to the shelf at a supermarket and browse the ten varieties of pasta sauce available, you soon notice that each one has its own brand image and product message. The images and words, the packaging, and the product placement all are bits of the overall message designed to entice you to select the product and place it in your shopping cart.

Selling your own product or service works in much the same way. You have to make a clear case for who you are and what you represent before a potential employer can determine if you are a good fit for the job. The goal is to be very clear about who you are and what you can offer to the marketplace and then deliver that message successfully.

Branding is not about trying to be all things to all people. On the contrary. It's about being yourself—your best self in word, print, and deed. Branding allows you to stand out from the crowd, to be the first person that the potential employer thinks of when a project comes along that would be a perfect fit for someone like you. In other words, you clearly position yourself in the minds of others. This clarity lends credibility to your message and, in turn, causes people to let down their guards and make impulse hiring decisions based on what "feels right." That is the ideal scenario, where the employer makes an impulse purchase; your services seem like an easy choice, and together you quickly strike a deal.

You craft your brand by making careful choices about the following factors that reflect who you are and what your business is *really* selling:

- **Your business name:** Is your business name conservative or irreverent? Either may be appropriate depending on your product or service and your market.

- **Your business title:** Do you anticipate being a consultant or projecting an image of being the head of a thriving corporation? Your title tells the potential employer before you do. Choose the title that seems best for your business.

- **Your business location:** Does your office have a fancy address in an upscale business district, or do you use a P.O. Box in suburbia? Does your address matter to potential employers? Is your office sleek and modern or cozy and eclectic? Which is a better fit with your would-be clientele?

- **Your marketing materials:** This includes your logo, business card, Web site, and brochures or leaflets. For example, a linen business card on heavy stock delivers a different message from one printed on a home computer. Linen might be too intimidating to some potential customers, whereas homemade cards might be too unprofessional for others. Likewise, a Web site chock full of too many bells and whistles may scare away some but draw others in. Knowing your audience is critical.

- **Your niche:** What do you do better than anybody else? Where do you focus your attention? Are you passionate about something? Are you an expert in one specialized area of the industry? Your niche should be at the heart of your brand—literally and figuratively.

- **Your style:** The way you dress, groom, speak, and carry yourself all play an important role in the branding process. We each have our own style. What's yours? How can you leverage your style to your professional advantage? Because every product or service has a brand, and because the most successful ones are those where the brand and the product become interchangeable (think Kleenex, Band-Aid, or Q-tips), consider which of your own personal characteristics you want to put "out in front" for an employer to associate you with. Adjectives may include reliable, ethical, upbeat, consistent, low-maintenance, exceptional, well-dressed, accessible, fun, energetic, professional, driven, and so on.

The overall goal of branding yourself is to clearly define yourself and your product or service and to reinforce the credibility of both.

Lead with a Good Story

My pitches almost always include a good story, carefully rehearsed well in advance. The stories are always true accounts of one of my unique experiences, another reason that collecting unique experiences is a worthwhile endeavor. A good story that is presented well can be one of the most useful tools in your toolkit. A good story makes you engaging and memorable, and it allows you to exhibit confidence because you are talking about something you know really well. Your story can separate you from the pack, if others are in the running for the same vacancy. Your story also offers a potential employer the opportunity to learn more about your personality and to see glimmers of you talking in a relaxed, "just being yourself" manner. I always feel like this is where I make it or break it during a pitch; I can see it in the decision maker's eyes.

The story you choose to tell must be presented at the right time in the conversation. There is often a moment when the employer will say something like, "Tell me a little bit about yourself," which you should consider your cue to lead in to your well-rehearsed story. The purpose of the story is not just being distinctive; more importantly, your story is an opportunity to reveal the key qualities or abilities that you most want the employer to know about you.

The goal is to make the story somehow relatable to the work at hand, but not in an overtly obvious way. Take my travel stories, for example. I am one of those high-adventure travel types. What I mean by that is that, given a choice, I'd skip the opportunity to sip fruity drinks poolside if I could instead walk through the rainforest knee-deep in mud. And it is these "deep-in-the-mud, somewhere-in-the-rainforest" stories that you can turn into one of those relatable stories that depict leaping into the unknown, taking on new challenges, a lifelong quest for learning new things, or adapting to ever-changing situations. Do you see where I am going with this? Give me the opportunity to tell you *one* story about how I trekked through the jungle, up the side of a cliff, or to the bottom of the ocean floor, and I can talk your ear off in a way that relates any proposed project to one of those unique experiences.

Now, think about your own life experiences and pluck out a few that are especially interesting. As you review each one for story potential, reflect on how you felt, what you learned, and how the overall experience represented one or more personal qualities that you can translate into strengths on the job. Then, rehearse different approaches to introducing these stories to potential employers.

> **Know What Not to Talk About**
>
> Generally speaking, employers never want to hear emotionally gut-wrenching stories, or anything gross, scary, too religious, too political, or too personal. Keep your stories interesting but appropriate.

Do *you* need to have an adventure travel story under your belt to wow the decision makers? No! That is just my hook. Everyone has a story to tell, so dig deep and find your own. If you need a good reason to set off on a trek around the world with only a backpack and a Nalgene bottle in your possession, however, then by all means please use this section of the book as total justification for spending the time and money on your adventure. (And invite me along, will you?)

Love the Work

Have you ever watched an episode of the popular television show *The West Wing* or a similar depiction of life as a White House staffer? The pace is brutal. The decisions are impossible. It's a pressure cooker 24/7. And yet those people *love* it! They live and breathe it—gladly. They are obviously passionate about the work and connect with their *flow*. Have you heard about flow? Mihály Csíkszentmihályi introduced the concept of *flow*, which can be summed up like this:

> Flow is completely focused motivation. It is a single-minded immersion and represents perhaps the ultimate in harnessing the emotions in the service of performing and learning. In flow the emotions are not just contained and channeled, but positive, energized, and aligned with the task at hand.…The hallmark of flow is a feeling of spontaneous joy, even rapture, while performing a task.[2]

Can you relate this description to some area of your life? Do you lose track of time when you're reading, running, painting, sewing, whittling, or working on your car or in the garden? That is a sure sign of connecting with your flow. There are generally three motivations for working: money, ego, and joy. Flow is doing work that connects with your joy.

Ideally, that type of work is the primary type of work you will do as a Patchworker. Your work is your decision, so choose projects that make you joyful and let the employer know that the available job is a good fit for you, that you would love it. If appropriate, mention how your career framework is based on selecting work that *you* believe is an especially good fit for you. Explain that you only consider taking on work that you love and that the job being discussed is one that you really believe is a great match for both you and the organization. Most people just need a job, period. But you—the Patchworker—you are selective; you work on purpose. "Name it and claim it," I say; name the work you love to do and then go out there and use your pitch to claim it.

Be Bright and Salty

Salt was the oil of ancient times. It was a commodity bought and sold, used as currency, and traded across great distances. In Rome, for example, people depended on salt to preserve meat to sustain themselves on long journeys, and they were paid in salt (hence the phrase "not worth his salt"). Both then and now, salt was and is a critical part of life. Salt adds flavor to anything it encounters. It releases the flavor of other things around it. It cleanses. It sustains us. It enriches us.

Your own personal "salt" is that extra bit of unique spice that you bring to the interview; it is best coupled with your enthusiasm, your bright inner light. This compelling combination of being bright and salty prompts the employer to think of you beyond the interview phase, to consider how plugging you and your talent into the organization may add something positive to it or release the talent of those around you. Be salty! It can be the secret to getting hired, the missing ingredient that no one else brings to the table.

> **Temper Your Enthusiasm**
>
> Being too bright or too salty can actually be a bad thing. Temper your enthusiasm in order to be appropriate. Also, remember that co-workers may react badly to someone exuding too much enthusiasm because, after all, the light reveals what is lurking in the darkness.

Being salty is about showing off your excitement about a project, about the prospect of working on the project, or for the organization. It is allowing your inner light to shine. And who isn't drawn to light? It draws every eye toward it with interest and sometimes with fascination. Does the light go up when you walk in the room during the pitch? It should. That is part of what you are selling—your enthusiasm! Sell, Baby—sell!

Look the Part

Maybe this goes without saying, but looking the part matters. If you are pitching to someone in person, then dress and groom to match the style of your audience. If you are pitching online via a service such as Skype, be sure that both you and the on-screen area of the room look the part. Remember that in these online interview situations, it is critical that you minimize both noise and clutter as much as possible in order to make a good impression. If the interview process is strictly an exchange of e-mail messages, which can be the case in some job board environments, be sure that your online presence (your Web site or Twitter page) properly reflects your professionalism.

Exude Confidence and Competence

Remember that the pitch is all about selling your personality, skills, and abilities. Take the advice of Dr. Seuss and be yourself, which he of course expresses in rhyming fashion: "Today you are you! That is truer than true! There is no one alive who is you-er than you!"[3]

Be prepared to talk about your career lifestyle, which is what will interest people! Drive home the fact that you chose this career design; you're not simply unemployed and making ends meet until you get a "real" job. The decision makers need to know that you're dependable and will be there consistently throughout the project's term (or into the future if this arrangement promises to be a regular part-time assignment).

Enthusiasm counts in this situation as well. Be excited about your career lifestyle. If you are, you may just find the decision maker wanting to know how you got started, what motivated you, and more. Use this opportunity to lead into your *elevator speech* (also known as your *personal positioning statement*), which is a compelling overview of what you can offer to a potential employer that you present succinctly enough to take place during a short elevator ride. You need to know your elevator speech backward and forward long before you go in! The keys are to make it short, on point, and memorable.

Now that you know how to fish and pitch, let's talk about how to lock in a deal and make it official. Let's move on to the fun part: negotiation! This is where it all comes down to brass tacks, as they say. Negotiation is a challenge that can give you an adrenaline rush and can raise your level of income, training, and exposure to new experiences if you play your cards right. If you are hesitant to embrace this next step because of previous experiences with negotiating salary or benefits, rest assured that the intensity level of these meetings are going to be much cooler. Less is at stake, from the employer's point of view, when the position is temporary, part-time, or both. Hurrah! What's not to love about being a Patchworker?

Endnotes

[1] Rory Sutherland, "Life Lessons from an Ad Man," TED Conferences, July 2009, www.ted.com/talks/rory_sutherland_life_lessons_from_an_ad_man.html (accessed August 20, 2010).

[2] *Wikipedia*, s.v. "Flow (Psychology)," http://en.wikipedia.org/wiki/Flow_(psychology)#cite_ref-1 (accessed August 20, 2010).

[3] Dr. Suess, *Happy Birthday to You!* (New York: Random House Children's Books, 1987), 44.

CHAPTER 14

Negotiate—Everything!

Negotiating with the world around us can be intimidating—until you get your bearings. I learned this firsthand one autumn day at a state park in Australia. I was with a small group of fellow graduate students, and we had all signed up to go "canyoning," which I understood to be a modified hiking adventure. So I laced up my hiking boots and jumped into the rented van along with everyone else that morning.

Hours later I found myself midway up a canyon wall, clinging to the frail, craggy rock. Any subtle movement caused the thin outer layers of rock to break off and race toward the canyon floor. The hot sun was beating down, and I was completely alone. I was terrified, dehydrated, and suffering from a complete lack of experience. I was in trouble. Where were my fellow hikers? It turns out that they were experienced canyoneers who had scaled the side of the cliff with ease and continued to the next stage of the trek. It was nothing personal; they were simply enjoying their own experiences, oblivious to my predicament.

I knew that this was a defining moment. I had to get my emotions under control, take an objective look at the situation, and then figure out a way to negotiate the terrain. Calming myself down was the biggest challenge. Once I did that, the rest was just creating a plan and putting it into action.

That experience taught me so much about myself and about negotiating the terrain in the world around me. After all, no matter what the situation, successful negotiation begins with remaining calm, keeping your eyes on the prize, and taking action appropriate to the situation at hand. Although hanging from the side of that cliff was a stressful experience, negotiating the terms of your employment doesn't have to be. In fact, you may even come to see it as an exciting challenge once you have a little practice (and a few victories) under your belt. It's time to negotiate—*everything!*

The Negotiation Mindset

Negotiating is the name of the game when you're a Patchworker. Whereas 9-to-5ers generally are able to negotiate only their salary, you have the ability to negotiate everything: time, rate, location, and more. This negotiation process is *the* opportunity to shape your work in order to create the lifestyle you have in mind. Know your priorities as you go into a negotiation, not just the money but also the other factors that are critical to you. For example, if you want to spend the month of July backpacking through Europe, then negotiating that time off would be critical to you. Alternatively, if you want to make some fast cash in order to purchase a new car, then getting the best rate possible would be your top priority. If you have young children at home, then perhaps working from home is at the top of your list.

The negotiation is your chance to carve out work and terms that fit your Lifestyle Design, but keep in mind that negotiation is a two-way street. Be sure to listen to the potential employer's needs as well to ensure that everyone walks away satisfied. And don't forget to sell, sell, sell the skills that you bring to the table during this very important conversation. If you're like me, negotiation sparks an adrenaline rush that can turn you into a freelance junkie.

Stepping into a negotiation process can be a little bit like competing in the Olympics—okay, that may be a slight over-dramatization, but in some ways it is true. Both in a job negotiation and in Olympic competition, all parties step onto the playing field ready to throw it all down and go for the gold. The gold in this case is what each party defines as "getting everything they wanted" from the deal. For example, perhaps you go into a negotiation wanting a specific dollar figure and the freedom to complete the project within a flexible timeframe. If you walked away from the table with a deal that gave you both of those things, wouldn't it feel like it was a winner-take-all situation? Okay, so these are the things that dreams are made of the night before a big negotiation.

But did you know that Olympic bronze-medal winners, on average, are *happier* with their finishes than silver medalists after the competition is said and done? It's true! Researchers say, "Take silver and you tend to fixate on the near miss. Score bronze and you are thankful you were not shut out altogether."[1] Going for the gold and falling short both in the Olympics and within the context of business negotiation doesn't have to result in winning gold (getting absolutely everything you wanted from the process).

Simply being a finalist has its payoffs, which in a business context includes

- Actually landing the account instead of being passed over

- Gaining the satisfaction that comes from knowing you were able to agree on the most important points (and if not, having the freedom to walk away from the negotiation process knowing that your livelihood does not depend on securing any single job)

- Getting in the door, earning some money, and becoming familiar with the organization and its members

As you begin to think about negotiating your time, rate, title, location, and other freedoms, be sure to remember that the best outcome is one where everyone walks away feeling like a winner. Although driving a hard bargain may result in you getting what you want, it may leave a negative and lasting impression on the decision maker, who may hesitate to contact you in the future. From a business perspective, it is best to negotiate fervently for those factors most critical to you and to allow the decision maker to "win" on other points in order to strike a balance that satisfies both parties.

Negotiating Your Time

Time is the most valuable commodity in the world. Managing your time wisely allows you to cultivate new experiences and maximize profits. Study after study shows that time is the one thing that people will gladly accept in lieu of money, and as a Patchworker you are in a position to negotiate for both!

When it comes to negotiating your time with a potential employer, it can be useful to think about the negotiation process like a game of chess:

- Negotiation involves two players.

- There is a finite amount of space with which to work (chess board, calendar).

- It requires concentration in order to do well.

- It seems complicated until you have a good strategy.

- Strategy and experience are the keys to knowing what works best.

Negotiating for time, just like chess, requires two worthy opponents to sort out how to use the space on the calendar. The more experience you have with mapping out your own schedule, the easier this exercise becomes.

You will become familiar with the schedule configurations that are to your greatest advantage both economically and personally. Some configurations allow you to maximize your profits, such as scheduling work with multiple employers in a single day, whereas others allow you to maximize your free time, such as working for concentrated periods in the morning, which gives you an afternoon of leisure time. Knowing what your goals are before you go into any negotiation about your time is the key to feeling satisfied with the outcome.

If you were to head in to a negotiation at this moment, what would your goals be? Consider the following options and then write about your goals in the space that follows:

- Working in short bits of time in order to minimize the time your child is at daycare?

- Working in concentrated periods of time to free up the rest of your week for something else?

- Working days, nights, or weekends only?

- Working at least twenty-one hours each week in order to qualify for company benefits or perks?

- Working on a flexible schedule instead of a regimented schedule?

Write About It

_____

_____

_____

The goal of the negotiation process is to honor your Lifestyle Design by striking the balance you seek between work and the rest of your life. Negotiate with a win-win solution in mind to help both you and your potential boss feel good about the outcome, which can be critical to the health of your new business relationship.

Negotiating Your Rate

Years ago I was floating around the Cho nôi Cái Răng, the most famous floating market in Cân Thó, Vietnam—in the whole Mekong Delta, for that matter. Local merchants were gathered in a variety of makeshift boats with their wares in tow, ready to deal. They were selling mostly what we Americans would consider exotic fruits, such as mangoes, durian, and pomelos. Those fruits are plentiful in that region, and the prices reflected how common they were at mere pennies on the dollar compared to what I paid back home in the snowy Midwest, where these fruits were rare and impossible to grow. Therefore, I was more than willing to pay an inflated rate (by Vietnam's standards) that merchants offered upon seeing an obvious tourist.

But my guide was not about to let that happen. He was a seemingly fierce negotiator, although for me much of it was lost in translation. He would flail his hands around, shake his head, sit in silence for moments, and paddle away from the merchant as if the deal was off—all in the name of getting the best rate possible on whatever it was that I wanted to buy. This guy was shrewd! He was negotiating the best rate possible out there on the open market. The price associated with these items or any other product or service on the open market, be it in Cân Thó or in your own city, is a reflection of its quality, its uniqueness (or lack thereof), and the marketing pitch of the seller. Let's put this in perspective relative to negotiating a rate for your own skills and services out on the open market.

Determine the Worth of Your Skill Set on the Open Market

How do you determine a reasonable amount to ask the would-be employer to pay you for your skills and services? What is your time worth? Are you uniquely available, flexible, and risk-free? Yes, you are! Can you close the sale with a great sales pitch? Yes, you can, because you give that speech often, and practice makes perfect! Let's answer each of these important questions. To get you started, here are two unscientific but key considerations for developing a price you would like to pitch during the negotiation:

- **Know what number makes you feel valued.** Going in, you need to know what rate of pay would feel emotionally satisfying. What number would make you feel like getting up in the morning and doing fantastic work for Company X? What number would make you feel like you have life by the tail?

- **Know what number you absolutely need in order to pay your bills.** To determine this number, look back to Chapter 6, "The Framework—Lifestyle Design," where you wrote down the annual amount you need to earn in order to pay for the basics. Prior to each negotiation you must ask yourself how that specific job fits into your larger financial earning strategy and then come up with a "bottom-line number" before talking with the decision maker. After all, the job of the decision maker is to get you to sign on for the lowest possible price, so be prepared; know your lowest possible price as well and be willing to walk away if it doesn't make sense for you financially. As Richard Branson says, "Business opportunities are like buses. There's always another one coming."

As you can see from the preceding points, determining the value of your skill set requires a combination of practicality and emotion. Armed with that information, you are ready to develop a pricing strategy.

Develop a Pricing Strategy

Figuring out how to price your skill set is daunting for some people. Some will price themselves too low; others will overprice. The key is to figure out what is reasonable and then adjust your pitches based on the situation. For example, in the case of an emergency situation where the employer needs your specialized skills that same day or week, perhaps you charge a premium, whereas when it's a normal hiring situation you charge your standard rate. But how do you figure out that standard base rate? There are a few commonly used frameworks:[2]

- **Hourly rate:** There is an old standard called *The Rule of Thirds* that can dictate the hourly rate you charge as a Patchworker. To start, determine your hourly rate (including benefits) for your skills and services as a traditional 9-to-5 employee. Then triple it, essentially. Of that number, one-third is attributed to your wage, one-third to your expenses, and one-third to administration. Therefore, if your hourly wage for someone with the same skill set in the 9-to-5 world is $30 per hour (refer back to Chapter 6 for the calculations you made about your hourly wage as a 9-to-5er), then your freelance rate would be $90 per hour ($30 x 3).

  > **Determine Your Worth**
  >
  > To review wage rates across occupations and geographic locations, visit the U.S. Bureau of Labor Statistics Web page on wage data: www.bls.gov/bls/blswage.htm.

- **Daily rate:** You can calculate your daily rate simply by taking your hourly rate and multiplying it by the number of anticipated hours in a standard workday. However, you may wish to offer a modest discount for being hired for a block of time to encourage the employer to hire you for larger chunks of time (and money!) in the future. Give a little, get a lot!

- **Project-based rate:** The project rate is a pricing strategy based not on your time necessarily but instead on what getting the job done would be worth to the client. This requires that you have a clear idea of how much time would likely be involved in completing the project and then charging accordingly. If you underestimate, then you have to live with your miscalculation and do the work anyway. However, if you overestimate, then you're golden. Ideally, you want to be somewhere in the middle, but err on the side of overestimating when in doubt.

  A classic example of project-based pricing comes from Niels Bohr, a Nobel Prize–winning physicist. He priced out a project years ago in a way that has become the stuff of legends. When asked to help fix a client's machine, he went into the business, drew an X on the side of the machine, and then proceeded to hit the X with a hammer. That caused the machine to come to life and begin working properly. He promptly mailed the client an invoice for $10,000. Upon receipt of the invoice, the client was outraged and protested the charge. In response, Bohr sent an itemized invoice that read, "Drawing an X on the side of your machine: $1. Knowing where to put the X: $9,999."[3] The moral of the story is, sometimes a project-based pricing strategy is your best bet!

Choosing the most suitable framework in each employment opportunity that arises will become easier over time. Experience will guide you and make the decision effortless.

Managing the Negotiation Process

When I begin negotiating, I always like to break the ice with conversation that includes something along the lines of, "What is it like to work for you?" The answer and the nonverbal cues tell me a lot about how much money I *need* to work for *that person*. I like to fall silent during that part of the conversation because people tend to fill the silence with nervous chatter that can reveal more about the topic than a long line of formal questioning ever could. This moment is usually when the potential employer will make a series of off-the-cuff remarks that he or she will later regret because of revealing too much information. It's marvelous and gives you some amazing leverage in an instant. Try it; it works!

As you sit down to negotiate your rate, there are five cardinal rules that you must keep in mind:

1. **Let *the client* make the first offer.** The first offer tells you a lot. For example, if the offer is an unreasonable lowball offer, carefully observe the body language of the person delivering it. Is that person uncomfortable or confident? If the person confidently names a rate that is 50 percent less than market value, you may be dealing with someone who is simply looking for a bargain and may not be a good match for you. If the individual is uncomfortable, then perhaps he or she figured it was worth a try to start low and work up the pay scale.

2. **Their first offer is *never* their best offer.** This is an important point to keep in mind. If the first offer you hear is not what you were hoping for, don't despair. This process is a negotiation, after all, and the job of the potential employer is to hire you for the best price possible. Therefore, simply view this initial offer as a starting point, not the bottom line.

3. **Know what rate you are willing to accept.** Doing a little research about what the position likely pays and what your absolute lowest rate is can really pay off. *Knowing your bottom line is critical in the negotiation process.* Going into the discussion without that knowledge can cause you to flounder and become dissatisfied with the terms. Keep in mind that your rate of pay now needs to account for the fact that you are a no-risk hire, benefits-free, short-term commitment. There is a premium to be paid by the company for those advantages that greatly favor *them!*

4. **Name *your* price with confidence.** Know your dollar number and state it confidently. If this is your standard rate, then say so; if this is less than your standard rate, then be sure to inform the client. The delivery tells the employer a lot about how much wiggle room exists. Name your price with confidence, smile, and sit in silence, looking the person in the eye in a polite, relaxed manner.

5. **Don't settle for less; be willing to walk away politely.** Don't be afraid to walk away. You can always call back at a later date and agree to the lower wage, but keep the "happiness" factor in mind. If you go in working for peanuts, working long hours or some other configuration of factors that causes you frustration, you are falling right back into the 9-to-5 lifestyle trap. Don't do it. Also, keep in mind that under these circumstances you will likely not be the stellar employee with the

great attitude that you need to portray in order to get a callback in the future. Bad behavior could tarnish your reputation, causing poor word-of-mouth marketing about you to other potential clients. If the terms are not a match for you, enjoy the freedom of walking away from the table—politely, of course.

During the negotiation process, remember to really sell what you have to offer, including not only your skill set but also your unique Patchworker advantages such as immediacy and a simplified employment situation that is at will, with no strings attached. Most importantly, negotiate for a price that makes you feel good about working for the organization. Be willing to walk away from the table if the organization's offer is unreasonable. Know your absolute bottom line number going in; do your best to negotiate for that number or better and be willing to walk away if the negotiation process does not yield the rate of pay you need in order to work happy.

Negotiating Your Title

Billy Joel had it right when he sang, "Just like a boxer in a *title* fight, you got to walk in that ring all alone." When it comes time to negotiate for your title, you have to walk into the room ready to go to the mat for the designation that serves you best. The negotiation doesn't necessarily need to be a contentious situation, but sometimes it can be.

Because a Patchworker is a nontraditional employee, the title that fits the work being done is not always a foregone conclusion. In my own experience, there often comes a moment when the would-be employer looks at me and asks, "Would you like to be classified as an employee, an independent contractor, or a consultant?" In some instances this is because the boss doesn't care which title I choose; in other cases it is because he or she has no idea how to categorize the anticipated work.

The first few times I was asked this question, "Which title?" I looked back at the decision makers with a blank expression. Over time, however, I learned that answering that question one way or the other has definite advantages, with each employment situation being unique. Today, I deliberately research the pros and cons in advance and bring the topic up in conversation if necessary. The questions I research *ahead of time* cover the following topics:

- **Benefits:** Does the organization offer a benefits package for part-time employees, and if so, what are the eligibility requirements?

- **Union dues:** Do any of the job classifications require this payment?

- **Latitude:** Does one classification receive a significant amount of latitude over the others (punching the clock versus flexible hours, for example)?

- **Tax benefits:** Are the non-employee tax benefits associated with mileage or expenses significant?

- **Bounce:** Is one classification better for my resume than the other? This is what I often refer to as "bounce"—will the decided-upon classification help me spring up and out to bigger and better opportunities?

- **Acceptance:** Will individuals in the organization more readily accept one job classification over another?

- **Closure:** Is one classification more likely than another to close the deal?

Beyond these talking points, it is important to understand the fundamental differences between the three classifications: employee, independent contractor, and consultant. Let's take a look at the pros and cons of each.

The Employee

Being an *employee* is the classification with which we're all most familiar so I will gloss over the description, but I will mention that holding this status as a Patchworker has these major pros and cons:

> **Pro:** You are on the payroll and get paid like clockwork each pay cycle. This classification eliminates the need for invoicing (billing), which is heavenly.

> **Pro:** You may qualify for limited benefits from the organization if you meet the minimum thresholds. These benefits are the equivalent of cash-in-hand compensation.

> **Pro:** The organization calculates your tax deductions and withholds them from your check automatically. This saves you from the rigmarole of having to set aside a predetermined amount of cash in savings and ante it up during quarterly tax periods.

> **Pro:** You reap the benefits of being affiliated with the organization if there are sporting events, health clubs, or other community vendors that provide discounts for employees.

> **Pro:** You may enjoy some additional "buy in" from co-workers who see you as a part of their team.

Con: You likely will not be paid as well as you would be under the other two titles. Job classification standards likely set the boundaries for the upper range of pay allowable.

Con: This classification requires you to fill out a mountain of internal forms and walk through other administrative procedures those first few days or weeks on the job.

Con: The title implies a long-term commitment to a specific job, which may not be your intention as a Patchworker.

If a long-term, ongoing commitment is not a good fit for your Lifestyle Design, then consider working as an independent contractor.

The Independent Contractor

An *independent contractor* is hired to perform a specific function in an at-will capacity. In other words, the contractor is someone who is hired for a purpose with no strings attached; the job can end at any time for any reason if either party walks away. There are no benefits offered and no liability is in play. In my experience this title is the most common among those positions you find advertised in job search engines and at freelance sites. It's a generic term that means "we need short-term help."

Although the title itself is lackluster and the position does have drawbacks, it also affords you some unique opportunities. Let's take a look at them.

Pro: The position may pay higher than the typical employee rate for the same work. This classification is not constrained by a pay range, like an employee position would be.

Pro: The position allows you to sample the organization and learn about the culture and key players.

Pro: The position may lead to other opportunities within the organization if your boss and other decision makers like you.

Pro: Unlike the other two classifications, employees within the organization are unlikely to feel at all threatened by the title and, therefore, may be more welcoming and cooperative.

Pro: You can write off your expenses for tax purposes.

Con: You alone are responsible for setting aside required tax contributions from each payment you receive. Failure to pay these contributions at quarterly tax deadlines will result in hefty fines from the Internal Revenue Service.

Con: You are responsible for pursuing funds from organizations that do not pay on time or at the agreed-upon rate.

EDUCATE YOURSELF

The job classification of independent contractor has come under scrutiny recently with the government cracking down on companies that wrongfully classify some workers as independent contractors instead of employees in order to avoid paying Social Security, Medicare, and unemployment insurance taxes. Because of this crackdown, both companies and workers are more cautious about the use of this job classification. Therefore, it's important to educate yourself about what constitutes an independent contractor.

Workers are generally considered employees when someone else controls how and when they perform their work. In contrast, independent contractors are generally in business for themselves, obtain customers on their own, and control how they perform services.

By this definition, most work you do as a Patchworker will likely fall within the parameters of this job classification. However, it is wise to spend time educating yourself about its legal description, effective as of the date that you read this book, by visiting www.irs.gov/businesses.

The Consultant

Last but not least is the classification of *consultant*. At some organizations hiring a consultant is commonplace, whereas at others it is unheard of. Consultants are often seen as temporary, project specific, and having little impact on the standard departmental budget because funds traditionally come out of special budget lines such as endowments, gifts, or grant money. *I love those organizations; I seek them out!* Those organizations typically pay consultants generously and hire them quickly. Additionally, these organizations usually hire teams of consultants repeatedly over many years.

In my own life, these short stints often last for a few months and pay me at a rate that is equivalent to working my old 9-to-5 job for the entire *year!* When they call, I always find time on my schedule, even if it means postponing work with another organization. Consulting work that pays well and comes around consistently is like finding the pot at the end of the rainbow, and it can evaporate just as quickly if you have limited availability. When I am on the job as a consultant, I do my best work, deliver on time, and am enthusiastic and pleasant at all times to all people, no matter what the circumstances.

I am the dream employee on purpose. But please note that I am officially not an employee; I am a consultant!

You can think about a consultant as you would an independent contractor; you won't receive benefits such as paid vacation leave as you would if you were an employee. However, one tangible benefit that you *do* enjoy is operating outside of the politics and everyday drama of the workplace. Even if you physically work on the premises, you are happily insulated from some of the workplace dynamics that affect traditional employees.

For example, for several years I worked for a small organization. For some of those years my formal status was "consultant," and for a few years it was "employee." *I* negotiated each classification for various reasons that were meaningful to me. Throughout my entire tenure with that organization, with little exception, I worked in isolation from my colleagues. I don't mean that I ran into my office and shut the door during my office hours, but after socializing a bit, I could get to work and not be subject to the standard staff meetings, performance reviews, and budget meetings. It was fantastic!

Being a consultant also affords you a higher status in many organizations because you are hired based on some specialized skill that no one else has in the organization. You are a rock star and enjoy a little fame (and fortune!) while on the job. Also, consultants that do well are often traded like playing cards, where one department will hire you when your assignment in another department ends. Consequently, you can have a lengthy assignment within an organization if you "play well with others," as they say.

Also worthy of mention is the fact that executive-level managers sometimes share the name of an excellent consultant with their colleagues. This word-of-mouth referral can result in the Patchworker receiving unsolicited calls from organizations that are ready to hire immediately and pay top dollar. What's not to love?

Although you can attribute many positives to being a consultant, you must contend with some negatives as well. Not all that glimmers is gold, after all. Here are some considerations worthy of note:

Pro: The rate of pay should be fabulous. Negotiate and make it so.

Pro: The emotional payoff is great; you get to be a rock star within the organization.

Pro: You can write off your expenses for tax purposes.

Pro: You can flaunt your consulting history to future employers as evidence of your known expertise in the field.

Con: People expect to get what they pay for, and sometimes they experience buyer's remorse; therefore, you must dress, act, and perform like a superstar at all times. This can be a bit costly, in terms of wardrobe expenses, for example, and more tiring than working in the capacity of an independent contractor.

Con: Others within the organization may become resentful of your pay rate, which in some organizations is public knowledge. This higher compensation can cause tension between you and those regular employees.

Con: The work can be demanding because the employer may want to be sure to get his or her money's worth by giving you little downtime during your work schedule. The expectations are also high, which requires you to constantly perform and churn out stellar work.

The "consultant" is the most coveted of job titles because of the accompanying prestige and generous rate of pay. As a result, the title places great expectations on your ability to perform at exceptional levels, so your boss and your co-workers may carefully scrutinize your performance. Consultants usually garner the highest rate of pay among the three titles, making it the most attractive for many. You need to decide if the consultant title is a good fit for you and advocate for yourself when it's time to sit down and start negotiating your title.

Choosing Your Title Wisely

Whichever title you choose, it is to your benefit to become educated about the pros and cons of holding the title of employee, independent contractor, or consultant ahead of the meeting with your potential employer. Most businesses have a Web site that outlines any benefits extended to part-time workers with "employee" status, along with a definition of what qualifies as a part-time employee for each perk. If the organization you are courting does not have this information available online, simply contact the human resources office and make a blind inquiry. It is time well spent.

Negotiating Your Location

If you have been working "down on the farm," out of a 6' by 6' office cubicle for most of your life, the idea of being what cubicle dwellers refer to as *free range* is highly attractive. Imagine if you could work from home in your pajamas (people do that!). Or work from a remote location, such as a white sand beach in Thailand (people do that, too!). Or maybe it's something altogether different from these two simple scenarios. Whatever your aspirations, negotiating the terms of your location is an important component of the overall compensation package. Let me share a real-life example that illustrates just how important the location factor can be:

> For two years I worked as an independent contractor at a nearby college. Going in, I negotiated the terms of my location, namely that I wanted to work from home via the Internet. The supervisor was pleased to agree to these terms; it was an easy sell. I regularly enjoyed taking my laptop outdoors to work in the sunshine while I basked in the sun and tanned or to a coffee shop where I could sip a latte and listen to jazz. It was wonderful, and it made me more productive; I looked forward to the hours that I spent working on that project.

> My colleague, however, did not enjoy the same location luxury. He had to report to the office during his assigned hours in a windowless office where the temperature gauge was set to "freezing" year round. While he was stuck in the office doing work that was quite similar to mine, I enjoyed working from home. Fortunately for me, he was a nice guy who was never resentful, and the arrangement was a great success for several years.

Negotiating where you work is worth the time and effort. It's a key component to living your lifestyle by design. What did you map out in the Lifestyle Design section (refer to Chapter 6) as your ideal location scenario? Keep that picture at the front of your mind when you head in to negotiate the terms with a would-be employer. The boss may be eager and willing to make a concession about location in lieu of being able to offer you other perks or a rate of pay that would normally be expected to recruit you. This can result in a win-win situation that is good for all involved.

Negotiating Some Extras

There are many miscellaneous freedoms that are worth rolling in to the negotiation process, when applicable. These can add value to the work experience and be the equivalent of an increase in pay, in some cases. In other cases, some factor may be worth (dare I say it) even *more* to you than the money. Let's look at a few examples to get you thinking about what the "extras" are that you may wish to bring in on your mental list of demands to a future negotiation for a Patchwork position:

- **Deadlines:** Let's face it: Deadlines can be the bane of your existence, especially if you are juggling multiple projects for multiple employers in multiple locations and time zones. Events in your personal life, such as unexpected emergencies or important family events, can also cause deadlines to go off track. The ability to negotiate away deadlines in exchange for approximated end dates is well worth your time and effort. It takes the pressure off of accomplishing a project or set task by a specific date and instead gives you a general timeframe to keep in mind. This can be marvelous, unless you have trouble keeping yourself on task, in which case you need that definite end date to keep you motivated.

- **Learning while you earn:** One of the *major* advantages of working for a variety of organizations is the opportunity to expose yourself to new technologies and other industry-specific advances that you simply couldn't afford on your own or would have little reason to invest in for your own purposes. That's where "learn while you earn" comes in! In advance of sitting down at the negotiating table, troll the company's materials and Web sites and perhaps even make some innocent inquiries of your soon-to-be boss and co-workers during the interview process about on-site equipment or training programs that could help shape your resume and build your knowledge base.

  The idea is to cultivate professional development programs for yourself at their expense. In most cases the training programs, for example, are run by salaried personnel from within the organization, which means that the organization bears no additional costs for allowing you to attend. Therefore, the boss sitting across the table from you during the negotiation will probably not even flinch at the idea, because it doesn't cost him a cent. However, for you the retail cost of attending the training from an outside vendor may be significant and makes this opportunity one that may even be worth taking a slight reduction in pay if it means closing the deal. Learning while you earn can be your key to staying current at an affordable price.

- **Noteworthy experience:** Sometimes opportunities come along that can catapult you into an entirely new career field or a new *level* of your current career field or somehow shift the tectonic plates of your career background in such a way that it signals a new era of opportunity in your Patchwork career. These opportunities are worth grabbing with both hands, almost regardless of the anticipated rate of pay. They can include exposure to new work environments that may open doors of opportunity in the future to additional work in those settings, access to people who could catapult your career in new directions, or other credentials and experiences that could have a lasting, positive effect on your resume far into the future. Sometimes these experiences are worth it, even if you have to work for a greatly reduced rate of pay, because you reap the dividends in the months and years after the job ends; the money is earned at future organizations.

Negotiation is the fine art of blending what you want *and* what the boss wants into a finished product: the terms of your employment. Each person has an *ideal* in mind. However, despite the letter *i* before the word *deal*, the end game is to reach a "deal" where neither person's goals are alone fulfilled but instead both parties are satisfied in some respects and mildly disappointed in others. The goal is reaching a deal where everyone walks away a winner to some extent.

ℛ

This wraps up the "Make It Happen" section of the book, which spells out in practical terms what you would need to do to make your dream a concrete reality. You have a lot to think about and even more to do to get started, but before you do, let's take a moment to think it through. The next section provides an opportunity for you to reflect on the demands of being a Patchworker before you make the big leap and start setting up shop.

Endnotes

[1] Steve Wieberg, "Analysts: Bronze Medal Leads to More Happiness Than Silver," *USA Today*, February 2, 2010, www.usatoday.com/sports/olympics/vancouver/2010-02-22-bronze-vs-silver_N.htm (accessed August 20, 2010).

[2] Retire and Consult, "Setting Consultant Rates," http://retireandconsult.com/cm/consultant-center/setting-consulting-fees.html, (accessed April 5, 2010).

[3] Consultant Journal, "Consulting Fee Rates," Trustmode Marketing, May 26, 2006, www.consultantjournal.com/blog/setting-consulting-fee-rates (accessed August 2, 2010).

PART V

Think It Through

CHAPTER 15

Do You Have What It Takes?

Before you dive in and try out this new career lifestyle, let's take a moment to determine if the Patchwork model is really the right choice for you. After all, being a Patchworker means owning your own business and running the show, which is new territory you are wading into if you are currently part of the 9-to-5 world. There are many important considerations to weigh; let's take a look at some of them.

The Mindset

A mindset is "a fixed state of mind."[1] In other words, it is a way of thinking to which you are fully committed. The *Patchworker mindset* is that of a mindful entrepreneur, committed to operating a successful business within the parameters of Lifestyle Design.

Your mindset will determine the limits of your success as a Patchworker; therefore, carefully consider the following characteristics (keeping in mind that you should possess most but not necessarily all of them):

- **Do you have the energy?** Do you have the energy required to complete all of the initial startup tasks? Are you too burnt out from your current or past job to do the work? Starting a business *is* work. In fact, you may work more than anticipated in the beginning in order to get the wheels of your business turning. Are you willing to put in the time and effort?

- **Do you have the focus?** Do you have the mental focus necessary to open, operate, and maintain a new business? When you are self-employed, you don't have a boss keeping you on task and sending you reminders about approaching deadlines. You have to coach yourself, to motivate and propel yourself forward by staying on task. Can you do that?

- **Do you have the dedication?** To be a successful Patchworker, you need to be committed to following through on all promises you make to yourself and your clients. Consistency is vital in order to be successful as a business; it takes discipline. You will sometimes have to do things that are mundane, time-consuming, or uninteresting in the course of maintaining your business. Do you have the dedication necessary to stay on task?

- **Do you have the organizational skills?** Running a business requires basic organizational skills, period. You need not be a perfectionist—in fact, that may hinder your success. However, your clients will expect you to be on top of things related to the work you do for them, Uncle Sam will expect you to maintain records and pay taxes as required by law, and if you ever expect to get paid, you will need a good way to keep track of who to invoice, when, and for how much. The nutty professor style of filing with numerous stacks of dog-eared papers leaning over in a dangerous balancing act on your desk doesn't cut it when you manage your own business. Can you start and stay organized?

- **Can you multitask like a pro?** If there is one thing that being a Patchworker requires, it is the ability to multitask. And to be a Patchworker, at times you may have to be an über-tasker as you manage multiple projects for an array of organizations simultaneously in a single week. Then there is invoicing, recordkeeping, collecting, advertising, and more. Do you have the will to keep a handle on it all? Can you play the part of CEO, secretary, accountant, and driver all in a single day? More importantly, are you willing to?

- **Can you work independently?** Even if you work on-site at your employer's workplace location, there is still some amount of paperwork, such as invoicing, that you must do independently in your home office setting. Do you have the space, even if it is only a corner of the room, from which to run your business? Most Patchworkers spend most of their time working out of their home office, but there are exceptions—like me, for example! Could you stay on task, feel energized, and remain motivated if you worked independently at home? The location aside, could you simply work independently on the projects or tasks for which you are responsible? Could you stay focused?

- **Can you drum up your own leads?** To be a successful Patchworker, you absolutely need to scout out new opportunities and then determine if they fit into your lifestyle framework. Drumming up new business must be a regular part of your routine as the business owner. Can you get out there and sell? Before you say, "No way!" let me mention that selling doesn't have to involve the traditional approaches such as in-person cold calls or telemarketing-like approaches. I have never made a single cold call or done any telemarketing to drum up a lead, just to reassure you.

In today's modern world, selling often means marketing yourself online via e-mail and social media sites such as Twitter. Because my business approach seeks work mostly from local businesses in my geographic location, I could walk in and talk with decision makers, but I find e-mail to be a practical, effective medium for making my pitches. Each business is different, so test out the waters and see what works best for you.

- **Can you make your own decisions?** The great thing about being a 9-to-5 employee is that you can always blame any misguided initiatives on the boss. Whatever goes wrong, you name it and the boss is a prime target at which to hurl criticism. However, when you are the boss of your own Patchwork business, the buck stops with you. Any and all decisions are yours to own. You must take full responsibility for the ideas, the execution, and the outcomes. When things go really well, it's nice to bask in the glow and take full credit. However, when things go awry, you have to be able to deal with the consequences. Can you handle it?

- **Can you keep learning?** Lifelong learning is a prerequisite for most everything in life that is worthwhile; work is no exception. Although you will settle into a routine related to recordkeeping and other mundane tasks, you will likely never fully enjoy the "cruise control" mentality that you may now know in your 9-to-5 world. In contrast, as an entrepreneur you will be growing and learning in many directions at once. You alone will need to determine when you need to seek out a book, class, or mentor to guide you when you encounter new topics related to running your business, either to keep up with the industry in which you work or as you strive to honor your lifestyle framework. Are you able to ask for help when the need arises? Can your ego handle it? Are you willing to climb the learning curves that you will inevitably encounter?

> **Consider the Reality of Being the Boss**
>
> To get a better picture of what it's like to be your own boss, both during the startup process and once you've established yourself, talk with fellow entrepreneurs in your area. Places to find such people include the following:
>
> - Local chamber of commerce meetings
> - Business networking groups
> - Online via Twitter twibes, Facebook groups, Yahoo! groups, or Meetup. com clubs

Although the preceding points are only the main points of consideration, it is important to take some time to seriously consider the realities of being the boss. Being in charge is a much different experience from being a subordinate. Some people love it; others do not.

The People Skills

Emotional Intelligence (EI) counts for a lot in business, especially when you are self-employed. Your ability to work and play well with others can determine the reaches of your success on some levels. Are you familiar with this concept of EI, introduced by Daniel Goleman? EI has a long and controversial history of evolving into what we know it to be today, but generally speaking the term refers to a person's ability to manage his or her own emotions and the emotions of others. Goleman believes there are five fundamental elements to EI:

- Knowing your emotions

- Managing your emotions

- Motivating yourself

- Recognizing and understanding the emotions of others

- Managing relationships (managing the emotions of others)

Ultimately, these elements all boil down to a few fundamental people skills—inspirational, interpersonal, operational, cultural, and "crazy"—you must master as a Patchworker.

Inspirational Skills

Inspirational skills are the skills you need to land work, keep it, and get called back in the future. These skills include the following:

- Exuding confidence when you pitch your ideas

- Performing under pressure

- Keeping your emotions under control if a client makes unreasonable requests or behaves badly

- Maintaining the relationship well enough to be someone the client would want to hire again in the future

You must inspire the individuals who consider hiring you, dazzle them with the work you do, and maintain a good working relationship throughout each project.

Interpersonal Skills

Each work environment has many different personalities to contend with, and your Patchwork career will take you to multiple organizations and require you to interact with an even *greater* number of people than a typical 9-to-5er. Can you handle the great variety of personalities with which you must contend? More importantly, are you *willing* to do so? Let me answer this one for you: YES! You must. The opportunity to work with a variety of people at an array of organizations makes your work more interesting, increases your opportunity to network, and makes the day more interesting.

As you might anticipate, the more clients you work with, the greater the likelihood of encountering a difficult personality. If this person is your direct supervisor, the situation can prove challenging. However, unlike a 9-to-5 worker, you can remove yourself from this work environment immediately after the project or short-term assignment ends and never return to work for that difficult supervisor again. Although a Patchworker is in the enviable position of being able to decline offers from clients they dislike, this knowledge often (and unfortunately!) comes only after having worked with the person.

One of the tough realities that you must face as a Patchworker is that if you sign on for a project only to discover that the client is difficult or unreasonable in some way, you must ride out the remainder of your contract as promised. Could you do this? Let me rephrase: You *need* to do this in order to protect your reputation. Although you may never want to work for that same person again, you may want to work with someone else within the organization. Alternatively, you may not like the company but may want a recommendation from this person as you bid for a similar project at another organization.

> **Steer Clear of Conflict**
>
> If you tend to be a hothead who lets your temper get the best of you when interpersonal conflicts occur in the workplace, consider seeking off-site employment that allows you to minimize your level of contact and exposure with co-workers. Working off-site can, at the very least, allow you to more readily measure your responses when you are communicating through a medium such as e-mail or fax than you can in a face-to-face conversation.

Operational Skills

One type of people skills critical to your business is the ability to interact productively with clients, including those who help you to sustain your business (accountant, banker, or webmaster, for example) and the employees in each of the key administrative offices at the organizations you work with (human resources or payroll personnel, for example).

The most heated situation among those that occur in this realm of operational management is related to receiving timely payment from a client. The bottom line is that you have done the work and now you want to receive payment. What's the problem? In my experience, delayed payment is most often a communication breakdown that happens within the organization. For example, perhaps your supervisor forgot to send a directive to payroll or the payroll office is awaiting an approval from someone in human resources. These administrative tasks can cause frustration for the Patchworker, who is perhaps off-site and unfamiliar with the people working in these administrative offices. Navigating the waters within each organization when a problem occurs requires some finesse. If you create a big stir that leaves a lasting impression on your supervisor and perhaps others in the organization, it may leave an indelible mark on their memory. Take this snippet from one of my real-life adventures, for example:

> Eight years ago, while working as a consultant, I was having trouble collecting payment from a rather wealthy organization. When the first pay cycle did not produce a check, I notified the boss in a calm way with a "by-the-way" tone. She assured me that the first check was delayed simply due to paperwork processing that plagued all new hires.
>
> When the second pay cycle came and went without producing a paycheck, I decided to inquire directly with the administrative offices to be sure that I had completed all of the necessary paperwork and to make them generally aware of the situation. They, too, assured me that this was routine and I need not be concerned.
>
> When the third pay cycle rolled around and there was no check in sight, I had a decision to make: Should I storm out of my office and down the hall to the boss's office to demand immediate payment? Should I send out an e-mail message to everyone involved threatening to quit for lack of payment? Should I simply

let things continue the way they were going and hope that it all worked out? Or should I do something altogether different?

These are the moments when the right move or the wrong move can be a defining move. I'll tell you that I did get paid eventually, and because I remained calm under pressure, this account ended up being one of my biggest and best for the next three years. And yes, I was paid on a predictable and consistent basis once it was discovered that payroll had simply failed to add my electronic record to the check-cutting system to which they farmed out the work. Someone had simply goofed, and I got paid once it was figured out. Just imagine if I had stormed down to the boss's office back then. What a financial loss that would have been for me, not to mention the hit my reputation would have taken within that industry. Yes, there are moments when you may have to lay down the law a little bit, but they should be rare and carefully crafted events.

Are you wondering how I handled this situation, three pay cycles (six weeks) of nonpayment? I scheduled a fifteen-minute appointment with the boss and explained in a pleasant but firm way that I would finish out the remainder of the week and then put the project on hold until the paycheck problem could be resolved. Right there, on the spot, the boss got on the phone and demanded a resolution from payroll. Within hours the situation was resolved, and I had a check for the entire outstanding amount by the next morning. I walked away looking like a professional with my reputation intact and a check in hand. Most importantly, I didn't have to skulk around for the remainder of my assignment feeling like I had behaved badly. That counts for a lot in my book.

Cultural Skills

If you have ever traveled overseas to a country completely different from your own, you know that the experience can conjure up a potluck of emotion, including feelings of disorientation, elation, isolation, or fascination. New people and new perspectives challenge our deeply held beliefs and invite us to stretch and grow in new directions. Some people are good at navigating through the experience; some are not. Which category do you lean toward? Although you may think that this question is silly, because the topic of this book is not overseas travel, it is still quite relevant because overseas travel can in many ways be likened to working for an unfamiliar company.

Every organization has its own culture. In other words, each business community has its own unique values, norms, assumptions, acceptable behaviors, and tangible artifacts (such as awards on display or paintings in the hallways). Just walk into the headquarters at Google and look around at the people and the environment; then compare that with any conservative accounting firm. The people act and dress differently. Behaviors at one place may be encouraged, whereas at another place those actions are grounds for dismissal. Some artifacts may seem outrageous and out of place to one company, but not to another. For example, Google has a shiny corkscrew slide that employees can ride between floors as an alternative to taking the elevator or stairs. Show me any accounting firm that has one of those!

This discovery of new organizational cultures is an inherent part of being a Patchworker. You will have many different accounts, each representing a different organization. Each organization, in turn, has its own culture that you must observe and respect if you want to fit in and do well. However, sifting through the many cues and clues about what the culture reveres and abhors can require careful observation and thoughtful questions phrased carefully to sort it all out. Although the obligatory New Employee Handbook is available to reference, this guide often does not address many (or any) of the subtleties that are of greatest interest to you as a new part of the organization. Instead, you must sort out these nuances one day, one interaction at a time. Can you do this? Do you typically do this well? Can you refrain from being outspoken if your opinions about a topic are quite different from those of others in the organization? These are tough questions that only you can answer.

Crazy Skills

Some people are crazy, they just are. And sometimes those people are your clients. When this happens you have no choice but to sing and dance in order to appease them, at least until the project or short-term assignment that you committed to reaches a conclusion. This song and dance can be a challenge, but you must persist—you *must* honor your agreement with the client. You can do this simply by keeping your head down and charging ahead as you might do each day in your current 9-to-5 job.

To really excel as a Patchworker, however, you want to do more than just survive the experience. You want to learn how to get an otherwise grouchy decision maker who has unreasonable expectations to come over to your side. You want to groom the person into someone who could be tolerable in the long term. Now, this may be too tall an order in some cases or simply not worth the work if, for example, the likelihood of future work at the company seems unlikely based on a dwindling budget or some other relevant factor. However, for accounts that could be a veritable goldmine for you if only the decision maker was a bit more reasonable, you may wish to make note of a simple lesson spoken in an old Tamil saying that is well known in many parts of India:

> Sing and milk if the cow sings,
> Dance and milk if it dances

Put another way, sing the song or dance the dance of difficult clients in order to produce the most good from the encounter. To better understand the mindset and framework that the difficult decision maker operates within, stretch your way of thinking, ask questions, or befriend the person within professional boundaries; do *something!*

Engage with the person and find out why he or she is a bundle of nerves, a red-hot ball of anger, or whatever. You need to find out how to neutralize the person for the good of your working relationship if a future with the client is going to be feasible. Can you do this? Can you muster up the courage to approach a hothead and attempt conciliation? Can you manage your own temper when faced with a rage-a-holic? Will you have the determination to attempt transforming a dud of an account into one that has great potential? Sometimes an account is a diamond in the rough, so polish it up and reap the rewards.

The Fiscal Discipline

Yes, it has come to this. I am going to have the same conversation that your father had with you in third grade when he pointed to the piggy bank and suggested that you learn how to save your nickels and dimes. But instead of talking about money, let's talk about marshmallows. They're a lot more fun and, as it turns out, a bit more interesting to talk about than porcelain pigs.

In the 1970s a researcher at Stanford University conducted what is now famously referred to as *The Marshmallow Experiment*. He and his colleagues, with permission, invited one four-year-old at a time into a small room that contained only a chair and a desk. Placed on the desk was a single marshmallow. The researcher told each toddler that if he or she could wait to eat that marshmallow until the researcher returned from running an errand, he would reward the child with a second one. The researcher then walked out of the room and observed the child behind a two-way mirror for fifteen minutes. Some children ate the marshmallow immediately, some waited for a few minutes but then gave in, and some distracted themselves or covered their eyes in order to avoid the temptation and were successful. About one-third of the children grabbed the marshmallow right away, another one-third were able to wait until the researcher's return, and the remaining group fell somewhere in the middle along the larger spectrum.

Although the results were interesting, the fascinating part of this longitudinal study is really what happened years later. Researchers followed up with the toddlers during adolescence and found that those toddlers who demonstrated an ability to resist the marshmallow (demonstrating self-control) had grown up to be more positive, self-motivating, and able to delay gratification in pursuit of their goals. These children had these and other habits of successful people, including happy marriages, higher income, and career satisfaction. Those toddlers who were unable to resist the marshmallow (demonstrating lack of self-control) were troubled, stubborn, and indecisive with impulse guiding their decisions, and they demonstrated habits of unsuccessful people, resulting in inverse lifestyle outcomes.[2]

This study went on to draw a number of conclusions related to delayed gratification, but let's stop here and extrapolate in a way that is meaningful and relative to your decision about leaping into the world of Patchworking. Let's consider self-identity. If you were a four-year-old, would you be able to resist the marshmallow? As an *adult*, are you able to resist the marshmallows that cross your path? Seriously, are you? Is having the latest and greatest of everything part of your current lifestyle? If so, could you realistically make a change away from that impulsive lifestyle in order to, say, delay making unnecessary business-related purchases when money is tight? Or save a percentage of your income when business is booming so that you can weather leaner times by dipping into those reserves? If this is not the norm in your current lifestyle, the real question is, *could* it become the new norm for you? Are you motivated enough to change how you spend and how you save?

Embracing the 9-to-5 Cure is an opportunity to change the focus of your life. To pursue dreams. To regain personal and professional freedom. To make money in the process. However, be ever vigilant of the fact that poor spending habits are the trap that can send any entrepreneur into the red and back to a 9-to-5 job. Consider the proposition that living modestly empowers you. It allows you to honor all of the other wishes of your lifestyle framework. Debt, conversely, traps you and robs you of that lifestyle.

Ultimately, your fiscal discipline determines a lot about the longevity of your business, so be sure to take stock of your spending habits, your financial resources, and your willingness to make a success of this business venture before you get started.

The Courage to Change

Change takes courage. For some, change can be invigorating. For others, change can be terrifying. If you find yourself wanting the 9-to-5 Cure described in this book but feel resistant to making the necessary changes, then I suggest that you take a moment to look back at your life to this point. Are you frustrated with your career or your lifestyle (or both) but fear of the unknown causes you to stay stuck? If so, isn't that exhausting? Take the leap into the unknown already—just do it! An expert on change, M.J. Ryan offers some thoughts on change resistance:

> Resisting change wears down our bodies, taxes our minds, and deflates our spirits. When we resist change, we keep doing the things that have always worked before—with depressingly diminishing results. Frustrated, we expend precious energy looking around for someone to blame—ourselves, another person, or the world. We worry obsessively. We get stuck in the past, lost in bitterness or anger. Or we fall into denial—"Everything's fine, I don't have to do anything differently." We may engage in magical thinking—"Something or someone will come along to rescue me from having to change." We don't want to leave the cozy comfort of the known and familiar for the scary wilderness of that which we've never experienced. And so we rail against it and stay stuck.[3]

If you feel frustrated with your 9-to-5 lifestyle, then I invite you to jump out and make the changes necessary to free yourself from the captive career lifestyle you now lead. Here are a few pointers for riding out change in a productive way, based on Ryan's philosophy:

- **Stay focused on the outcome.** Keep the goal in mind and use that as a motivator for moving forward.

- **Prioritize.** Determine which of the many tasks that lie ahead are the most important and then work on them one at a time in that order.

- **Schedule.** Plan time to stop and tackle your worries. Limit your worrying to this isolated period of, say, fifteen minutes of time each week.

- **Fake it.** If you doubt your ability in some area of the business startup process, just fake it 'til you make it. This approach "has validity in brain science. The thoughts we hold and actions we take really do create new pathways in our brains," according to Ryan.[4]

One of the biggest challenges of starting a business is not always knowing what's around the next corner. There is much to learn, and that all-important question of "How much can I earn?" can keep a new Patchworker awake at night. However, know that like anything else in life, experience is the remedy that soothes us. With each passing day, week, and year, the questions you now hold at the front of your mind will retreat and ultimately disappear altogether as each one is answered in turn.

The most pressing question that I encounter when people ask me about becoming a Patchworker is how to handle periods of time when business may not be booming. This is the biggest concern for many; is it for you? It may well be because before you make the leap into the unknown you want to know you can pay your bills on the other side. I won't mince words in this regard: In the beginning of your business startup, you may have periods of time when you are not working as much as you would like to be. It's true. But before you slam the book shut and walk away, let me give you a look back at my own startup experience with my Patchwork career.

The first week on my trial run of being a Patchworker, I landed work. How did I do it? I played the numbers. I was interested in teaching a specialized computer class, and I approached decision makers at a large number of organizations in my area via personalized e-mail messages. That first week I landed a few interviews that were scheduled for the following week; one group hired me on the spot just days after the initial inquiry. By the end of that month, I was employed by seven organizations.

> **Evaluate Your Personality Type**
>
> The endeavor requires remarkable focus and sincere dedication, especially in the beginning. You have to take a good look at your personality and determine if you have the attention span of a goldfish, which is three seconds, according to the cap on my Snapple bottle, or a sloth, which has to be the world's most patient animal.

I put myself out there and it worked, practically overnight. And all of these years later, being a Patchworker still works, like a charm. I can't promise that it will work for you this quickly, but it very well *could*. What's important is mustering the courage to step out into the unknown and see what happens. To echo a Michael Jackson song, "Make that change!"

The Nerve to Tackle Your Fears

Becoming a Patchworker takes some nerve. I'm not going to sugarcoat it; there is some hard work and risk involved. Your reputation is on the line, and some start-up money may be as well.

Does the prospect of being your own boss and calling all the shots invigorate you or cause you to shudder like a hairless polar bear? Do you enjoy learning many new things on a regular basis or does the thought of that make you feel like you're back in middle school where, let's face it, no one had much fun. Most importantly, you have to take inventory of your fears and look down the road at what may lie ahead for you as a new entrepreneur. Although it is unlikely that you have a real "fear" of the situations included in the following list, it is worth considering to what extent you are willing to step out of your comfort zone in order to move your business forward. Join this logophile (word lover) as I take you on an unconventional walk through a list of important thinking points for budding yet timid Patchworkers:

- **Allodoxaphobia (fear of opinions):** Everyone has an opinion, especially when you are the boss. Suddenly, people are not afraid to tell you what they think of every minute decision you make. Those who are most vocal may include your significant other, your immediate family, your friends, your lovely in-laws, and absolutely everyone who is negotiating with you about your pay rate. The question is, can you handle it? Do you have the confidence required to stand tall and defend yourself and your business? Being in business is not for the faint of heart, especially when your business model is unconventional.

- **Chronophobia (fear of time):** How well do you respond to deadlines? Are they motivators, do they paralyze you, or do you ignore them altogether? Deadlines are a very real factor to contend with in any work environment. But when you are the boss, no one is sending you a series of increasingly alarming reminders. Managing deadlines well is critical; I cannot overstate this point. If you fail to pay your quarterly taxes on time, you *will* face a penalty from Uncle Sam. If you fail to deliver a product by the agreed-upon deadline, the client likely will *not* hire you again. You have to be able to self-monitor when it comes to deadlines if you want to maintain and grow your business.

- **Decidophobia (fear of making decisions):** You're the boss. If you don't make the decisions, who will? If making decisions and owning them are not part of your makeup, then you need to dedicate great time and effort cultivating these skills—beginning immediately! The inability to make decisions is a nonstarter for any entrepreneur; look yourself in the mirror and decide if you have the courage to make choices and stand by them.

- **Enissophobia (fear of criticism):** Undoubtedly, some opinions are steeped in criticism and require you to develop a thick skin. Can you do it? Can you hear someone tell you that your business idea is crazy/horrible/stupid or some other descriptor and still hang in there? The ability to believe in yourself and your abilities even if and when few others do is crucial to your success.

- **Hippopotomonstrosesquippedaliophobia (fear of long words):** C'mon, you have to admit that this is a cool-looking word, even if it is impossible to pronounce. It highlights the fact that learning a variety of new jargon is only the beginning of the learning curve that lies ahead for any new Patchworker. There are new government terms and forms to learn, new computer skills to master, new accounting routines to set up, new marketing strategies to develop, and more. Learning comes with the territory, and being hungry to learn is a real asset.

- **Isolophobia (fear of solitude):** Can you handle spending long stretches of time by yourself? The answer to this question needs to tend toward "yes" if you are going to make it as a Patchworker, because you need to spend a great deal of time thinking, reading, creating, writing, and doing other rather solitary activities. Although the actual work you do to earn money can be very people oriented if you so choose, the invoicing and other recordkeeping work you do, for example, requires that you be productive when spending time alone.

- **Macrophobia (fear of long waits):** If instant gratification is important to you, then you just might have trouble facing this entrepreneurial reality: Things take time. You will apply for a federal employee identification number (EIN)…and wait. You will pitch an idea…and wait. You will mail the client an invoice…and wait. Waiting is an inherent part of most businesses. This concept goes back to the discussion about the marshmallow experiment. Can you resist the marshmallow and be productive in the meanwhile?

- **Soteriophobia (fear of dependence on others):** In the beginning and to varying degrees throughout your tenure as a Patchworker, you will be dependent on others for their advice, resources, contacts, and more. Your ability to reach out and ask for help from the right people at the right time, a willingness to accept assistance graciously, and an ability to reciprocate will determine a great deal. Can you put your ego aside and reach out for help at key moments?

- **Xenophobia (fear of strangers):** How well will you be able to approach people in positions of power and pitch your ideas to them convincingly? Will you be able to stand up and negotiate your salary, even if it takes some doing? Even if you tend toward introversion, do you have the nerve to walk into a negotiation and do what needs to be done to close the deal? If the thought of pitching your idea in person and negotiating across a table seems terrifying, you may be able to remedy this by changing environments. What I mean by this is taking advantage of online marketplaces where discussions take place by phone or live chat. Although this does limit your potential client base significantly, many people make a successful living this way.

If ultimately you suffer from ergophobia (fear of work), well then, it's an easy call. Otherwise, take this alphabetized list into consideration going forward, but don't let it hold you back. The best strategy for overcoming apprehensiveness about tasks or situations previously listed or any others that occur is simply jumping in and tackling them head-on.

℘

And while we are discussing the practical realities of being a Patchworker, let's take it one step farther. The next chapter describes the personal and professional drawbacks of this career lifestyle in a no-holds-barred fashion.

Endnotes

[1] *Merriam-Webster Online*, s.v. "Mindset," www.merriam-webster.com/dictionary/Mindset (accessed August 30, 2010).

[2] Jonah Lehrer, "Don't! The Secret of Self-Control," *The New Yorker*, May 18, 2009, www.newyorker.com/reporting/2009/05/18/090518fa_fact_lehrer (accessed August 30, 2010).

[3] M.J. Ryan, "Learn to Be a Master of Change," The Women's Conference, www.womensconference.org/learn-to-be (accessed August 30, 2010).

[4] M.J. Ryan.

CHAPTER 16

Consider the Drawbacks

Everything in life has its drawbacks. There is just no way around it. The key is to weigh the good with the bad and march in the direction that best suits you. So, too, with the Patchwork Principle are there advantages and disadvantages to consider, both personally and professionally. In order to take an honest look at this career paradigm, this chapter is dedicated to what the rest of the book is not: discussing the drawbacks of the Patchwork Principle as a career lifestyle. Knowing the true nature of this lifestyle will give you an opportunity to make an informed decision and, if you so choose, to march confidently in the direction of your dreams.

Personal Drawbacks

There are personal drawbacks to Patchworking, and there is no way around this simple truth. You may not get the respect you deserve in certain situations, you may be subject to more distractions than you would like, and it may even take a toll on your physical fitness if you're not careful. Fortunately, you can control all of these factors, at least to some extent, and of course you always have a choice as to how you react to those realities that you cannot change.

For example, years ago I lived next door to a family who loved to listen to the sound of their car alarm for reasons that I still cannot figure out. Each time the alarm would sound, I would get upset and become fully consumed by the situation. After a while, however, I realized that it was them or me. I had to suck it up and learn to concentrate despite the car alarm or else surrender.

Although being a Patchworker definitely has advantages, let's take a moment to consider these personal disadvantages:

- **You will encounter many distractions while working.** There is television, Facebook, neighbors who come knocking at your door, piles of laundry that beg to be washed, and a friend who calls to invite you to an afternoon round of golf on a day that you face a can't-be-missed deadline. Having the ability to stay focused can be challenging at times.

It requires setting clear boundaries for yourself as well as for your neighbors, friends, and family members.

- **People may not take your career seriously.** Because your career will be new and unfamiliar to people in your life, they may mistakenly believe that you are doing this work until a "real job" comes along. You will be challenged at times to seemingly defend and most certainly explain your new career lifestyle. People will inquire out of curiosity and sometimes disbelief, which can require patience and a thick skin on your part.

- **People may not take your office hours seriously.** Family, friends, and neighbors may not recognize your office hours as those off-limits times of the day when you are unavailable for socializing. Although these people in your life would never dream of barging into your 9-to-5 workplace setting unannounced, they may show up at your home office door expecting you to drop everything and spend the rest of the morning or afternoon chatting, driving them to the airport, or accompanying them to the farmer's market. Drawing clear boundaries is critical to the success of your Patchwork career. Be firm but kind and establish the ground rules early on.

- **There is no built-in social network.** The water cooler talk that you may have regularly enjoyed with 9-to-5 co-workers will no longer be available in its traditional format. You will need to seek out and cultivate new ways to build a social network, and it's even better if these connections are relevant to your business. Online communities or local entrepreneurial associations are good ways to do this. Likewise, if you are used to being on the corporate softball team or some other sponsored group activity formerly coordinated through work, you will need to seek out a suitable substitute in your local community through a recreation department or another source.

- **You may not be able to enjoy the same amenities that you enjoyed when the company was paying.** Finer hotels and first-class airline tickets may take a back seat to standard accommodations and coach-class flights, at least initially. Likewise, membership to the best gym in the city that was subsidized by your former 9-to-5 employer may no longer be practical at full price. These expenses affect your bottom line and can add up quickly if travel is a regular part of your business model. However, this is not to say that you have to say goodbye to these luxuries forever—just until it makes sense based on your business's bottom line. Or perhaps you may want to use your profits for something else altogether.

> **Negotiate Additional Perks**
>
> As you negotiate with potential employers, consider haggling for extra amenities, such as gym discounts, that the employer already offers to its full-time employees. The result can be the enjoyment of a few extra perks, completely free of charge!

- **Managing your waistline can be challenging.** If you work at home, the refrigerator is readily available, and mindless snacking can pose a challenge to your figure. Likewise, doing work that is not physical in nature (computer-based projects, for example) cuts down on the number of calories you burn during the workday. That inactivity can show up on your waistline. However, a simple remedy is to balance your day out by scheduling some time to hit the gym and get your body moving.

- **You may feel like you never leave the house.** Many people in the 9-to-5 world long for the opportunity to work from home. What you may not consider is the fact that if you work from a home office, you rarely need to leave the building. This can have implications for your physical fitness, your mental health, and your social life. Working from your home office can cause you to feel stuck in the house day after day. The simple fix for this is to deliberately schedule regular outside activities, such as signing up for extracurricular activities or meeting friends outside of the house and socializing. It's your life, so remember to get out there and live it!

- **Your house may feel smaller.** Whether you work out of your home office on a regular basis or simply use the space for filing and bookkeeping purposes, part of your former living area will be dedicated to a new function: work. Think about how to carve out a place in your house that allows you to feel cheerful and motivated without compromising too much of your primary living space. An effective home office for some people is a dedicated room with a door, whereas for others it is simply a desk on wheels positioned in the corner of a room. Have an open mind and make the most of your available resources.

When you are a Patchworker, you have to contend with both personal and professional drawbacks. However, none of these is insurmountable. Your attitude is the key to success when faced with one of these unavoidable realities.

Professional Drawbacks

Now, having looked at the personal drawbacks, let's take a look at the professional drawbacks that have implications for your career and your lifestyle:

- **There is no paid time off, period.** Paid vacation days are not part of the Patchworker's reality. If you choose to take time off to hop aboard a cruise ship headed to the Bahamas, you must factor lost wages and perhaps paying a substitute into the overall cost of your vacation. Likewise, there is no sick leave allotment from which you can draw from, so be sure to take an objective look at your health history. Sometimes you will need to work despite minor illnesses in order to provide seamless service to your clients.

- **Your income is less stable.** For the 9-to-5er, income is like a water faucet; either it's flowing from the employer to the employee or it's not. As a Patchworker, you assume some financial risk because your income is based on landing new accounts and maintaining existing ones. Therefore, income is not as certain as it is for a 9-to-5 employee, at least on a day-to-day basis. However, it is no surprise either. Whereas 9-to-5 employees may be subject to sudden job loss due to redundancy, Patchworkers are well aware of their current income and future prospects from their many clients. Therefore, although income may appear more sporadic for the Patchworker, it is in many respects more stable than it would be in a traditional career. However, it takes time to get used to drumming up your own leads consistently enough to feel comfortable making new, substantial purchases such as a house or car.

- **Your nontraditional career carries less prestige than a traditional one.** If you carry the title Vice President of Sales with a local company, people know how to rank that role within the 9-to-5 hierarchy. However, if you are president and CEO of your own Patchworker business, your title is an enigma for the traditionally minded. Although you may earn more and ultimately enjoy more freedom as a Patchworker, an automatic endorsement from those in the 9-to-5 world is atypical.

- **There is no corporate insurance plan.** When you are a Patchworker, you must shop for and apply for your own

> **Secure Loans Before You Plunge into Patchworking**
>
> If you are considering the purchase of a new house or car, make the purchase before you take the plunge into Patchworking because lenders will require that you demonstrate a history of earning before approving a mortgage or car loan. However, once you are an established Patchworker, your earning history will speak for itself.

health and life insurance plans. This topic will be addressed in greater detail in Chapter 19, "Meeting Uncle Sam and Other Necessities."

- **You must be able to handle high-tech headaches.** This is not to say that you must know how to fix all of your technical issues, because you can always call an expert to make a house call to your home office. However, you must have the ability to remain calm in the face of a technical snafu and create an action plan to remedy the situation.

- **Sometimes clients will not pay for services rendered.** Some clients will not be stellar. It's a business reality, no matter what business you are in. It's rare, but there may be some clients who will not pay even long after you invoice them. In such cases, you will need to get tough with them, and in the event of complete noncompliance, you'll have to research your options and perhaps consider taking them to small claims court. These experiences are very educational because they teach you how to spot a red flag when you see it in the future, so you can cut your losses more quickly.

- **Paperwork and recordkeeping can be tedious.** When you are a Patchworker, you wear many hats and, as a result, find yourself responsible for recordkeeping activities such as invoicing, payroll (yours!), and tax filings. Getting organized and keeping your records current are the best strategies for making this part of business ownership feel manageable.

- **You will pay more taxes than you did as an employee.** Welcome to the harsh reality of being independently employed—your tax bill will increase. In addition to the standard income taxes you are used to paying, you will have to pay both the employer and employee portions of the Social Security and Medicare taxes.

- **You must seek out and finance your own professional development opportunities.** The days of signing up for rounds of training sessions on the company's dime are not typically part of the Patchworker's reality. Budgeting for needed training will be required, and it can sometimes be costly, depending on your profession. However, you may find opportunities to negotiate for training as part of or in lieu of compensation through a client's organization.

- **Managing your cash flow responsibly is a must.** You will need to create and maintain a cash reserve during boom times to counterbalance lean times. Failing to do that can cause your business to go bust in the event of a slowdown, an unexpected leave of absence such as maternity or paternity leave, or an emergency situation such as a prolonged medical absence. Saving for a rainy day is critical for peace of mind and survival.

- **You will be responsible for maintaining and upgrading your own equipment.** Gone will be the days when the latest technology gadget or upgrade magically appeared on your desk, configured and paid for by the company. You alone will be the one making decisions about which equipment is a must to purchase, upgrade, and maintain when weighed against the related costs. On the other hand, you are in complete control of what you purchase, when, and why. There is no more petitioning the boss or the budget manager for the funds to purchase a necessary item, which can be very liberating.

Although the seemingly endless list of professional drawbacks can appear daunting to the Patchworker, consider the benefits that are plentiful, substantive, and much more advantageous to your overall career and well-being.

℃

So, what do you think? Can you handle the drawbacks? Can you accept them as part of your Patchworker reality and make a break from the 9-to-5 work world in spite of them? Although drawbacks are by nature unpleasant, you do have to take the good with the bad if you want to dive into this new world. Can you negotiate the drawbacks, or will you call it quits at this juncture? Only you can answer the question. Make a decision and decide if now is the right time to begin planning your escape.

CHAPTER 17

Plan Your Escape and Get Out of There

A re you ready to get out of Dodge? Are you ready to escape the rat race of the 9-to-5 and take control of the reigns that guide your life? If so, congratulations! If you plan to jump in and become a full-time Patchworker, you will see results much more quickly than if you start on a part-time basis. However, this chapter looks at both the full-time and part-time options and related considerations. Most importantly, I will share important considerations for you to reflect on as you prepare to exit the 9-to-5 world once and for all.

Part-Time Patchworking

If you are currently employed and hesitate to leave your current job in order to pursue the lifestyle and the career of your dreams, you're not alone. After all, the security of a 9-to-5 job, where the boss reels in the work and you get paid no matter how the company does, is pretty enticing from a distance. However, *adding* freelance work to your already-overwhelming workload can be a recipe for disaster, so you should approach this scenario with caution.

First, consider that you may need to bring your personal laptop or other equipment to work with you in order to do some of your freelance work after hours or during break periods in order to meet pressing deadlines. As a preemptive move, depending on your circumstances, you may want to broach the subject with your boss to avoid a potentially sticky situation. For example, your current employer may react badly to the idea of having you work on the premises if you get caught doing so and haven't sought prior permission. I don't recommend that you work covertly, but if you do, make sure you have a foolproof plan for keeping the work a secret. Translation: Don't get caught! I've seen people in this situation get fired on the spot; don't be one of them.

Second, when running a business, you will need to interact with your clients during normal business hours when they, too, are at work. This can cause any number of sticky situations. For example, imagine if you are on the phone talking to a client and your boss walks in and decides to wait until the call ends in order to speak with you. What will you do? On the one hand, you may want to keep this endeavor a secret from your boss. On the other hand, you don't want to rush the client off of the phone, which may leave a bad impression. Each workplace environment is unique, so be sure to think through your situation before diving in. Here are some important tips:

- **Take on work cautiously.** Be sure the work is a good fit with your available resources, such as time or equipment.

- **Be up front with your clients.** Let your clients know that you are currently working full time and may not always be readily available during normal business hours.

- **Separate your phone and e-mail communications from your current workplace systems.** Electronic communications routed through your workplace network are subject to monitoring by the network administrator. You may want to invest in a smartphone, such as an iPhone, to manage all of your communications during work hours exclusively and independent of your employer's network.

Finally, be forewarned that this full-time plus part-time work arrangement may cause you to feel like you are working day and night. This is because it will, in fact, likely require attention both at night and on the weekends in order to manage the business end of things (invoicing, for example) and the project itself during the hours you are not attending to your full-time job. Consider this fair warning. This lifestyle can quickly lead to burnout and ultimately cause you to call it quits, robbing you of the chance to experience truly living the career lifestyle of your dreams.

Although these are a few of the noteworthy entanglements among many, there are certainly advantages to trying out a part-time approach at first. One advantage is getting the opportunity to test out the idea and see whether you are cut out for handling the various aspects of owning and operating a business. Another advantage is that you get to find clients and work directly with them. Then, when you decide to make the leap to a full-time Patchwork career, you already have a few clients to refer back to for references or additional projects.

Leaving the Door Open

When you know that your 9-to-5 days with the company are numbered, it is easy to find yourself feeling a bit cocky. You have a nothing-to-lose attitude that can transform your previously mild-mannered personality into one of a loudmouth know-it-all. We all know the type. After countless years of carefully crafted business interactions, people often go renegade in their last few days on the job and tarnish their image forevermore. Don't make this mistake! It could undermine your new business startup before it even begins. You worked hard to build your reputation into what it is today, so handle it with care right up to the moment when you exit the building on the last day of work and drive off toward your dreams.

As the old saying goes, "People hire people." In other words, every contact that you have at this moment is valuable to you from a business standpoint, even if you can't see the potential just yet. Walk away from your 9-to-5 job on good terms with the boss, co-workers, and clients, and you can reap the networking and referral benefits. Walk away on bad terms and it can haunt you by driving down the number of available opportunities within your geographic location, your industry, and your networking circle.

Leave your current job like a true professional. Give the appropriate notice, help train the replacement, make personal contact with each co-worker to let them know how much you enjoyed working with them, and so on. Do whatever is necessary to leave your boss and your co-workers with these positive memories firmly embedded in their minds.

Leaving a Trail

Have you heard of "breadcrumb navigation"? Derived from the Germanic fairy tale of Hansel and Gretel, this Internet term refers to tools that help users keep track of their location within a program like a Web browser. It gives users a sense of where they have been and where they are currently, which aids them in calculating their next move. An everyday example of this is the Forward and Back buttons in a Web browser. Where am I going with this? Like breadcrumbs, give your current list of clients and business contacts this same option of navigating to you at your new location and in your new Patchworker capacity. Although you may want to shake the dust from your heels and fall off the map when you leave your 9-to-5 job, it can be to your great advantage to leave a trail instead.

Let your clients and other important business contacts know what your plans are and how to get in touch with you should they want to work with you in the future in another capacity. Sometimes this is best accomplished through a series of telephone calls and casual conversations prior to your departure. Sometimes this communication is simply a mass mailing by e-mail or post. Only you can decide what is appropriate for your own business community.

If possible, on the last day at your 9-to-5 job, set up an auto-reply for your e-mail account that indicates you are no longer working with the company but can be reached by phone or e-mail should someone wish to get in touch with you. Then, proceed to list your new contact information, including the name of your new business and job title when possible. Sometimes work comes from the most unlikely sources!

> **Review Your Non-compete Agreement**
>
> Some businesses prevent employees from working with the same clients for a period of months or years after leaving the organization, as outlined in a non-compete agreement that employees may have signed upon joining or exiting the company. To avoid legal action, be careful to honor such agreements. Contact the Human Resource office to obtain a copy of the signed agreement on file if you have misplaced your own copy.

So, did you think it through? Do you feel like you have what it takes on some level and are willing to accept the challenges and drawbacks that come along with this career lifestyle? If you still have some doubts, that means you are perfectly normal and, in fact, are truly considering the practical realities of this paradigm shift. Leaping out of the traditional 9-to-5 framework and into something different takes courage. So muster up some courage and let's talk about taking the first concrete steps toward establishing your business. Get ready to set up shop!

PART VI

Set Up Shop

CHAPTER 18

Get Your Move On

Congratulations! You've decided to pursue a Patchwork career. Now it's time to set up shop. This is the exciting phase of establishing your business in concrete terms, and it includes establishing a workspace, naming your business, setting up a phone line, selecting a business structure, and more. This is that moment when you sit down and get to work putting systems in place to make everything else possible. It's a time full of excitement, adrenaline, steep learning curves, and sweet release from your 9-to-5 world.

Journaling Your Journey

Before you get too far into the setup work, you may want to begin journaling your experiences—both to help you process everything and to serve as a record of your progress that you can look back on over time. Here are some excerpts from my journal during those first few days of setting up shop at my home office:

> Well, today is Day One of my adventure into self-employment! I hope that I can really make a go of this. I have an amazing chance to change my career path, and I want to do it!

> What a great day! I'm really getting things done, and it feels amazing—freeing!

> Today is even more exciting than yesterday! So many new ideas are rushing through my mind. I am reading every book that I can get my hands on, and the ideas I came in with seem more and more possible. I'm starting to develop action plans and lists, which is my personal key to success in any work environment. Progress!

> It's the end of the first week of working for myself. I feel like this is the right direction for me. Do what you love, and the money will follow, right? Off I go into the world of self-employment! This IS going to work—I can feel it!

On that first day in my home office, when I took the first steps toward building my Patchwork business, I remember the excitement and the long to-do list that appeared the moment my fingers hit the keyboard. I was off and running in a flash. For me, the number of items on my to-do list was invigorating! However, if all of the tasks that lay ahead do the opposite for you—if they leave you reeling—then take these important factors into consideration before you become too overwhelmed:

- You don't have to figure it all out right away.

- You can purchase many reasonably priced tools to make many of your most complex tasks (accounting, for example) very manageable.

- Many federal, state, and local small business associations can advise you during the startup process free of charge.

- You can always hire experts to direct you or do much of the specialized work (accounting, for example) for you if you would rather focus on fishing for leads.

- Countless people have waded through the startup process successfully. You will, too.

Making big changes can cause anyone to feel a little nervous. Just stay focused on the next step, keep the big picture in mind, and make slow, deliberate moves.

Startup Costs

If you think that having limited cash flow is an insurmountable problem for your business, let me be the first to tell you that it could quite possibly *improve* your likelihood of success rather than detract from it. If that statement seems outrageous, consider the fact that a limited cash flow keeps you "hungry," which feeds your determination and drive. It also allows you to realize a profit more quickly because you are not paying down large amounts of debt (or ideally, any). Seeing your bottom line turn from red to black builds both emotional and financial

> **Invest in Yourself, Not in a Franchise**
>
> The Patchworker business model is accessible to just about everyone! And it's is a pretty good alternative to starting up a Krispy Kreme donut store, estimated to cost $2 million to get started, not including a $40,000 non-refundable franchise fee and then an ongoing percentage of sales.[1] (However, I wouldn't mind being a Patchworker at one of their stores for one hour a week in exchange for all of the donuts I could carry home at the end of my shift!)

momentum quickly and can grease the proverbial wheels of your entrepreneurial endeavor during that first crucial year.

Unlike the purchase of an established franchise, being a Patchworker is founded on the premise of building your business at the pace that you determine to be appropriate, based on a number of factors, including your financial wherewithal. There are no big financial demands outside of some basic office equipment, an Internet connection, and a reliable mode of transportation.

Spend with Caution

I'm cautious when it comes to spending on business startup expenses. However, this wasn't always the case. When I opened my first business, a national seminar company, I went straight to an office supply store and bought a fancy office chair, glass-top desks, a new computer, linen business cards, and more. I bought a multiline phone; ordered phone and fax lines; and purchased a fax machine, copier, and printer. I got the works!

I also went through my startup cash in a flash because my mentality was that in order to succeed I *had* to first pay out for these big-ticket items. I was under the impression that this was just what you "do" to get a business up and running, that the business wasn't legitimate unless you had all of the equipment and supplies in place. This false assumption was a costly mistake. I learned, but it cost me. I spent that first year staring at the bottom line that was as red as an apple despite all the money coming in.

When I started my Patchwork business, however, I did the opposite. This time, I had zero dollars in startup cash—none. I had to earn it as I went. And do you know what happened? This time I spent wisely, out of necessity. What follows are some tricks that I learned along the way. Depending on your financial circumstances, the work you anticipate doing, and a number of other important factors, you may wish to minimize your costs or go all out on each of these expenditure categories. Whatever your intentions, make your first step a logical one by using the resources you might already have on hand and take inventory. Secretary of State Hillary Clinton uses this same tactic; here is a supposed excerpt from a staff meeting:

> And it reminded me of what I occasionally sometimes do, which I call shopping in my closet, which means opening doors and seeing what I actually already have, which I really suggest to everybody, because it's quite enlightening. (Laughter.) And so when you go to the store and you buy, let's say, peanut butter and you

don't realize you've got two jars already at the back of the shelf—
I mean, that sounds simplistic, but help us save money on stuff
that we shouldn't be wasting money on, and give us the chance
to manage our resources to do more things…"[2]

Now think about your much-smaller-than-the-Department-of-State-budget
that is available to start up your own business and apply Secretary Clinton's
strategy to your own business venture. Make the most of what you have in
order to maximize the reach of your startup money. If you have no funds to
speak of, then dig deep into the resources already on hand.

Checklist for Setting Up Shop

Are you ready? This is when you jump in and officially begin setting up shop
for your new Patchwork business. Let's discuss the following core components:

- Your office
- Office equipment
- Office supplies
- Business phone
- Web site
- Business identity

The following sections are dedicated to discussing the logistics and related
considerations.

Your Office

Although it is absolutely necessary to set up
an office *somewhere*, think carefully before
committing to a lease. This expense can
easily be your most costly fixed expense, so
proceed with caution. The real questions to
ask in determining if leasing a space is critical
to your startup plan are these two:

> **Get Started Now**
> You can do these steps incrementally
> well ahead of your official leap out of
> your 9-to-5 job.

- **Will receiving clients into your office be a core piece of the work?**
  For example, if you will be operating as a life coach for part of each day,
  then securing an office space may be necessary in order to make your

clients feel comfortable. However, if you will be doing graphic design work, then perhaps a laptop and a café are all that you need to conduct successful client meetings. The acceptable norms of each industry are unique, and you have to determine for yourself what is appropriate for you, your business, and your clients. Also, keep in mind that the work you do may change over time as you identify viable sources of income and learn more about the type of work you most enjoy doing.

- **Will working from home ultimately result in you sitting on the couch in your pajamas and watching infomercials for hours on end?** In other words, if you know going in that you lack the discipline to focus on the work at hand and ignore the television, refrigerator, and other distractions, then you may want to consider leasing some space. However, remember that you will need to be a helluva lot more productive at bringing in business to cover the costs of your lease each month. Leasing can be exactly the right choice for some people, exactly the wrong choice for others. Proceed with caution; decide what's right for you.

Ultimately, these choices boil down to two basic options: the home office or the leased space. Let's take a moment to consider each in a bit more detail.

The Home Office Option

Keep in mind that for many Patchworkers, the work does not require receiving clients. Instead, you can maintain a home office for your own purposes but meet the client on-site, at an appropriate off-site location, or online via Skype or a similar video conferencing technology. For example, if your business will likely be working with clients via the Internet, then running a business from your home office seems tenable, keeping a few things in mind:

- **Minimize noise pollution.** If you will be speaking with your clients by telephone, you will need an area free of household noises in order to maintain a professional atmosphere. In other words, avoid a situation where an important meeting is interrupted because your dog starts barking wildly at the mailman.

- **Create a conversation corner.** If you will be talking to clients via video conferencing, be sure to create a neat, clean, and appropriately decorated area of your office that can be used for these virtual face-to-face (f2f) meetings. For example, in your home office you may wish to dedicate one corner to virtual f2f meetings, complete with a small table for a webcam, a comfortable chair, and a lamp that provides appropriate lighting. Be sure to evaluate any photos, artwork, or other decorations that would be in view of the client for appropriateness based on your industry. For example, if you are working within the music industry, having a framed KISS poster on the wall might be acceptable, but if you are working with a conservative group of economists, then perhaps that poster is best kept out of view. Remember, when you work with people in a virtual environment, these few images they see may be the only evidence they have available to build a mental picture of who you are in real time. Serve up the images with care.

- **Look the part.** Although you may be sitting around in your track suit all day long, it is important to dress and act the part of a professional when on camera. Clients will develop an image of who you are based on those brief on-camera interactions, so be prepared to dress and act the part of the consummate professional, however that is defined within your industry.

The home office option is the most affordable and most immediately available; however, it may or may not be the best choice for you depending on your circumstances. Consider working from home, but keep reading as the discussion turns to considering a leased office space.

The Leased Space Option

If your anticipated daily routine will require you to welcome clients to your office space, then you may wish to consider scouting for shared office space. This is a hot new trend among startups that allows you to lease office space in noteworthy, high-end commercial real estate locations on a month-to-month basis or on an annual contract.

However, it's not just the space that you're renting. The fee you pay includes a fully equipped office environment complete with the following desirable amenities:

> **Learn More About Shared Office Space**
>
> To learn more about shared office space, visit the Web sites of these companies that have a national presence: Regus (www.regus.com) and Instant Offices (www.instantoffices.com).

- A high-profile business address for sending and receiving letters and packages
- A private, nicely furnished office space
- A receptionist to receive, screen, and forward your calls

- Local phone number and voicemail

- Access to a complete line of expensive office equipment and capabilities, including copier, fax, audio-visual equipment, and high-speed Internet access

- Luxurious, high-end meeting rooms such as board rooms or smaller conference rooms in addition to a lounge, café, and kitchen

- A fully trained, on-demand support staff (additional fees may apply)

Keep in mind that if you decide to leave this leased location, changing your business address and phone number months or years later can cost you clients. Those who call the defunct phone number or drop by your office only to find you have left the building may assume that you are out of business and not inquire further. If you do choose to start in a shared office space and move at any time, be sure to notify both your active and dormant clients.

Office Equipment

Whatever you do, don't rush out and buy an expensive copier, printer, and fax machine on the first day you set up shop. These pieces of equipment are affordable and readily accessible at any local copy shop or office supply store. The per-piece price is higher, but the overall costs are significantly lower.

Outside of owning my own computer, which is mission critical, and some standard software, the nature of my work most often means that I am using my client's equipment to carry out the work that I am doing for them. Owning my own office equipment is rarely necessary. But for the sake of convenience, over time I have purchased some used equipment through eBay and similar places for a fraction of the cost. Give yourself time to take inventory of what equipment you actually need before you run out and make any big purchases.

Office Supplies

One of my favorite places to go shopping is the office supply store. The entire place is full of fun tools and gadgets, and the air smells of pristine copy paper and wooden pencils. What can I say; I'm a teacher at heart. I can spend lots of time and money in those stores. The first time around with my seminar business, I sure did! I stocked up on everything from boxes of binder clips to stacks of Post-it Notes. However, the second time around I was wiser. I purchased only the items that I absolutely needed—and only as

I needed them. Aside from perhaps a stapler and a few pens, the only mission critical office supply tool that you need is a calendar.

Now, many people will gasp at the mere mention of a paper calendar. Who uses such things in this day and age, right? Certainly not a cutting-edge professional! However, keep in mind that although electronic calendaring is surely wonderful (and I love Google Calendar), a sudden loss of data can spell catastrophe if you haven't backed it up properly or recently.

I have a simple calendar that fits nicely in my business satchel, and I carry it with me everywhere. Many times, opening a paper calendar is more useful than an electronic one, such as when I'm talking with a client and he or she wants to glance at my calendar as we discuss upcoming meetings and deadlines. If you decide to maintain both an electronic calendar and a paper calendar,

> **Back Up Your Paper Calendar**
>
> Even a paper calendar needs to be backed up just in case you misplace it temporarily or lose it altogether. Photocopy your paper calendar regularly and store the copies securely for your peace of mind.

the redundancy is well worth the effort. Alternatively, you may choose to maintain only an electronic calendar and print out a daily or weekly snapshot as needed.

Business Phone Line

There is no way around it; you will need a business phone line. Using your home phone or personal cell phone to conduct business can lead to complications that may tarnish your reputation as a solid, full-time business professional. However, having a business line doesn't necessarily have to be a big drain on your bottom line. Instead, you may wish to forego setting up a costly land line, at least initially. You can opt for something as inexpensive as a prepaid cell phone that includes voice mail. I ran my entire business with a T-Mobile prepaid cell phone for the first two years at a cost of about $200 per year, after which time I ported the number to a smartphone (for example, my iPhone) that could access the Internet and run advanced applications. This prepaid plan worked so well that it inspired several people I know to adopt this same strategy!

If you opt for a smartphone right from the start, you will have to weigh the costs of this costly overhead expense against its usefulness early on in the life of your business. The nature of your work will also drive how

> **Send Faxes by E-mail**
>
> For an instant fax line, consider using an Internet-based service that allows you to send and receive faxes as e-mail attachments. No equipment required. No additional phone line to maintain. Start by visiting RingCentral (www.ringcentral.com).

critical a smartphone is to you at this early juncture, including the ability to instantly reply to incoming e-mail messages, watch critical-to-your-business Internet sites in real time, utilize relevant business apps, and so on. Whichever option you choose, the bottom line is that having a dedicated phone line for your business is mission critical. It also prevents clients from ringing your home phone at odd hours of the night, weekends, holidays, or other times that would prove to be an unacceptable interruption to you or your family.

Web Site

Do you really need a Web site? A Web presence can be a costly business product to have designed and *maintained* for you. Keep in mind that you should refresh the content of your Web site regularly, which can be as often as once a day or as infrequently as once every few months, depending on the nature of your business and how integral this tool is to your overall identity in the virtual and face-to-face marketplace. Depending on the services you are selling to potential employers, you may opt out of this expense in the beginning or altogether. However, if you do choose to throw your hat into the virtual ring, here are some of the basics to get you started:

- **Domain name:** This is your business's online real estate, and the same rule of thumb applies: location, location, location! Select a short, memorable, easy-to-spell, easy-to-speak domain name from those that are available (such as www.FunDesigns.com). You can browse the available names at a reseller such as Network Solutions (www.netsol.com). Prices vary depending on the reseller's perceived value of the domain name. Ideally, you should purchase a domain name from the same company you plan to host with to avoid transfer fees, and you should purchase the .com, .net, and .biz domains (if available) to avoid any competition from parallel sites (such as www.fundesigns.com, www.fundesigns.net, www.fundesigns.biz). Be sure to register the site in your business's name and use your corporate mailing address, phone number, and e-mail address to maintain your personal privacy.

- **Hosting:** For hosting purposes, I recommend that you host your Web site offsite through a reliable online provider. This eliminates the need to purchase and maintain your own Web server, which is costly and complicated. To save more money, opt for "shared" hosting instead of "dedicated" hosting. Shared hosting essentially means sharing a machine, known as a *Web server*, with a number of other Web sites.

In other words, you *share* the cost of the server with other Web site owners as opposed to "dedicated" hosting, which means you rent the entire server. Dedicated hosting makes the most sense for high-volume Web sites, which is not the case for your business in its early stages, generally speaking. When shopping around, be sure to ask the hosting company the following questions:

1. How many Web sites reside on each server?

2. What is the volume of traffic seen by other sites on the server where your site would be hosted?

3. What are the "uptime" guarantees and statistics?

> **Explore Google AdWords**
>
> Many hosting plans offer new users a promotion that includes free Google AdWords credit. If you have this option, be sure to use the credit to explore advertising your business in search engine result ads. This option makes more sense for some products and services than others. Visit http://adwords. google.com for more information.

4. Does the company support the anticipated technical requirements of your Web site (Cold Fusion, Java, or Access, for example)?

5. What are the setup fees or other initial costs? If month-to-month plans are available, which is the best option from a quality-control standpoint?

Because hosting companies seem to appear and disappear quickly, I hesitate to recommend any one company. However, the well-respected CNET (www.cnet.com) is a good resource for up-to-date rankings of hosting companies.

- **Design:** If you choose to create a Web site and know your way around a WYSIWYG (What You See Is What You Get) Web design program such as Adobe Dreamweaver or Microsoft FrontPage, then you may wish to shop at a template site. These online businesses offer intricately designed "canned" Web sites that include the corresponding .HTML, .PSD, .FLA, .SWF, or other relevant files you need to create and display your site. These canned Web sites are fully customizable with all of the code, layers, and script included for a flat rate. The site I recommend is Template Monster (www. templatemonster.com). I have pur-

> **Choose the Month-to-Month Hosting Option**
>
> Don't let a few dollars in savings lure you into prepaying for a year of hosting service. Instead, choose the month-to-month plan just in case the service does not live up to your expectations.

chased many templates from them for my own use and for my clients with great success. However, here are some words of caution:

1. If having a *unique* Web site design is imperative to the strength of your business identity (if you are an artist, for example), then a template may not be the right approach.

2. If you purchase a template that is beyond your skill level and need help troubleshooting or perhaps a bit of coaching, you must rely on live chat or the online help center. (Or if all else fails, you can open up a help desk ticket, but in my experience you are not able to speak with anyone by phone.)

Template Monster sells practically every type of Web product, including Flash, SWISH, and e-commerce templates, to name a few. Keep in mind that the content of some Web site formats can be difficult for search engines to catalog, so do some research about this topic before making a final selection. You most definitely want the

> **Test Drive Your Web Site Skill Set**
>
> If you want to just mouse around and test your skill level at Web site design, or if you want to preview the organization of files, layers, and so on, Template Monster offers a free template that you can download from the home page.

search engines to catalog and rank your Web site in order to increase the visibility of your business. That was the secret to the rapid growth of my seminar business early on.

• **Optimization:** Search engine optimization (SEO) is the business of embedding keywords and employing other strategies in order for your site to be ranked higher in the search results displayed by search engines such as Google, Yahoo!, and Bing. SEO is referred to as "organic" improvement of a site in order to rise in the ranks, as opposed to paid marketing ads that appear alongside search results (Google AdWords, for example). Optimizing your site requires technical tweaks and enhancements in order to "place" well in the search engine rankings among other sites that market products or services similar to your own. This placement can be mission critical or completely irrelevant to your business depending on how much you depend on the search engines to drive visitors to your Web site. For the Patchworker, this is typically not critically important because you are actively seeking new accounts instead of passively waiting for them to find you. On the other hand, why not draw in any new lead that you can with your Web site, right? Every client counts.

Creating a Web site can be beneficial and in some cases even necessary, depending on the nature of your work. If you choose to create a Web site for your business, prepare for an initial learning curve, but know that it is possible for a beginner with a technology bent to acquire these skills and improve with time and practice. Maintaining full control of your Web site allows you to make both subtle and bold changes to your business identity at any time. Let's take a look at various virtual and printed business identity items.

> **Optimize Your Web Site with an App**
>
> Search the Internet using the keywords "SEO tools" to locate free or nominally priced applications that can evaluate your published Web site and make recommendations about how to improve the ranking.

Business Identity

This checklist item of *business identity* is about developing a visual aid for clients in order to help them understand your business and the products or services you offer. Your business identity includes such tangible products as your logo, business card, online social media profile, and so on. Consider that you may work in multiple fields (programming and teaching, for example) and wish to brand each product or service you sell independently of the other, especially if the fields are completely unrelated. When you come at the marketplace with a portfolio of individual brands, this is called *multibranding,* whereby each brand has its own image. I use this approach, and it works very well for me. However, you do lose some momentum if you try to be too many things to too many people, so if you decide to take this approach, proceed with caution.

Let's review the various printed and virtual materials that you can choose from in order to solidify your business identity in the marketplace.

Printed Materials

As a Patchworker, you may manage multiple brands for multiple areas of specialization, such as immigration work and computer work. And each brand that you put forth into the marketplace (ComputerPro, Inc., for example) requires some basic business identity products, such as business cards and stationery. However, forget the expensive graphic design firms or office supply print shops to initially get your brand(s) out into the marketplace. Instead, purchase business cards, matching stationery, and other necessary products from a reliable online print shop.

I highly recommend Vistaprint (www.vistaprint.com). This print shop is an amazing asset to any small business owner. You simply browse the thousands of preformatted layouts and choose one that suits your business. Just fill in the blanks of a business card, for example, and see an immediate rendition of the full-color product. For less than $10, you can have a box of 250 business cards printed and delivered to your door within days. You can't beat it! Sign up for their mailing list to have promotions e-mailed to you offering discounts of as much as 90% off many popular products.

Along with business cards, take some time to browse the other *matching* business products, such as letterhead, envelopes, and greeting cards. Using the Vistaprint templates allows you to brand your newly founded company with quality business identity and promotional products in an instant—and for rock-bottom prices. I have ordered products from this company for ten years, sometimes 10,000 pieces at a time. The quality is always fantastic, and the customer service is excellent. Check them out and see for yourself.

> **Make Photoshop Your Friend**
>
> One of the best investments of time and money you can make is learning how to use Photoshop. From business cards to logo design and everything in between, it allows you to customize your business's printed materials how and when you choose. Photoshop files are accepted at nearly every face-to-face and online print shop in the country; it is the gold standard. However, keep in mind that this software is costly and has a steep learning curve. Consider purchasing the software secondhand and prepare to spend a significant amount of time learning how to use it. Photoshop is not for the technologically faint of heart, but the investment of time and money will pay dividends for many years to come.

Virtual Materials

Nearly every business can benefit in some way from creating a virtual profile on select social networking sites. These online communities present an opportunity to engage with both like-minded people and those with opposing views, with businesses that are similar as well as those that are complementary. All of these sites are free to use and can provide a greater exchange of ideas about any given topic than any networking event that you might ever attend. It is thrilling! Twitter (www.twitter.com) in particular is a wonderful way to exchange ideas, keep up with the latest trends in your field, and network with people in your area or halfway around the world.

> **Remember That First Impressions Are Lasting**
>
> Although Vistaprint offers free business cards, I suggest that you choose the option to pay for the cards because doing so removes the Vistaprint logo and the mention of their free promotions from the back of the cards. Cards bearing this "freebie" label can leave potential employers with the impression that you are a fly-by-night operation, so spend the $10.

Post Like a Pro

If you want to discuss your personal views about controversial topics or leave comments for your friends about your weekend adventures, open a second Twitter account to do so. Keep your business profile professional and separate from your personal exchanges.

Creating a virtual identity, also called a *profile page*, and navigating around the sites requires some dedicated time and effort. You must visit each site, create an account, populate it as necessary, learn your way around, and then acquaint yourself with the netiquette associated with each community. Although you have many sites to choose from, entrepreneurs benefit most from using the resources of Twitter and LinkedIn (www.linkedin.com).

Finally, you may wish to consider blogging about topics of interest to your potential customer base in order to further build your brand. This avenue can help you to stand out as an expert about a specific topic. To get started, register with a well-known blog hosting service provider such as Blogger (www.blogger.com) or WordPress (www.wordpress.com).

Setting up shop is the first step toward making your dream a reality! Have fun, spend wisely, and enjoy this part of the start-up process. It is a special time where your dreams and reality intersect and begin moving your business forward. If you feel overwhelmed by all the details that require your careful attention, simply prioritize and focus on one item at a time. Slow and steady wins the race.

Endnotes

[1] Carlye Adler, "Would You Pay $2 Million for This Franchise?" CNNMoney.com, http://money.cnn.com/magazines/fsb/fsb_archive/2002/05/01/322792/index.htm.

[2] Farhad Manjoo, "State Department Workers Want Firefox!" Farhad Manjoo's page on the Internet, http://blog.farhadmanjoo.com/post/141748401/state-department-workers-want-firefox (accessed August 18, 2010).

CHAPTER 19

Meeting Uncle Sam and Other Necessities

Let me begin this section by saying that I am not a legal expert, a financial planner, or a tax professional of any kind. However, I *have* made my way through a number of business startups without having hired any of these experts to date—all while remaining on good terms with the federal government. I learned the old-fashioned way: by reading, researching, working with successful business owners, and asking tons of questions. I tell you this because if your business is starting out small, you may want to consider doing the legwork yourself and saving a few thousand dollars.

One of the best tips I can give you is to visit your local library and search for books dedicated to the legalities of starting a small business. Alternatively, you can search online for reputable treasure troves of information such as the U.S. Small Business Administration (www.sba.gov) or the Internal Revenue Service (www.irs.gov). There are endless printed directives, video instruction, materials you can have shipped to your door—the works! Let me hit some of the highlights to get you started, but please keep in mind that this list is not exhaustive.

Establishing Your Business

This is an important section of the book, walking you through each of the mandatory steps for establishing your business as an official entity. From choosing a location for your office to setting up your records, the following steps will get you up and running:

1. **Choose a location.** Choose an official location for your business: a home office, a leased space, or some other place (see the previous chapter for more information on this topic). If you choose to run the business from your home, check local zoning requirements to be sure that your intended business activity is permitted in a residential area.

2. **Determine your business mailing address.** Once you know the location of your business, it's time to think about whether you want your actual location to be your business mailing address. Even if you anticipate working from a home office or leasing office space on a trial basis, it is still a good idea to open a P.O. Box to use as your official mailing address in the name of anonymity and continuity. However, keep in mind that this will require you to drive to and from the post office on a regular basis, so choose the location nearest you. Once you have an official business mailing address in place, you are ready to choose a legal structure.

> **Think Twice Before Using Your Home Address as a Business Address**
>
> If you run a business out of your home and use the house address as your official mailing address, you may find that customers and solicitors will knock on your door unexpectedly and fill your residential mailbox with supply catalogs and other junk mail for many years to come.

3. **Choose a legal structure.** This sounds complicated, but if you are willing to do a little reading on the IRS Web site, you can readily determine which structure is the best choice for your business. Legal structures range from sole proprietorships to S corporations to limited liability companies (LLCs) and more, and each structure has its own legal and tax considerations. Once you decide on the structure that is right for your business, you can apply for your Employee Identification Number (EIN).

> **Spend the Money for a Larger P.O. Box**
>
> If you're setting up a P.O. Box, choose a medium-sized P.O. Box instead of the smallest box available. Although the small box seems best in the beginning, a year from now your box may be overflowing, causing mail to be returned to the sender. This can be embarrassing, be confusing for the client, and cause checks to become lost in the mail. And changing boxes down the road means changing all of your printed business materials and requiring all of your clients to update their records as well. Buying a larger box now will save you and your clients time and hassle.

4. **Apply for an EIN.** This number, also known as a *Federal Tax Identification Number*, acts as an identification number for your business, and you will use it for paperwork filing and to receive payment in much the same way that you use your Social Security number. The EIN is a necessary form of identification for banking, tax, and payroll purposes. Most importantly, the EIN makes it possible for clients to pay you! As soon

> **Learn More About EINs**
>
> For more information, read IRS Publication 1635, *Understanding Your EIN.*

as you are serious about getting your business started, you need to visit the IRS Web site and apply for your EIN. Having this number makes it possible to open business bank accounts and more.

5. **Open a business checking account.** Once you have your EIN, you will be able to open a business checking account from which you can write checks to pay for business expenses and receive checks from clients for deposit. Opt for a free business checking account that is separate from your personal accounts to get started. Maintaining a separate account for your business prevents personal items from inadvertently becoming mixed up with business items and makes it easier to view your business cash flow.

> **Search for Checking Plans with Unlimited Deposit Plans**
>
> Look for a business checking plan that allows for unlimited deposits with no additional fees. Because you will be working for multiple employers, you will be receiving and depositing a great many checks each month. You earned it; hang on to it!

6. **Set up your recordkeeping.** Last but not least, you'll need to determine if you will pay taxes based on a calendar year (12 consecutive months beginning January 1 and ending December 31) or a fiscal year (12 consecutive months ending on the last day of any month except December). Then mark your calendar with your important must-pay-by federal and state tax deadlines. Missing these deadlines means paying penalties and doing additional paperwork. Also, you'll need to set up your recordkeeping system either on paper or with a program such as Quicken and determine whether you will use a cash or accrual accounting method. (To learn more about these methods, consult the IRS Web site.) Meticulous recordkeeping is critical in order to have an accurate picture of your income and expenses, to make adequate tax payments, and to answer to Uncle Sam in the event of an audit. Finally, look ahead to April 15 and think about how you can best organize your records to make tax filing as seamless as possible. Quicken and TurboTax pair nicely together; do the research and determine if they are the right solution for your new business.

> **Learn More About the Business of Accounting**
>
> For more information, read IRS Publication 538, *Accounting Periods and Methods*.

Congratulations! You are officially in business. Now it's time to protect yourself and your business by taking a look at the various forms of insurance.

Taking Steps to Safeguard Yourself

Insurance is a necessary expense for any small business owner. The purpose is simply to transfer risks that you can afford (the premiums) to cover risks that you cannot afford (such as a client breaking his leg when slipping on the ice on your front steps). The necessity for any of these forms of insurance will be driven in part by the type of work in which you engage. As a Patchworker, you may want to consider a few different types of insurance:

- **Liability insurance:** Does your business need liability coverage in case you make a grievous error while on the job? For most people the answer will be no, but due diligence is in order.

- **Renter's insurance:** If you lease office space and store your computer and other office equipment there, you will want to get a quote on renter's insurance.

- **Upgrade on homeowner's insurance:** If you run your business from your home, you may want to upgrade your current insurance policy to reflect the additional equipment stored in the home and other business-related considerations.

- **Health insurance:** Let's face it. Health insurance is the big sticking point for a lot of people when they consider leaving the security of the 9-to-5 world. The next section details health insurance concerns in more detail.

- **Life insurance and disability insurance:** These forms of insurance may have previously been arranged through your 9-to-5 employer and are yours to shop around for going forward.

Insurance is essential to your long-term success. You should contact a certified insurance agent for more information about these products and what is best for your business needs. Among the many forms of insurance that you must consider purchasing, health insurance is the most critical.

Health Insurance—More Affordable Than You Think

Millions of Americans get up and go to their 9-to-5 jobs each day for the sole purpose of maintaining their health insurance eligibility. I used to be that person, so I understand where you are coming from. The turning point for me, in all honesty, was when I one day discovered that the inflated health insurance premium that I was paying at my 9-to-5 job for basic coverage was only *$20 per month less* than it would have cost if I opted to leap out on my own and purchase coverage independently. It was a revelation.

Alternatively, you can investigate your eligibility for COBRA group health continuation coverage through your most recent 9-to-5 employer. Under certain circumstances, you may be eligible to purchase coverage through the group plan for up to thirty-six months. Prepare yourself for the fact that COBRA coverage may be pricey, but it can prove to be a viable and guaranteed form of coverage for individuals with certain preexisting health conditions.

> **Acquaint Yourself with Insurance Jargon**
>
> A great place to begin educating yourself about the business of health insurance, including the terminology, is Freelancer's Insurance Company (www.freelancersinsuranceco.com), which is owned by Freelancers Union (www.freelancersunion.org). Just click on the FAQ (Frequently Asked Questions) link. However, please note that the health insurance products that they offer are available to New York state residents only.

When was the last time that *you* shopped around for health insurance? Have you *ever* done that before? Do you know what the *actual* costs are to purchase coverage outright for yourself and your family? Shop around! You might be pleasantly surprised.

To begin your quest for insurance, you can request insurance quotes online through a portal, such as www.healthinsurance.org, or enlist the help of a local certified, professional insurance agent who can evaluate your needs, educate you, and shop around on your behalf.

Health Savings Accounts

Opening a Health Savings Account (HSA) is a smart option for managing health-related expenses when you choose a high-deductible insurance plan. The HSA is a tax-advantaged repository established by the U.S. Department of Treasury to encourage saving for health-related expenses. You can withdraw money from the account to pay for health-related expenses such as medical bills, medication, or your deductible. According to the official Treasury directives:

- Amounts contributed to an HSA belong to the account holder and are completely portable.

- Funds in the account can grow tax-free through investment earnings, just like an Individual Retirement Account (IRA).

- Funds distributed from the HSA are not taxed if they are used to pay qualified medical expenses.

- Unlike amounts in Flexible Spending Arrangements (FSAs) that are forfeited if not used by the end of the year, unused funds remain available for use in later years.

Purchasing a health insurance policy with a high deductible and then building up an amount in the HSA equivalent to that deductible can give you peace of mind, knowing that in case of a catastrophic accident or serious illness your deductible can readily be met and a large portion of the costs will be covered. Contact a health insurance expert or the U.S. Department of Treasury (www.ustreas.gov) for more information.

Cash Discounts

It is unorthodox in our society to haggle with someone about the costs of a retail good or service being provided in a store, much less a medical setting. However, most medical professionals do have a separate pricing category for someone who has a high deductible and is essentially paying cash, minus the in-network discount. For routine procedures this can provide a moderate discount that can add up to a great deal of savings over the course of a year. For major procedures, such as newborn delivery, the discount can be as much as 50 percent off of the inflated retail sticker price. That can really add up to a lot of savings. Ask the question of the billing specialist at the medical office—you may like the answer!

Retirement Savings

Saving for retirement is critical, period. Just because you're no longer contributing to a company-sponsored 401(k) doesn't mean you can forget about saving for retirement. After all, retirement is a metaphor for the biggest journey of your life. The journey will be to places you have always dreamed of living or visiting and in the manner you have always envisioned. It is a trip that will last for many years, and the path you travel as well as the level of luxury you enjoy will be determined by your careful and disciplined preparation. Effectively saving for retirement will empower you. Failing to save for retirement sufficiently will result in a long, difficult journey.

To plan for and ensure a safe, pleasant journey into your golden years, you should first check out an online retirement calculator to determine the approximate amount you need to save in order to enjoy the lifestyle you have in mind. Most brokerage companies, such as Vanguard, offer excellent, free, and easy-to-use online tools for the general public. Use this information as a starting point for a conversation with a certified financial planner in your area.

ॐ

Attending to these necessities is critical in order to ensure your health and the health of your business. Take your time and build a strong foundation that will safeguard your future success.

CHAPTER 20

Parting Thoughts

So, that's it! You now have all of the tools necessary to create your own personalized 9-to-5 Cure! First, remember to create a lifestyle that is meaningful to you, making careful note of your priorities and then honoring them as much as possible. Second, be sure to take an inventory of your skills and abilities, surveying the landscape both online and offline for opportunities that are in alignment with who you are and what you value. When you combine those two core components, you create the formula that lets you live the life of your dreams!

> **THE 9-TO-5 CURE EQUATION**
>
> *Lifestyle Design + The Patchwork Principle = The 9-to-5 Cure*
>
> *or*
>
> *Quality of Life + Enjoyable Work in Abundance = The 9-to-5 Cure*

You are ready to charge out into the world headlong. This is your moment. What are you waiting for? Get out there and start making some changes in your life. Begin by creating a list of dreams and goals that you have in mind as you near the end of this book—Patchworker-style! Develop the following goal sheet to reflect the direction you envision for your life from this point forward. Use it as a foundation for the action plan you formulate after you close this book and begin to chart your course for success.

FIRST PATCHWORKER GOAL SHEET

CAREER	EDUCATION
_____	_____
_____	_____
_____	_____
_____	_____
_____	_____
_____	_____
_____	_____
_____	_____
_____	_____

RELATIONSHIPS	FINANCES
_____	_____
_____	_____
_____	_____
_____	_____
_____	_____
_____	_____
_____	_____
_____	_____

Compare the preceding Patchworker goal sheet with the preliminary goal sheet you created in Chapter 3, "Charting a New Course." Can you identify any shift in your goals or priorities when comparing the lists? Consider what those changes mean for your career and your life. Are you feeling more empowered now than you were when you picked up this book? If the answer is yes, then this book served its purpose.

My hope is that the chapters of this book have equipped you with empowering tools that allow you to embrace your true purpose as you charge out into the world once more. As you set out on your journey, I would like to leave you with a few parting thoughts about lessons I have learned as a veteran Patchworker. I share these with you so that you, too, may enjoy all that the 9-to-5 Cure has to offer and find your own path to true success and happiness.

ℰℭ

Be Willing to Make Some Big Mistakes

Do you know what Scotchgard, potato chips, Coca-Cola, and Silly Putty all have in common? They were invented by mistake![1] Each of these wonderfully successful products came about completely by accident while the inventors were focused on creating something totally different. The lesson for all of us in life and in business is to be willing to take risks and make big mistakes. The twentieth-century Irish novelist James Joyce once wrote, "A man's errors are his portals of discovery," a timeless statement that can readily be applied to Patchworkers who are willing to forge new paths and see where they might lead. "To boldly go where no man has gone before." (Okay, so maybe this *Star Trek* quote is a bit over the top, but you get the idea.) Nothing is a waste of time if you use the experience to your advantage by evaluating and incorporating the lessons learned in order to leverage your future endeavors.

You must be willing to take action, test new theories, and be bold. Action is what separates the dreamers from the achievers. All of the famous business people of our time seem to believe this idea to be true as well. Take, for example, Conrad Hilton, American hotelier and founder of Hilton Hotels, who once attested to this very same philosophy: "Success seems to be connected with action. Successful people keep moving. They make mistakes, but they don't quit." Or the famous quote by Albert Einstein, who requires no introduction: "Anyone who has never made a mistake has never tried anything new." These two men and many other notable people in history all collectively shout to you, the reader, "Be willing to make mistakes!" Or, as Nike says, "Just do it!" Get out there and don't let a few mistakes, big or small, along the way deter you. Learn and move on all the wiser.

Never Underestimate Yourself

Recently I came to the realization that if you pitted the philosophy of iconic cultural anthropologist Margaret Mead against the iconic American Dilbert cartoonist Scott Adams, it would be a draw. Mead believes "…a small group of thoughtful, committed citizens can change the world," while Adams believes, "You can never underestimate the stupidity of the general public." Well, which is it? Perhaps both are correct.

Sometimes it's difficult to estimate how intelligent decisions are when made by a group, hearkening back to the conversation about the scores of sometimes ineffective committees. Groups are complicated organisms. However, when it comes to making decisions independently, with no one else evaluating the decisions, it can be daunting at times. It is at those times that I remind myself what Wilma Rudolph, the first American female runner to win three gold medals at a single Olympics, once said, "The potential for greatness lives in each of us." Her words are so true and serve as a helpful reminder on days when running your own business feels like a challenge too great for you (and there will be those days). Just like Rudolph, we all begin at the starting line and look toward the finish with a hopeful spirit. Sometimes we race around the track and enjoy an effortless lap; other times we stumble or face an unexpected hurdle. Whatever may come, the secret is to believe in yourself and keep your lifestyle by design at the forefront. You *can* achieve—just believe!

Cultivate a Community of Colleagues

Don Quixote said it best: "Tell me thy company, and I'll tell thee what thou art." Whom we choose to associate with makes a statement about us and shapes the way we see ourselves and the world around us. Choose wisely, especially as you venture into the world of entrepreneurship.

When you are struggling, the jackals in the business world can smell blood. They will try to welcome you into their schemes and invite you to join their pack in exchange for some easy money. Don't do it. When you hit your stride and feel like the wind is finally at your back, well, that is when everyone else will come calling, asking you to spend money in order to optimize some facet of your business or partner with them in their own business ventures. Proceed with caution. Surround yourself with colleagues who are also in the startup phase of their own businesses and share information about all of the mundane but perplexing topics that new business owners need to know. Lean on each other. Share ideas. Laugh. Go out for coffee. Build a community of colleagues.

Likewise, seek out experienced entrepreneurs, including veteran freelancers, to mentor you. They can help you when you can't see the forest for the trees. Because the dynamics of entrepreneurship are quite different from those of being a 9-to-5 employee, finding seasoned, self-employed guides is especially constructive. They understand the importance of marketing, daily operations issues that arise, and the emotional ups and downs of being the boss.

In her book *Ten Things I Wish I'd Known—Before I Went Out into the Real World*, Maria Shriver makes a strong case for cultivating mentors when they appear in your path. Mentors can be experienced guides that help you get to the next level in some aspect of your career, colleagues who excel in the same field, retirees who know what it takes to walk the same path that you are starting on, or someone else who can inspire and guide you. As Shriver mentions in her book, mentors may not always look or act like the sage you are expecting, so "keep your eyes open."[2] Mentors can be long-term confidants or momentary counselors who appear in the right place and at the right time. Be on the lookout!

Mentors are extremely important not only for your professional development, but also for personal growth. "You are the average of the five people you spend the most time with," according to entrepreneur Jim Rohn, which means that you had better choose those five people carefully. It's the same principle in many ways as a study in the *New England Journal of Medicine* that found that our friends influence our weight, with either fitness or fat spreading from person to person like a virus.[3] Essentially, we look at our friends and set our own standards based on what we see, whether it is about our body image or our professional aspirations. We exchange ideas and share networks that help us refine our ideas, hear about new ideas, and leap ahead as a result. Finding like-minded mentors who also value the quality of their life is important for the same reasons. "The quality of your life is a direct reflection of the expectations of your peer group," says motivational speaker Anthony Robbins, so choose wisely.

Go Easy on Yourself

Let's face it; life is a bowl of cherries, and once in a while you're in the pits. There is no way around it. Occasionally, we all have a meltdown. I'm not giving you no-holds-barred permission to walk into a client's office and lash out at someone in a completely unprofessional manner. But I am saying that it's okay if sometimes you need to take yourself out for a latte and rethink your life plan because you feel like the wheels have come off of the tracks. I'm telling you, thoughts like this are okay! In fact, they can be defining moments where, in a moment of clarity, you have the ability to see what is wrong with the current strategy and what you need to change going forward. These are opportunities to take your career to the next level.

Give yourself permission to feel confused, frustrated, or anything (and everything!) else once in a while. Cultivate acute awareness about your emotions related to work (and life); this will help you to further define what matters most to you as you design a career that matches your ideal lifestyle.

It will be those obstacles in your path that cause you the most grief, but remember that while you are not in control of them, you *are* in control of how you react to them. Don't take my word for it; heed this advice from über-successful entrepreneur Mary Kay Ash, founder of Mary Kay cosmetics:

> When you reach an obstacle, turn it into an opportunity. You have the choice. You can overcome and be a winner, or you can allow it to overcome you and be a loser. The choice is yours and yours alone. Refuse to throw in the towel. Go that extra mile that failures refuse to travel. It is far better to be exhausted from success than to be rested from failure.[4]

So be gentle with yourself on those days when you are frustrated and feel like chucking the whole idea of being a Patchworker. You will encounter roadblocks, and some of them will frustrate you, which is completely understandable. Once in a while you will need to vent your frustration on the golf course or the basketball court. That is perfectly normal. What you do after that, the way you handle your frustration, is what counts. It can define you. Choose to be a success—by definition.

Lead with Kindness

In some business circles, kindness is seen as a form of weakness. After all, there is any number of sayings akin to "It's a dog-eat-dog world," and we all fall for it. We believe that if we aren't fighting for our piece of the pie, then we're just not going to "win." However, in my experience kindness pays dividends.

When you seek out forms of employment that are both a public service and a source of income, others are attracted to your business and are eager to support its mission and tell others about you. An excellent example of leading with kindness was demonstrated by the founder of The Body Shop stores, Anita Roddick. She introduced the idea of ethical consumerism that embodied ideas such as animal-free cosmetics testing and fair trade with so-called Third World nations. She said, "The end result of kindness is that it draws people to you," which is a statement that I wholeheartedly agree with from my own experience in business.

For example, one area of my Patchwork business model is dedicated to serving senior citizens, and it has flourished with little effort, based mostly on the kindness of strangers who are eager to play a role in connecting this deserving group with quality services that just happen to be provided by me. It is a win-win for all involved, and it provides both emotional and financial fulfillment for me as well. Making money while you help people who are in turn grateful for the help and made happier by the services you provide is energizing. These happy customers sing your praises and spread the word about you to their family and friends. This word-of-mouth marketing is priceless and extremely effective.

A final note about kindness is a suggestion that you treat your clients like colleagues and friends. Ultimately, we are all just people who get up and work each day, longing to connect on a personal level with those around us. Although I'm not necessarily advocating that you become bosom buddies with every one of your clients, I would encourage you to learn about those things that matter most to your clients. Make a note of their birth date and send a card or give them a call on that date each year. Know the names of their children. Send them a thank-you note when they bail you out of a tight spot. Treat them with respect when they fall flat. Kind gestures go a long way and can cement your business relationship for the long term. Such gestures can also pay dividends in the form of feeling interconnectedness with your clients over time instead of leaving you with nothing but a series of sterile interactions.

At the intersection of our personal lives and our business lives is kindness. Mindfully demonstrating and cultivating it can determine how far we go and how we feel throughout the journey. Cultivating kindness is a valuable part of the business of life.[5]

Be Willing to Apologize

Apologies don't come easy for some people, especially in the business world. In the world of work, people are constantly posturing in an effort to dominate in some way, and an apology just doesn't fit neatly into that paradigm. However, in the world of Patchwork you *do* have the opportunity to shape your reality. You have the chance to let down your guard and apologize when you mess up. And apologizing can pay off.

If you think there is little economic value to be gained from apologizing, consider how it's paying off for the hospital system at the University of Michigan. In a radical departure from the status quo of "denying and defending" complaints, hospital officials began sitting down with patients and their lawyers to talk. In many cases, the doctors apologized directly to the patients for harm, and hospital administrators and lawyers were there to bear witness and quickly settle legitimate claims. This practice satisfied patients to such an extent that malpractice suits dropped by more than half. What the hospital administrators learned was that in some cases, patients just wanted the wrongdoing to be acknowledged, and barring a conversation, the courts were the only way that they could feel heard.[6] Think about the economic savings garnered by dropped suits, including lengthy and costly litigation. This has been such a successful model of savings (and decency) that hospitals all across the country are jumping on board the apology bandwagon.

Apologizing is economically viable and, in fact, can be critical to the success of your own business. For one thing it is far easier to take responsibility for your own bad behavior and begin to repair the existing relationship you have with a client than it is to drum up a brand-new customer. As a Patchworker, it is especially important to protect your integrity because much of your business may derive from referrals. Apologizing can demonstrate your maturity, honesty, and ability to handle a difficult situation well, which in turn may actually increase the employer's opinion of you.

Remember that mistakes will happen; they are inevitable. So have the strength and the courage to swallow your pride when it really matters and take responsibility for your actions.

Stay Positive

Happy people make it to the finish line. You just can't keep them down. I'm one of them. I am not naïve, but I am the eternal optimist. A positive attitude has its place in business, especially when you are a Patchworker. For one thing, clients like working with a positive person. After all, who wants to call up a grouch and invite him or her to join the team? Happy people draw others to them like a force of nature and, as a result, are more likely to close the deal. Also, people with positive attitudes are more memorable; they leave lasting impressions on the decision maker.

Your attitude should be an essential part of your brand, causing decision makers to conjure up positive images of the last time they worked with you, which may cause them to call you with subsequent offers. It can be a critical component of what drives the momentum of your business and also what drives you. With that in mind, give yourself permission to protect your time to occasionally enjoy the finer things in life that remind you about why you chose this lifestyle. For example, if you are working on an ongoing project that can wait an extra day, give yourself the day off to hit the links and golf eighteen holes on an unusually gorgeous summer day. Those moments will remind you of how wonderfully free you are to live your life on your own terms, and moments like these will feed your positive attitude for many days to come. These moments help to keep you feeling positive about your work, your lifestyle, and yourself, and positive people see reality differently from those who are negative or neutral.

Positive people can see the possibility in the impossible. They have boundless energy that thrusts them far ahead of their exhausted, stressed-out counterparts. This translates into people who can think more creatively, get more done, and, as a result, excel above and beyond the average person. In other words, "The positive thinker sees the invisible, feels the intangible, and achieves the impossible."[7] A positive attitude is underrated.

Keep Making Forward Progress

As you embark on your own journey of Lifestyle Design and Patchwork Principle earning, I wish you great success—however you define it for yourself. To make the 9-to-5 Cure work in your own life, just remember that at its core the Cure is simply a method for defining what it is that you want from your work and your life and then making small, calculated moves in that direction. Your direction may change over time as you reevaluate what it is you want from your work and your life; it is a continual process that marks your forward progress.

The Japanese call this *Kaizen*. It literally translates to "improvement," and, just like the 9-to-5 Cure, it has applications across both your personal and professional lives. In a business context, Kaizen is translated more specifically to mean "continuous improvement,"[8] which goes right to the heart of the 9-to-5 Cure: Strive to continually improve in small but meaningful ways in order to serve yourself and your clients well. Constantly test and improve yourself, your business, and your lifestyle in order to keep growing. Stay focused and remain in touch with your heart's deepest desires. Be brave. Take risks. And most importantly:

Work on purpose—always.

Endnotes

[1] Charlotte Foltz Jones, *Mistakes That Worked* (New York: Doubleday, 1991), back cover.

[2] Maria Shriver, *Ten Things I Wish I'd Known—Before I Went Out into the Real World* (New York: Warner Books, 2000), 33.

[3] Gina Kolata, "Obesity Spreads to Friends, Study Concludes," *New York Times*, July 25, 2007, www.nytimes.com/2007/07/25/health/25iht-fat.4.6830240.html (accessed August 16, 2010).

[4] Scott Allen, "Quotations from Famous Entrepreneurs on Entrepreneurship," About.com, http://entrepreneurs.about.com/od/famousentrepreneurs/a/quotations.htm (accessed August 23, 2010).

[5] Simran Khurana, "Kindness Quotations," About.com, http://quotations.about.com/cs/inspirationquotes/a/Kindness4.htm (accessed August 30, 2010).

[6] Richard McGill Murphy, "Why doing good is good for business," CNNMoney.com, http://money.cnn.com/2010/02/01/news/companies/dov_seidman_lrn.fortune/index.htm (accessed August 30, 2010).

[7] Sam Davis, "5 Quotes on Positive Thinking," Ezinearticles.com, http://ezinearticles.com/?5-Quotes-on-Positive-Thinking&id=4384791 (accessed August 30, 2010).

[8] Creative Safety Supply, Kaizen in the workplace, booklet, www.creativesafetysupply.com/Kaizen.pdf (accessed March 16, 2010).

Glossary

The 9-to-5 Cure Equation—A blueprint for a groundbreaking career strategy that combines Lifestyle Design with the Patchwork Principle for lasting personal and professional freedom and success.

balance—The sense of stability individuals experience when they determine what factors are relevant to them and to what extent they give each priority.

beginner's mind—Derived from Zen Buddhism, an openness to new ideas, free from assumptions or foregone conclusions.

business identity—Visual aids developed for a client to illustrate and define a business and the products or services offered.

career myopia—Loss of function in a person's imagination that results from an inordinate amount of time spent focusing on work life; a narrow field of vision fixated on surviving instead of thriving.

consultant—An employment classification assigned to an individual with specialized skills who is hired to complete or provide insights about a specific project.

crowdsourcing—The act of outsourcing micro tasks to a large group of people or community (a crowd), through an open call [to work]. Individuals perform narrowly defined tasks in exchange for per-piece payment.

cultural skills—The skills needed to interact with various business communities, each of which has its own unique values, norms, assumptions, acceptable behaviors, and tangible artifacts.

cure—A complete or permanent solution or remedy.

Eagle Eye approach—The Patchworker job search strategy in which the individual carefully analyzes a potential territory, identifies key opportunities, methodically researches to learn more about the organization, and then crafts a pitch that proposes a customized solution.

elevator speech—A compelling overview of what an individual can offer to a potential employer that the individual can present succinctly enough to take place during a short elevator ride. Also known as a *personal positioning statement.*

Emotional Intelligence (EI)—A person's ability to manage his or her own emotions and the emotions of others.

employee—An employment classification assigned to an individual with a regular and ongoing commitment from an employer.

Employee Identification Number (EIN)—A federal identification number assigned to a business that is used for paperwork filing and is required to receive payment from an employer; it is used in much the same way that a Social Security number is used by the traditional employee.

evaluation—The final step in the fishing process, in which the Patchworker sizes up opportunities and determines how closely they align with the priorities that matter most.

expert skills—Skills to which a person has dedicated 10,000 hours, either in concentrated amounts or in small chunks over the course of a lifetime.

fishing—To cast out inquiries in search of job leads. The four basic steps include reflection, observation, identification, and evaluation.

flow—Completely focused motivation in which emotions are positively aligned with the work being performed.

free range—Having the freedom to work outside of the constructs of an office cubicle.

Freelance Dance—Refers to the pace and predictability of a Patchworker's career and lifestyle, determined by how they choose to schedule work performed for multiple employers and likely in multiple position types.

Gigaverse—The bleak employment arena of a gigger.

Gigonomics—A career approach adopted by a once upwardly mobile workforce, known as *giggers,* in which individuals complete an ongoing series of gigs (such as freelance projects) that they "stitch together" in order to make ends meet.

identification—The third step in the fishing process, in which the Patchworker focuses on finding work that is both enjoyable and a good fit with their lifestyle framework.

independent contractor—An employment classification assigned to an individual hired to perform a specific function in an at-will capacity.

inspirational skills—Those abilities associated with securing work, maintaining it, and generating future business with the same client.

interpersonal skills—Those abilities attributed to interacting well with others.

Kaizen—A continual process that marks forward progress. Translated from Japanese, Kaizen means "improvement" and in a business context means "continuous improvement."

Lifestyle Design—A framework that prioritizes an ongoing quality of life over waiting until retirement to pursue one's wildest dreams.

location independent—A lifestyle choice that values the ability to move from one geographic location to another at will without it compromising one's work.

micro task—A crowdsourcing term used to describe small tasks that workers choose to do in exchange for per-piece payment. Examples include image tagging, image sorting, and data transcription.

mobile crowdsourcing—Micro task outsourcing that workers complete by using their cell phones.

mobile money—A crowdsourcing term that describes the compensation paid to workers in the form of credits redeemable for local currency or cell phone airtime.

momentum—Success that builds on itself, leading to results with ever-increasing ease. Within the context of the Patchwork Principle, it is a dynamic form of client building.

multibranding—Coming to the marketplace with a portfolio of individual brands, in which each brand has its own image.

No-Vacation Nation—A term used to describe the United States, which is the only advanced economy in the world that does not guarantee its workers paid vacation.

observation—The second step in the fishing process, in which the Patchworker strategically looks for and identifies unadvertised and unrecognized opportunities.

operational skills—The skills needed to interact productively with clients, including those who help you to sustain your business, and the employees in each of the key administrative offices at the organizations you work with.

The Patchwork Principle—A freelance career strategy based on the simple idea that working for a number of employers simultaneously presents unique business opportunities and insulates an individual from sudden and total job loss. Enjoyable work in abundance is the signature of this business model.

Patchworker—A freelancer who selectively accepts work based on lifestyle factors that they determine to be personally important.

Patchworker mindset—The mentality of a mindful entrepreneur, committed to operating a successful business within the parameters of lifestyle design.

pitch—The proposition a Patchworker makes to a potential employer.

The plug—A temporary, full-time, or part-time position born of a recent change within an organization due to a staff member's sudden departure.

The quick fix—An ad hoc position created with a well-defined purpose in mind. This position typically includes project-based work that is generally founded on immediacy.

re-entry shock—The phenomenon associated with individuals distancing themselves from a familiar environment and then coming back to it with new experiences for a unique perspective on familiar surroundings. Also known as *reverse culture shock*.

reflection—The first step in the fishing process, in which the Patchworker decides what kind of work he or she wants to find.

reverse outsourcing—An arrangement in which overseas companies hire American workers.

Seagull Scavenge approach—A Patchworker job search strategy in which the individual searches for opportunities among a wide array of businesses, getting the word out about themselves to a large number of decision makers in hopes that opportunities will present themselves.

soft skills—Interpersonal skills such as coaching, teaching, motivating, negotiating, leading, and socializing that enable a person to effectively interact with others.

The stand-in—A previously full-time position that is eliminated on one side of the books and added back in on the other side but without benefits and other costly perks.

The star—A position providing the Patchworker with an opportunity to perform a specialized task on an ongoing basis, for which the Patchworker charges a premium.

Survivalnomics—A desperate economic reality that people readily accept as the norm, whereby both employers and employees struggle to survive in a zero-sum business environment in which both parties are in a perpetual state of fight or flight and believe they must constantly prove themselves in the workplace if they are to survive.

telecommuter—An employee who works from a remote location, such as a home office.

thrive—To take hold of one's dreams in a literal sense; to prosper.

Type A personality—A theory describing a person who is often considered to be a high-achieving workaholic, who multitasks, drives himself or herself with deadlines, and is unhappy about delays.

Type B personality—A theory describing a person who is often considered to be patient, relaxed, and easygoing; generally lacking a sense of urgency.

Unretirement Index—A survey tracking the number of people who continue to work after becoming eligible for full retirement benefits.

Virtual Assistant (VA)—An entrepreneur who provides support services from a remote location. Services typically include general office support such as reception, executive assistance, word processing, and typing or specialized support such as bookkeeping, advertising, or paralegal services.

visualization—The idea of deliberately and carefully crafting an objective and then focusing one's energy and thoughts on that goal in order to achieve it.

The walk-on—A part-time or full-time position that a company creates on a trial basis.

INDEX